A COLLECTION OF RECIPES FROM THE FRIENDS AND FAMILY OF THE FRESH MARKET

25th Anniversary

THE FRESH MARKET & FRIENDS COOKBOOK

CELEBRATING **25** YEARS OF FAMILY, FRIENDS AND DELICIOUS FOODS

First Edition

Photography by D-Cube Studios, Greensboro, NC

Recipe Testing by Jason Rice of Terrabonne, Inc.

ISBN Number: 978-0-9723469-1-7

Library of Congress Control Number: 2007907200

© **Copyright 2007 By**
The Fresh Market, Inc.
P.O. Box 29567
Greensboro, NC 27429
(336) 272-1338

FOREWARD

. . . .

25 years ago my wife, Beverly, and I opened our first Fresh Market location – a small specialty grocery store dedicated to bringing family, friends and neighbors together to experience the joys of quality food and friendly service. We have grown immensely since that time due to the devotion of our customers and employees and are now celebrating our 25th Anniversary with over 70 stores in more than 15 states. To commemorate this milestone in The Fresh Market's history, we have asked you, our valued customers and employees, to submit your favorite time-honored recipes to create a unique collection that celebrates 25 years of bringing people together with great food.

We received so many excellent recipes and wish that we had room to include them all. Our selection process was rigorous: Each recipe was tested, sometimes more than once, then tasted by our panel of culinary experts who ultimately had some very difficult decisions to make. The result is a wonderful collaboration of tried and true recipes from your own personal collections. These are recipes to delight in and share with friends and family, recipes that are great for simple weeknight meals as well as recipes that take a little more time and are festive and celebratory, and, overall, recipes to light up the eyes of those around you and truly allow you and your loved ones to "experience the food."

I sincerely hope that you are pleased with the final result and find occasion to try out each and every one of these unique, well-loved recipes. We at The Fresh Market truly appreciate your contributions and have acknowledged all who contributed recipes on the back of this book. I wish you happy cooking from our kitchen to yours and hope you enjoy sharing these delicious recipes with family and friends as much as we have.

Ray Berry, Founder

CONTENTS

pre

APPETIZERS	17
SOUPS	59
SALADS	77

main

BEEF	125
PASTA	145
PORK	165
POULTRY	181
SEAFOOD	201
LAMB & VEAL	233
ACCOMPANIMENTS	245

post

DESSERTS	293
BREAKFAST	335
EVERYTHING ELSE	347

Gazpacho Salad, page 88

Smoked Salmon Pillows, page 48

Honey Roasted Butternut Squash Salad, page 93

Italian Turkey & Spinach Meatball Soup, page 69

Crab Crostini, page 26

Whiskey Chili, page 76

Creamy Tomato Basil Soup, page 66

Rosemary Shrimp Skewers, page 45

pre

APPETIZERS

SOUPS

SALADS

ASIAGO CHEESE DIP

Make 2 cups

1 cup mayonnaise

1 cup sour cream

1 cup Asiago cheese, shredded

2 green onions, sliced and white ends removed

$1/4$ cup white mushrooms, chopped

$1/4$ cup sun-dried tomatoes packed in oil, drained and chopped

Preheat oven to 350°. In a bowl, blend mayonnaise, sour cream and $1/2$ cup Asiago cheese. Fold in onions, mushrooms and sun-dried tomatoes. Pour mixture into a loaf pan. Sprinkle remaining cheese on top.

Bake for 20 minutes or until bubbly. Serve with crackers, TFM French Rounds or pita chips.

BACON-WRAPPED OYSTERS

• •

Makes 15 oysters

RÉMOULADE

1 cucumber, peeled and seeded

2 teaspoons fresh thyme

2 - 3 tablespoons mayonnaise

1 tablespoon citrus champagne vinegar

2 teaspoons lemon juice

1 teaspoon olive oil

¼ cup crème fraîche

½ teaspoon salt

¼ teaspoon pepper

OYSTERS

20 slices applewood smoked bacon

1 pound oysters (cut into 1 ½-inch pieces if larger)

toothpicks

¼ cup vegetable oil

3 tablespoons garlic, minced

Purée cucumbers in a food processor or blender. Strain through a mesh strainer for 30 to 35 minutes; discard strained liquid. In a small mixing bowl, add strained cucumbers to remaining rémoulade ingredients and stir to combine. Place in the refrigerator until ready to serve.

In a frying pan over medium heat, sear bacon slices for 3 minutes per side (bacon will be only partially cooked).

Wrap 1 to 2 slices of bacon around each oyster and secure with a toothpick.

Heat oil in a sauté pan over medium heat; add garlic and sauté until golden brown, about 3 to 4 minutes. Place bacon-wrapped oysters in the pan and cook until bacon becomes crisp, about 10 to 12 minutes. Remove from pan and drain on a paper towel. Serve warm with rémoulade.

BAKED BRIE BREAD BOULE

1 sourdough boule

3 tablespoons butter, melted

1 tablespoon garlic, minced

¼ teaspoon dried thyme

¼ teaspoon dried marjoram

16 ounces Brie cheese, rind removed and cut into cubes

Preheat oven to 350°. Slice off the top of sourdough boule and reserve; remove inside of the bread to create a bowl.

In a small mixing bowl, combine butter, garlic, thyme and marjoram; brush mixture inside bread boule, completely covering sides and bottom.

Place brie cubes inside bread boule and top with reserved lid. Place on a baking sheet and bake for 15 to 25 minutes or until cheese is melted. Cut bread into wedges and serve hot.

BOURBON PECAN
BRIE PASTRIES

¼ cup brown sugar, packed

2 tablespoons butter, melted

1 tablespoon bourbon

¼ cup pecans, chopped

24 mini pastry cups

16 ounces Brie, rind removed and cut
   into ½-inch pieces

Preheat oven to 350°. In a small mixing bowl, mix brown sugar, butter and bourbon until combined. Fold in pecans.

Place one piece of Brie inside each pastry cup and top with bourbon pecan mixture. Bake for 10 to 12 minutes or until Brie is bubbly.

Chipotle Black Bean Empanadas

2 garlic cloves, minced

$\frac{1}{2}$ teaspoon cumin

1 - 2 teaspoons chipotle powder (or chili powder)

1 tablespoon olive oil

1 (15 ounce) can black beans

1 (14.5 ounce) can diced tomatoes with liquid

1 cup chicken, cooked and cubed

2 green onions, thinly sliced including whites

$\frac{1}{2}$ cup Cheddar cheese, shredded

$\frac{1}{2}$ cup Monterey Jack cheese, shredded

1 egg, beaten

Empanada Dough

2 cups all purpose flour

1 cup cornmeal

1 $\frac{1}{2}$ teaspoons baking powder

1 teaspoon salt

10 tablespoons butter

13 tablespoons water

In a large sauté pan over medium heat, sauté garlic, cumin and chipotle powder in olive oil for 1 minute. Add black beans, tomatoes and chicken, simmer 10 minutes. Remove from heat and stir in green onions and shredded cheese and chill.

To prepare empanada dough, mix dry ingredients together. Add butter and mix well. Add in water and mix just to combine. If dough seems a little dry add more water 1 tablespoon at a time. Dough should hold together when pressed in your palm, but not crumble apart. Flatten into a disk and wrap with plastic wrap; place in fridge for 1 hour.

Preheat oven to 375°. Remove dough from plastic wrap and cut into about 20 pieces. Roll pieces out into 6-inch rounds about $\frac{1}{8}$-inch thick. Place approximately $\frac{1}{8}$ cup of black bean mixture in bottom half of the dough $\frac{1}{4}$ -inch from the edge. Brush with a small amount of egg wash and fold the other half to form a half moon shape.

Using a fork, crimp edges together to seal. Dipping the fork in flour from time to time helps to prevent it from sticking to the dough. Repeat with remaining rounds.

Brush empanadas with remaining egg wash. Place evenly on a parchment lined baking sheet and bake for 10 minutes. Check and bake an additional 5 minutes if needed. Empanadas should be golden brown and dough will be flaky.

Coquilles St. Jacques

½ cup breadcrumbs

5 tablespoons butter, divided

6 ounces Monterey Jack cheese, shredded

1 cup mayonnaise

¼ cup dry white wine

1 tablespoon fresh parsley, chopped

1 pound bay scallops, cut in half

½ pound mushrooms, sliced

½ cup red onions, diced

24 mini pastry shells, thawed

Preheat oven to broil. In small mixing bowl, toss breadcrumbs with 1 tablespoon melted butter; set aside.

In separate mixing bowl, combine cheese, mayonnaise, wine and parsley; set aside.

In medium sauté pan, cook scallops in 2 tablespoons butter over medium heat until opaque, about 5 to 6 minutes. Remove scallops from heat, drain and set aside. In same pan, sauté mushrooms and onions in 2 tablespoons butter over medium heat for 3 to 4 minutes.

Add vegetable mixture to cheese mixture; stir to combine. Add scallops to vegetables and cheese and spoon into individual pastry shells. Sprinkle with breadcrumbs and broil 4 inches from heat until golden brown, about 2 to 4 minutes.

CRAB CAKES WITH CUCUMBER SALAD

· ·

Make 16 cakes

CUCUMBER HERB SALAD

2 cups cucumber, seeded and julienned

2 teaspoons fresh dill, finely chopped

1 teaspoon fresh tarragon, finely chopped

1 teaspoon fresh Italian parsley, finely chopped

2 tablespoons lemon juice

3 tablespoons olive oil

salt and pepper, to taste

CRAB CAKES

¼ cup mayonnaise

2 tablespoons Dijon mustard

1 teaspoon sugar

1 teaspoon lemon juice

1 teaspoon Worcestershire sauce

2 teaspoons hot sauce

¼ red bell pepper, finely diced

¼ green bell pepper, finely diced

¼ yellow bell pepper, finely diced

1 pound jumbo lump crab meat

1 ½ cups Panko breadcrumbs

4 tablespoons olive oil, divided

In a medium serving bowl, mix cucumber, herbs, lemon juice and oil until cucumber is completely coated; season with salt and pepper to taste. Set aside until ready to serve.

Preheat oven to 375. In a large mixing bowl, gently combine all crab cake ingredients except olive oil. Using a ⅛ cup, measure out 16 cakes. Heat 1 tablespoon olive oil a large non-stick sauté pan over medium heat. Sear 4 to 6 cakes until golden brown, about 3 to 4 minutes. Turn cakes over and sear for an additional 2 minutes. Place on a parchment lined baking sheet. Repeat with remaining cakes. Bake in oven for about 6 to 8 minutes.

25

CRAB CROSTINI

● ●

Serves 10

8 ounces lump fin crabmeat

$^1/_2$ cup red bell peppers, finely diced

2 tablespoons mayonnaise

2 tablespoons fresh parsley, chopped

1 tablespoon chives

1 tablespoon lime juice

1 tablespoon Dijon mustard

2 teaspoons aged Monterey Jack cheese, grated

4 - 5 drops hot sauce

$^1/_4$ teaspoon Old Bay Seasoning

$^1/_2$ French baguette, sliced diagonally into $^1/_4$-inch slices

Preheat oven to 500° and place top rack in over 4 inches from broiler. Line cookie sheet with foil and set aside.

In medium mixing bowl, combine crabmeat, peppers, mayonnaise, parsley, chives, lime juice, mustard, cheese, hot sauce and seasoning. Spread one tablespoon of crab mixture on each slice of bread. Place crostini on lined cookie sheet and broil until golden brown, about 5 to 6 minutes.

CRAB PUFFS WITH LIME SAUCE

Makes 36

LIME SAUCE

¹/₄ - ¹/₂ cup olive oil

1 garlic clove, minced

¹/₈ cup fresh lime juice + zest of 1 lime

2 tablespoons honey

1 teaspoon Dijon mustard

6 tablespoons mayonnaise (substitute
    with plain yogurt, if desired)

1 teaspoon capers, chopped

CRAB PUFF

1 cup all purpose flour

¹/₂ teaspoon salt

¹/₄ teaspoon pepper

1 teaspoon baking powder

¹/₄ teaspoon cayenne pepper (optional)

2 tablespoons butter

1 cup milk

1 tablespoon lemon zest

2 teaspoons lemon juice

2 eggs

4 egg whites

¹/₄ cup green onions, chopped

¹/₄ cup corn

¹/₄ cup roasted red peppers, chopped

¹/₄ cup zucchini, chopped

¹/₄ cup red onions, chopped

1 tablespoon Thai chili pepper

¹/₄ cup fresh cilantro, chopped

1 pound crabmeat, finely shredded

Preheat oven to 425° and grease a baking sheet. In a medium mixing bowl, whisk together all Lime Sauce ingredients until well combined. Refrigerate until ready to serve.

In a medium mixing bowl, combine flour, salt, pepper, baking powder and cayenne pepper; mix and set aside.

In a medium saucepan over medium-high heat combine butter, milk, lemon zest and juice; bring to a boil. Add flour mixture, stirring constantly with a wooden spoon for about 30 seconds, until mixture forms a ball and pulls away from sides of pan; remove from heat. Transfer mixture to a large mixing bowl and add eggs one at a time, beating well after each addition. Add egg whites one at a time, beating well after each addition.

In a separate bowl, combine remaining ingredients; pour ingredients into puff mixture and mix gently to combine.

Spoon rounded teaspoons of mixture onto prepared baking sheet; bake for 10 minutes in preheated oven then reduce heat to 350° and bake an additional 15 to 20 minutes until crab puffs are golden brown. Serve with Lime Sauce.

CRUNCHY POTATO WEDGES WITH PECAN ROMESCO SAUCE

Serves 6 - 8

2 ancho chiles

³/₄ cup olive oil, divided

¹/₂ cup pecan pieces

2 tablespoons breadcrumbs

3 garlic cloves, chopped

1 pound tomatoes, chopped

1 cup green olives, pitted

2 tablespoons fresh Italian parsley, chopped

1 tablespoon fig balsamic vinegar (may substitute with balsamic vinegar)

4 tablespoons paprika

1 teaspoon coriander

2 teaspoons cumin

3 teaspoons fresh thyme

1 tablespoon salt

1 teaspoon pepper

4 pounds Yukon Gold potatoes, cut into wedges

Preheat oven to 450°. Soak ancho chiles in hot water for 20 minutes. Stem, seed and chop chiles; set aside.

Heat ¹/₂ cup olive oil in a large frying pan over medium heat, add pecans and breadcrumbs; toast lightly until golden brown. Place in food processor and pulse several times to combine. Add peppers, garlic, tomatoes, olives, parsley and vinegar and pulse into a coarse paste.

Meanwhile, in a large mixing bowl, combine remaining ¹/₄ cup olive oil with paprika, coriander, cumin, thyme, salt and pepper. Add potatoes and toss until evenly coated. Place potatoes on baking sheet, peel sides down and bake for 25 minutes on top rack.

Pour sauce over potato wedges or serve on the side

FIG MASCARPONE PIZZA

PIZZA DOUGH

1 cup warm water (100°)

1 packaged active dry yeast

3 cups all purpose flour

2 teaspoons sea salt

2 teaspoons olive oil

PIZZA FILLING

14 figs, quartered

1 cup red wine

2 teaspoons fresh thyme, chopped

2 tablespoons olive oil

2 small vidalia onions, cut in half and
thinly sliced

8 ounces Mascarpone cheese, cut into
slices

1 slice prosciutto, cut into 2 inch strips

Preheat oven to 400°. Combine yeast and water in a small bowl and let stand for about 15 minutes, or until it turns creamy and foams.

Meanwhile, in a large mixing bowl, combine flour and sea salt. Pour yeast on top of flour and mix on medium for 15 minutes with a mixer with a dough hook. If mixing by hand, mix in the bowl until combined. Remove dough from bowl and using a push-pull technique, knead the dough with the heel of your hand and fingers for about 20 minutes. Dough should be smooth and elastic.

Swirl olive oil around in a large bowl, place dough in bowl and cover with plastic wrap. Place in a warm spot (top of the preheating oven) for 1 hour or until it doubles in size.

Preheat grill to medium. In a small saucepan over medium-high heat, bring figs, wine and thyme to a boil. Reduce heat to medium and simmer for about 15 minutes or until wine is syrupy.

Meanwhile, heat a large sauté pan over high heat. Add olive oil and sauté onions for about 2 minutes. Turn heat down to medium and continue to cook for 5 to 8 minutes, tossing from time to time until onions reach a golden color.

Divide risen dough into 6 balls. Roll each ball out to about 6 inches and fold up the edges to create a $1/4$-inch lip. Evenly distribute onions among crusts, followed by figs and cheese. Brush edges with olive oil and transfer to a baking sheet. Generously grease grill with oil and place pizzas on grates. Grill for 10 to 12 minutes, rotating crusts from time to time.

GOAT CHEESE CANAPÉS

1 French baguette, cut into ½-inch slices

16 ounces Goat cheese crumbles

2 eggs, separated

½ teaspoon black pepper

2 tablespoons fresh chives, minced

pinch of salt

Preheat oven to 350°. Place baguette slices on a baking sheet and toast on one side for 15 to 20 minutes until golden brown. Remove from oven and set aside; increase oven temperature to 425°.

Place cheese, egg yolks and pepper into a food processor and process until well mixed; remove mixture to a mixing bowl and fold in chives. In a separate mixing bowl, whisk egg whites with a pinch of salt until they form soft peaks; fold into cheese mixture.

For best results, use a pastry tube with a star tip and pipe equal amount of filling onto the untoasted side of each baguette slice (approximately 2 tablespoons per slice). If not using a pastry tube, simply place a dollop of filling onto each slice using a tablespoon.

Place prepared canapés into preheated oven and bake about 10 minutes until cheese is golden. Garnish each canapé with the pointed end of a chive and serve warm.

GRILLED HALLOUMI
OPEN FACED SANDWICHES

Serves 4 - 6

1 tablespoon olive oil

1 (8.8 ounce) package Halloumi cheese

SOURDOUGH

zest of 2 lemons

1 teaspoon fresh thyme

$1/8$ cup olive oil

1 small sourdough loaf, cut into $1/2$-inch thick slices

HERBED GREENS

4 cups baby greens

$1/2$ cup fresh Italian parsley leaves

2 tablespoons chives, roughly chopped

1 teaspoon fresh tarragon, chopped

1 tablespoon Blackberry Balsamic with Fig (can substitute with balsamic vinegar)

$1/2$ teaspoon ground coriander

1 tablespoon olive oil

Preheat grill to high heat. Combine lemon zest, thyme and olive oil and rub on sourdough loaf. Set aside.

Meanwhile, combine baby greens, Italian parsley, chives and tarragon. Set aside in the refrigerator. Combine Balsamic Vinegar, ground coriander and olive oil and set aside.

Place bread on preheated grill. Toast for about 1 to 2 minutes, turn $1/4$ turn and cook another 1 to 2 minutes, making sure not to burn the bread. Flip bread over and cook for an additional 2 minutes. Set aside.

Brush grill with oil and grill cheese. Cook for about 2 minutes, turn $1/4$ turn and cook another 2 minutes. Remove from grill and place on top of bread.

Toss herbed greens and vinaigrette together and place on top of cheese and sour dough.

HERBED CHEESE CANAPÉS

● ●

Makes 30 canapés

1 (8 ounce) package cream cheese

1 tablespoon horseradish

$3/4$ cup Swiss or Gruyère cheese, shredded

$1/2$ cup walnuts, chopped

1 - 2 tablespoons fresh chives, finely chopped

salt and pepper, to taste

$1/4$ teaspoon ground mustard

30 phyllo pastry shells, thawed

Preheat oven to 400°. In a large mixing bowl, combine cream cheese, horseradish and cheese until well blended. Fold in walnuts and chives and season with salt, pepper and ground mustard.

Spoon mixture into phyllo cups and bake for 12 to 15 minutes or until golden brown and bubbly.

MAPLE RUM CHICKEN DRUMMETTES

Makes 12

¼ cup butter

¾ cup tomato sauce

¼ cup blood orange vinegar (can
  substitute with champagne vinegar)

¼ cup maple syrup

2 tablespoons brown sugar, packed

1 ½ tablespoons Worcestershire sauce

2 teaspoons yellow mustard

¾ teaspoon ground black pepper,
  divided

¼ teaspoon chili powder

¼ cup dark rum

1 ½ teaspoons kosher salt

½ teaspoon pepper

12 chicken drummettes

In a large mixing bowl, whisk together all ingredients except drummettes. Add drummettes, toss to coat and marinate 3 to 4 hours in refrigerator, turning occasionally.

Preheat grill to medium heat. Remove drummettes from marinade; reserve marinade. Place drummettes on grill and cook, turning frequently, about 25 minutes until skin is crisp and juices run clear.

Meanwhile, in a saucepan over medium heat, reduce marinade for 15 to 20 minutes. Remove from heat and serve as a dipping sauce for grilled drummettes.

MEDITERRANEAN SUN-DRIED TOMATO SPREAD

Serves 8 - 10

2 (8 ounce) packages cream cheese, softened

1 package Italian salad dressing mix

2 teaspoons onions, minced

1 tablespoon balsamic vinegar

2 tablespoons tomato paste

3 tablespoons horseradish

$^1/_4$ cup sun-dried tomatoes packed in oil

$^1/_4$ cup mayonnaise

pimento stuffed green olives, sliced

crispy prosciutto

In large mixing bowl, beat cream cheese until smooth and fluffy.

In separate bowl, combine salad dressing mix, onions, vinegar, tomato paste, horseradish and sun-dried tomatoes. Once combined, stir in mayonnaise and beat until well blended. Add this mixture to the cream cheese and chill overnight.

Prior to serving, garnish with crispy prosciutto and olives. Serve with crackers or TFM French Rounds.

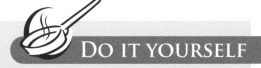 DO IT YOURSELF

HOW TO MAKE CRISPY PROSCUITTO?
Dice proscuitto and blanch by simmering in water for 5 minutes. Drain and sear in a small skillet over medium heat until crisp, about 8 - 10 minutes. Great as a topping for salads as well!

NEPTUNE'S SEA CAKES

Makes 12 cakes

1 ½ pounds cod

water (enough to cover fish)

1 lemon, sliced thin

2 tablespoons peppercorns (optional)

1 small potato, diced, cooked and
    mashed

4 tablespoons mayonnaise

2 teaspoons dried parsley

1 cup green onions, finely chopped

2 eggs, beaten

2 tablespoons olive oil

2 tablespoons all purpose flour

2 tablespoons butter

1 cup white wine

1 cup heavy cream

2 tablespoons fresh dill, chopped

salt and pepper, to taste

½ pound (21 - 25 ct) shrimp, peeled &
    deveined, rough chopped

caviar, for garnish (optional)

In a large sauté pan over medium-high heat, add cod and cover with water, lemon slices and peppercorns; bring to a boil. Reduce heat to simmer and poach fish for 10 minutes, or until it begins to flake. Remove from heat, drain excess water and place fish in a bowl. Using a fork, flake the fish and set aside.

In a large mixing bowl, combine flaked codfish, mashed potato, mayonnaise, parsley, green onions and eggs; stir to gently mix. Refrigerate at least 4 hours.

Preheat oven to 425°. Heat 2 tablespoons oil in a sauté pan over medium heat. Form sea cake mixture into 2 inch cakes about ½-inch thick. Pan-sear cakes on each side. Place in a baking dish and bake for 20 to 30 minutes or until golden brown.

Meanwhile, in a 4-quart saucepan over medium-low heat, mix flour and butter, continuously stirring until color reaches a light caramel. Whisk in wine, heavy cream, dill, salt and pepper; increase heat to medium-high and bring to a boil, allowing sauce to thicken. Add shrimp and cook for 5 minutes or until shrimp are pink.

To serve, place cooked sea cakes on a serving platter; ladle shrimp sauce over cakes and place caviar on top of each cake, if desired.

ONION APPLE TARTLETS

• •

Serves 8 - 10

1 tablespoon butter

2 sweet onions, cut into ¼-inch slices

1 tablespoon brown sugar, packed

2 (9-inch) pie crusts

½ cup apple butter

½ cup Feta cheese

Preheat oven to 350°. Heat butter in a large sauté pan over medium-low heat until melted; add onions and sauté 15 minutes stirring only once. Stir in brown sugar and increase heat to medium; cook another 10 to 15 minutes until onions are brown and very soft.

Meanwhile, gently roll out pie crusts and cut into 2-inch squares. Gently roll up a small lip on each side of the square and place on a greased cookie sheet; spread 1 to 2 tablespoons of apple butter in the center of each square. Once onions are caramelized, place an equal amount on top of apple butter in each pie crust square; sprinkle cheese equally over each square.

Place tartlets in preheated oven and bake 10 minutes until cheese is bubbling and crust is lightly browned. Remove and let cool slightly; serve warm.

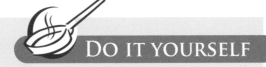 DO IT YOURSELF

HOMEMADE APPLE BUTTER
Peel, core and slice 4 Fuji apples. Puree in a food proceesor or blender until smooth. Add to a 4 -quart saucepan over high heat and bring to a boil. Add 1 ½ cups Demerara sugar, 1 teaspoon lemon zest, ¼ teaspon allspice and ⅛ teaspoon gound cloves; reduce to low for 3 - 3 ½ hours. Refrigerate until ready to serve.

ORIENTAL-STYLE CHICKEN DRUMMETTES

2 - 3 pounds chicken drummettes

¾ cup teriyaki sauce

¼ cup soy sauce

3 teaspoons sugar

¼ cup white wine

¼ teaspoon Chinese 5 Spice

2 garlic cloves, mashed

Whisk together all ingredients except drummettes in a resealable container. Once combined, add drummettes and refrigerate for 16 hours or overnight.

When ready to cook, preheat oven to 325°. Pour chicken mixture into a 9x13-inch baking dish and bake for 1 ½ to 2 hours.

PECAN DIP

· ·

Makes 2 cups

1 cup pecans, chopped

24 ounces Mascarpone cheese

1 tablespoon pimentos, chopped

1 small onion, grated

1 tablespoon Worcestershire sauce

$\frac{1}{4}$ teaspoon hot sauce

$\frac{1}{2}$ teaspoon salt

$\frac{1}{2}$ teaspoon pepper

$\frac{1}{2}$ cup mayonnaise

1 teaspoon garlic

Preheat oven to 300°. Spread pecans on cookie sheet and toast for 15 to 20 minutes, stirring occasionally.

In medium mixing bowl, combine pecans with all remaining ingredients. Serve with chips, crackers or TFM French Rounds.

PEPPERONI STUFFED MUSHROOMS

Makes 12

2 tablespoons butter

12 large white mushrooms, stems removed and chopped, caps in tact

1 medium onion, chopped

¼ cup green bell pepper, chopped

1 garlic clove, minced

1 saltine cracker, crushed

½ pound hard salami (capricola), chopped

3 tablespoons Asiago cheese, grated

¼ teaspoon dried oregano

¼ teaspoon salt

¼ teaspoon pepper

4 tablespoons chicken broth

water, for bottom of pan

3 - 4 tablespoons sherry

1 teaspoon dried tarragon, optional

Preheat oven to 350°. In medium sauté pan, melt butter over medium heat and sauté mushroom stems, onion, bell pepper and garlic until onions are translucent. Add cracker crumbs, salami, cheese and seasonings, stir to combine. Add enough chicken broth to form a stuffing consistency.

Fill mushroom caps with stuffing mixture and place in shallow baking dish. Fill bottom of baking dish with about ¼-inch water, sherry and tarragon. Bake uncovered for 25 minutes.

PHYLLO CHICKEN TRIANGLES

1 tablespoon olive oil

2 boneless, skinless chicken breasts
   (about 1 pound)

1 apple, diced

2 celery stalks, diced

8 ounces Brie cheese, rind removed,
   cubed

2 green onions, chopped

1 tablespoon lemon juice

1 cup mayonnaise

salt and pepper, to taste

1 package phyllo dough

1 stick butter, melted

½ cup pecans, finely chopped

Preheat oven to 350°. Heat olive oil in a medium sauté pan over medium heat and sear chicken 8 to 10 minutes, turning halfway through. Transfer chicken to a baking dish; place in preheated oven and bake for 12 to 15 minutes until done. Remove from oven, shred with a fork and then chill in refrigerator until cold (the chicken can be cooked a day ahead and refrigerated until ready to use).

In a medium mixing bowl, combine chicken, apple, celery, Brie, green onions, lemon juice and mayonnaise; stir until well coated and season with salt and pepper to taste.

Increase oven temperature to 375°. Lay 1 sheet of phyllo on a clean surface; brush with melted butter. Lay another sheet on top, matching edges; repeat with 2 more sheets, brushing with melted butter in between layers (should be 4 sheets total). Gently press phyllo together and cut into 8 equal squares (some trimming will be necessary to ensure that squares are all the same size). Repeat procedure 2 additional times, so you have 24 squares total.

Position a square in front of you so that it looks like a diamond; brush top 2 edges with melted butter and place 1 tablespoon of chopped pecans in the middle. Place 2 ½ tablespoons of chicken mixture on top of pecans; fold bottom corner of phyllo over chicken mixture until it meets the top corner (this should create a triangle shape) and press edges together to seal. Repeat with remaining 23 squares; place prepared phyllo triangles on a baking sheet and bake in preheated oven 20 minutes until golden brown.

PICKLED SHRIMP

¼ cup ketchup

½ cup vegetable oil

½ cup vinegar

2 teaspoons sugar

2 teaspoons salt

½ teaspoon dry mustard

2 tablespoons Worcestershire sauce

1 bay leaf

1 small yellow onion, thinly sliced

1 small white onion, thinly sliced

2 pounds (26 - 30 ct) cooked shrimp

In large mixing bowl, whisk together ketchup, oil, vinegar, sugar, salt, mustard, Worcestershire sauce and then add bay leaf (be careful not to crush bay leaf). Add onions and shrimp to marinade, cover and refrigerate for at least 2 hours before serving. Remove bay leaf before serving.

PROSCIUTTO & SWISS DIP

Makes 3 ½ cups

2 tablespoons olive oil

4 - 6 ounces prosciutto, cut into 1-inch
pieces

1 (8 ounce) package cream cheese,
softened

½ cup mayonnaise

2 cups Swiss cheese, shredded

1 medium yellow onion, chopped

Preheat oven to 350°. Heat olive oil in a frying pan over medium-high heat. Render prosciutto until crispy, about 5 minutes. Remove from pan and place on a plate with paper towels.

In a bowl, blend cream cheese, mayonnaise, Swiss cheese and onion. Spread into a 7x11-inch baking dish. Sprinkle prosciutto over top. Bake for 20 to 30 minutes or until bubbly.

Serve with crackers, TFM French Rounds or vegetables.

PORTABELLA PARADISE

Serves 10 - 12

3 tablespoons olive oil

2 medium onions, chopped

1 - 2 garlic cloves, minced

6 - 8 portabella mushrooms, sliced

½ lemon, freshly squeezed

¾ bunch fresh parsley, chopped

8 slices of crusty bread, toasted

5 - 6 ounces Gorgonzola cheese,
    crumbled (or Blue cheese)

Preheat broiler to 450° and place top rack 6 inches from heat source. Heat oil in a large sauté pan over medium heat; add onions and garlic and sauté 5 to 7 minutes until slightly brown. Stir in portabella mushrooms until coated evenly with oil; sprinkle with lemon juice. Sauté about 5 minutes until mushrooms are tender; stir in parsley and remove from heat.

Place bread on a baking sheet in a single layer; spoon an equal amount of mushroom mixture on top of each slice of bread. Sprinkle crumbled cheese on top and broil for 2 minutes or until cheese melts and is golden brown.

ROASTED RED PEPPER &
GOAT CHEESE APPETIZER

Makes 12 pieces

1 tablespoon olive oil

2 tablespoons garlic, minced

$\frac{1}{2}$ cup sweet onions, sliced

4 ounces Goat cheese, crumbled

1 roma tomato, seeded and diced

1 tablespoon fresh cilantro, chopped

1 tablespoon fresh parsley, chopped

$\frac{1}{4}$ tablespoon hot sauce

salt and pepper, to taste

1 red bell pepper

In medium sauté pan, heat olive oil over medium heat and sauté garlic and onions until translucent, about 5 to 6 minutes. Remove from heat and allow to cool to room temperature. Once cool, add Goat cheese, tomato, cilantro, parsley, hot sauce, salt and pepper. Stir to combine. Place in refrigerator.

Trim stem from red pepper and cut in half to from top to bottom; remove seeds. Rub sides of pepper with olive oil and season with salt and pepper. Bake for 5 minutes, until softened. Cool upside down to drain juices, about 2 hours.

Preheat oven to 350°. Fill pepper with Goat cheese mixture and bake in shallow baking dish for an additional 15 minutes. Cut pepper into wedges and serve immediately.

ROSEMARY SHRIMP SKEWERS WITH LEMON GARLIC PESTO

Makes 8

LEMON GARLIC PESTO

1/2 cup pine nuts

1 garlic clove, minced

juice and zest of 2 lemons

1/2 cup olive oil

SHRIMP SKEWERS

24 (21-25 ct) shrimp, peeled & deveined

1/8 cup olive oil

1/4 teaspoon red pepper flakes

2 tablespoons lemon juice

1 tablespoon fresh thyme, chopped

8 rosemary sprigs, leaves removed

Pulse all pesto ingredients in a food processor until they form a paste. Remove and set aside.

Place shrimp in a single layer in a baking dish. In a small mixing bowl, whisk together olive oil, red pepper flakes, lemon juice and thyme; pour over shrimp. Set aside for 30 minutes.

When ready to cook, preheat grill to medium heat and lightly oil the grates to prevent sticking. Skewer shrimp onto rosemary sprigs and grill for 5 to 6 minutes per side or until pink. Arrange skewers on a serving platter and serve with Lemon Garlic Pesto.

Shrimp Quesadilla Palenque

Makes 6 wedges

½ pound (26-30 ct) cooked shrimp, chilled and cut into quarters

3 tablespoons chipotle sauce

3 teaspoons smoked paprika

4 (6-inch) tortillas

8 ounces Mexican shredded cheese

½ cup fresh cilantro, chopped

1 small mango, diced

2 green onions, chopped

In a small mixing bowl, combine shrimp, chipotle sauce and paprika. Heat a large frying pan over medium heat; spray one side of first tortilla with cooking spray and lay greased side down in pan.

Place half of the shrimp mixture and half of each of the remaining ingredients onto the tortilla and place a second tortilla on top; spray top of second tortilla with cooking spray and flip once first side has browned, about 3 to 4 minutes. Cook on other side until second side is browned and cheese is melted; cut into 6 wedges. Repeat with remaining ingredients. Serve warm.

Smoked Gouda & Wild Mushroom Dip

Makes 6 cups

2 tablespoons butter

3 cups white, portabella or shiitake mushrooms, stems removed and caps chopped

1 tablespoon garlic, minced

2 cups half & half

4 (8 ounce) packages cream cheese

3 cups smoked Gouda, shredded

2 cups spinach, roughly chopped

salt and pepper, to taste

In medium sauté pan, melt butter over medium heat and sauté mushrooms and garlic until soft, about 6 to 8 minutes. Remove from heat and set aside.

In medium saucepan, combine half & half, cream cheese and Gouda over low heat. Stir constantly until ingredients have incorporated. Add mushroom mixture and spinach to cheese mixture.

Season with salt and pepper and serve immediately with crackers, TFM French Rounds or fresh vegetables for dipping.

SMOKED SALMON PILLOWS WITH OLD BAY AIOLI

. . . .

Makes 24

OLD BAY AIOLI

1 teaspoon Dijon mustard

1 tablespoon Old Bay Seasoning

1 teaspoon lemon juice

$^3/_4$ cup mayonnaise

SMOKED SALMON PILLOWS

4 ounces smoked salmon, diced

4 ounces cream cheese

5 ounces Goat cheese

1 $^1/_2$ tablespoons capers, drained

1 tablespoon dried dill

1 teaspoon dried tarragon

salt and pepper, to taste

1 package puff pastry, thawed

1 egg, beaten

In a small mixing bowl, combine mustard, Old Bay, lemon juice and mayonnaise. Chill until ready to serve.

Preheat oven to 425°. Combine salmon, cream cheese, Goat cheese, capers, dill and tarragon with an electric mixer; on medium speed for 1 minute. Season with salt and pepper to taste.

Place thawed puff pastry sheets on a lightly floured surface and roll out to $^1/_2$ the thickness. On one sheet of pastry, place about 8 dollops (2 tablespoons each dollop) of smoked salmon mixture. Brush egg wash around each dollop, then lay another pastry sheet on top, making 8 pockets. Cut into 8 squares, then repeat entire process using remaining 4 pastry sheets.

Transfer squares to a greased baking sheet and brush tops with egg wash; bake in preheated oven for 16 minutes. Serve warm with Old Bay Aioli.

Smokey Cheddar Mini Burgers

Serves 12

4 slices applewood smoked bacon

½ pound ground beef

½ pound ground pork

3 ounces aged Cheddar cheese, shredded

2 tablespoons onion flakes

1 teaspoon paprika

1 garlic clove, minced

1 Ciabatta loaf, cut in half then into 2-inch slices

Preheat grill to high. Lightly coat grill grates with olive oil to prevent sticking. Grill bacon slices for 2 minutes per side; remove from heat, crumble and set aside. Reduce grill heat to medium-high.

In a large mixing bowl, fold together ground beef, ground pork, bacon crumbles, Cheddar cheese, onion flakes, paprika and garlic. Use a tablespoon to form mini burger patties.

Grill patties over medium-high heat for 2 to 3 minutes per side, or until well browned. Meanwhile, toast Ciabatta bread slices for 30 to 45 seconds per side on grill.

Serve mini burgers on toasted Ciabatta bread and top with your favorite burger fixings.

SPICY BOMBAY SLIDERS

SAUCE

½ cup mayonnaise

½ cup Greek yogurt

1 tablespoon garlic chili sauce

2 - 3 tablespoons hot curry paste

1 tablespoon Demerara sugar

PATTIES

1 pound ground turkey

1 pound ground chicken

1 ½ tablespoons fresh ginger, minced

1 teaspoon cumin

1 teaspoon curry powder

1 garlic clove, minced

salt and pepper, to taste

In a small mixing bowl, whisk together mayonnaise, yogurt, chili sauce, curry paste and sugar. Refrigerate until ready to serve.

Preheat grill to medium heat. In a large mixing bowl, fold together turkey, chicken, ginger, cumin, curry powder and garlic until well combined; form ⅓ cup of mixture at a time into patties. Season patties to taste with salt and pepper; grill 4 to 5 minutes per side until done.

Excellent served over toasted baguette slices, inside a pita or simply on their own.

Spicy Panko Chicken Strips

1 pound boneless, skinless chicken breast, cut into strips

1 cup hot sauce

1 cup Panko breadcrumbs

½ cup all purpose flour

peanut or vegetable oil (for frying)

In medium mixing bowl, combine chicken and hot sauce. Cover and marinate overnight.

In separate mixing bowl, combine breadcrumbs and flour. Dredge chicken in flour mixture. Heat desired amount of oil in shallow skillet over medium heat and carefully place chicken in pan until thoroughly cooked, about 6 to 7 minutes per side.

SERVING SUGGESTION

Excellent served with Buttermilk Ranch Dressing, on page 82.

STUFFED BAKED PEARS

. . . .

Makes 16 pieces

4 medium pears, peeled and cut in quarters

½ cup olive oil

salt and pepper, to taste

3 tablespoons Wensleydale with Cranberries cheese, crumbled

½ pound prosciutto, thinly sliced

Preheat oven to 375°. In medium mixing bowl, toss pears with oil, salt and pepper. Place pears on cookie sheet, cut side down, and bake for 20 minutes. Remove from oven and set aside.

Place crumbled cheese in scooped out portion of pears and wrap with 2 to 3 prosciutto slices. Place scoop side up on baking sheet and bake an additional 20 to 25 minutes, or until cheese has fully melted. Serve warm.

STUFFED GRAPE LEAVES

1 cup long-grain rice

¼ cup pine nuts

¼ cup currants

1 cup olive oil

8 cups onions, finely chopped

¼ cup fresh parsley, finely chopped

¼ cup fresh dill, finely chopped

1 teaspoon fresh mint, chopped

juice of 1 lemon

2 jars grape leaves

2 cups warm water

8 ounces Feta cheese, crumbled

Preheat oven to 350°. Soak rice, pine nuts and currants in warm water for 30 minutes; strain well. In large sauté pan, heat olive oil and sauté onions, parsley, dill, mint and lemon juice for 10 to 15 minutes. Remove from heat, combine with rice mixture and set aside.

Rinse grape leaves and place small amount of rice mixture on each leaf. If desired, top with feta cheese at this point. Then, fold in the sides of each leaf so that the mixture cannot fall out. As each leaf is stuffed, place in a shallow baking dish very close together forming tight layers. Top baking dish with remaining grape leaves and place a heavy oven-safe plate on top, allowing the weight of the plate to keep the leaves tightly rolled as they are cooked. Add 2 cups of water to baking dish and allow to slowly simmer in oven for 2 hours. Remove to a serving platter and refrigerate. Serve cold.

DID YOU KNOW?

Working with Grape Leaves can sometimes be difficult. Grape Leaves typically come in two styles. The first style is solid all the way across the leaf with peaks at the end. These are the best to use for sutffing. The second style of leaf looks similar in shape to New England oak leaf. These are more challenging to roll. Use the second type of leaf to line the bottom and sides of the pan. Remember: Rolling grape leaves is a skill, the tighter the rolls, the better the stuffed grape leaves will come out.

TOMATO PESTO TART

2 ½ cups + 3 tablespoons fresh basil, divided

1 garlic clove, minced

¾ cup pecans, toasted

¼ cup fresh Italian parsley, chopped

2 - 3 ice cubes

¾ cup Parmesan cheese, divided

¾ cup olive oil

salt and pepper, to taste

1 (8 ounce) frozen pie crust, thawed

3 tablespoons water, ice cold

2 cups Mozzarella cheese, shredded

5 plum tomatoes, sliced

½ cup mayonnaise

½ teaspoon black pepper

Preheat oven to 425°. Combine 2 ½ cups basil, garlic, pecans, parsley, ice, ½ cup Parmesan cheese, olive oil, salt and pepper in a food processor or blender; process until well combined (mixture should still be fairly chunky). Set aside.

Place pie crust in a 12-inch pie pan (roll out first if necessary); brush outer 1-inch of pie crust with water, fold edges over and crimp. Prick the bottom of the crust several times with a fork and bake in oven 8 to 10 minutes until golden. Remove from oven and sprinkle 1 cup Mozzarella cheese over bottom of pie crust; arrange tomato slices decoratively on top of cheese and set aside.

Reduce oven temperature to 375°. In a medium mixing bowl combine remaining Mozzarella, mayonnaise, ¼ cup Parmesan cheese, pepper and ⅔ cup prepared pesto; spread mixture evenly over tomato slices. Bake in preheated oven 20 to 25 minutes until cheese melts; sprinkle with basil and serve with remaining pesto on the side.

SHORT CUT

TIP FOR MAKING PESTO
When making pesto, add an ice cube to your food processor prior to processing. The ice will help to keep the basil leaves green when the food processor is turned on and becomes hot.

TROPICAL SHRIMP FIESTA

Serves 12 - 15

1 ½ pounds (26 - 30 ct) cooked shrimp

2 tablespoons jerk spice blend

3 tablespoons olive oil

4 ounces pineapple, diced

4 green onions, thinly sliced

¼ cup red bell peppers, diced

¼ cup yellow bell peppers, diced

2 garlic cloves, minced

½ mango, diced

juice and zest of 2 limes

½ cup coconut flakes

Place shrimp, jerk spice blend and oil in an airtight container; mix thoroughly and store in refrigerator for 24 hours.

In a medium mixing bowl, combine pineapple, onion, bell peppers, garlic, mango, lime juice and zest. Place shrimp on a serving platter, pour pineapple mixture over shrimp and sprinkle coconut evenly on top.

Serve with toothpicks.

Turkey Burgers with Goat Cheese

Makes 10 small burgers

$1/8$ cup pecans, chopped

1 $1/2$ teaspoons lemon zest

1 tablespoon fresh thyme, chopped

6 tablespoons peppered Goat cheese

1 pound ground lean turkey

$1/2$ teaspoon salt

In a small mixing bowl, mix pecans, lemon zest, thyme and Goat cheese until well combined; set aside.

In a large mixing bowl, fold together turkey and salt. Divide turkey into 20 equal portions then flatten each portion to 3 inches around. Place about 1 tablespoon of Goat cheese mixture onto 10 of the burger patties then top with an additional patty, making 10 stuffed burgers total.

Heat olive oil in a large non-stick frying pan over medium heat, cook for about 8 to 10 minutes per side.

VEAL STUFFED MUSHROOMS

2 tablespoons butter

2 tablespoons olive oil, divided

4 shallots, finely chopped

1 pound ground veal

⅓ cup breadcrumbs

1 egg

¼ cup Parmesan cheese

2 tablespoons fresh parsley, finely chopped

½ teaspoon dried thyme

½ teaspoon dried chervil

30 white mushrooms, reserve and chop stems

Preheat oven to 400°. Heat butter and 1 tablespoon olive oil in a sauté pan over medium-high heat; add shallots and sauté until translucent.

In a large mixing bowl, combine remaining ingredients including chopped mushroom stems but not mushroom caps; add shallots and mix until well combined. Stuff equal amount of mixture into each mushroom cap. Brush 1 tablespoon of olive oil on baking dish; place mushrooms in a single layer on dish and bake in preheated oven 30 minutes. Serve warm.

WATER CHESTNUT DIP

Makes 2 cups

1 cup mayonnaise

1 cup sour cream

¼ cup onions, finely chopped

¼ cup fresh parsley, chopped

½ pound water chestnuts, finely
   chopped

2 garlic cloves, minced

1 tablespoon soy sauce

⅛ teaspoon salt

In a medium mixing bowl, combine mayonnaise and sour cream; stir in onion, parsley, water chestnuts, garlic, soy sauce and salt, mixing until well combined. Cover and refrigerate overnight; transfer to a serving bowl and serve chilled.

Excellent served with vegetables, crackers or TFM French Rounds.

pre

APPETIZERS

SOUPS

SALADS

Butternut Squash & White Cheddar Soup

4 tablespoons butter

1 medium onion, diced

2 celery stalks, diced

1 (4 - 5 pound) butternut squash, peeled, seeded and diced

4 tablespoons all purpose flour

$\frac{1}{2}$ teaspoon ground nutmeg

1 $\frac{1}{2}$ quarts chicken broth

1 cup half & half

1 cup white Cheddar cheese, grated

In large saucepan, melt butter over medium heat and sauté onion, celery and squash for approximately 10 minutes. Add flour and nutmeg to vegetable mixture to form a roux and cook over medium heat for 5 minutes, stirring often. Add chicken broth and bring to a boil, reduce heat and simmer on low for 5 minutes. Add half & half and cheese and purée with a blender until smooth. Serve warm.

CILANTRO CHICKEN SOUP

Serves 4

2 split chicken breasts

6 cups chicken broth

$\frac{1}{4}$ cup olive oil

$\frac{1}{4}$ -$\frac{1}{2}$ cup thin spaghetti, broken into bite-size pieces

salt and pepper, to taste

1 large avocado, pitted and diced

1 - 2 tablespoons cilantro, chopped

4 green onions, finely chopped

In Dutch oven, cook chicken breasts in chicken broth over medium-high heat until tender. Once cooked through, about 25 minutes, remove chicken, cut into bite-size pieces, removing bones, and set aside; reserve broth.

In large stockpot, add oil and pasta and gently sauté until slightly brown, approximately 8 minutes. Add reserved chicken broth to pasta and cook until al dente, according to the package directions. Add chicken and simmer for 10 minutes. Season to taste with salt and pepper.

Top with avocado, cilantro and green onions prior to serving

COLORADO GREEN CHILI

1 tablespoon olive oil

½ pound applewood smoked bacon, diced (about 10 slices)

2 pounds pork loin, cut into 1-inch cubes

1 large yellow onion, chopped

3 garlic cloves, minced

2 anaheim chiles, chopped

1 ancho chile, chopped

2 jalapeños, chopped

1 banana pepper, chopped

2 cups vegetable broth

2 cups chicken broth

2 cups water

1 (16 ounce) can chopped tomatoes, including liquid

3 (4 - 5 ounce) cans chiles, chopped

4 tablespoons unsalted butter, softened

4 tablespoons all purpose flour

salt and pepper, to taste

8 ounces shredded cheese (Cheddar, Colby Jack or Monterey Jack)

In large Dutch oven, heat oil over medium-high heat. Add bacon and cook for 10 minutes. Remove bacon from pot, set aside. In same pot, add pork and sear for 3 to 5 minutes, until browned on all sides; remove from pot and set aside. Add onion, garlic, chiles and peppers to same pot, cook for 10 to 15 minutes. Add vegetable broth, chicken broth, water, tomatoes and chiles to pot and bring to a boil; cover and reduce heat to low. Simmer for 1 ½ hours, stirring occasionally.

In separate bowl, combine butter and flour with a fork. Stir mixture into soup, increase to medium-high heat and bring to a boil. Add pork and bacon, reduce heat and simmer for an additional 15 minutes.

Season to taste with salt and pepper and ladle into individual bowls. Garnish with shredded cheese.

CORN CHOWDER

Serves 6 - 8

1 pound ground Italian sausage

3 garlic cloves, minced

½ cup onions, chopped

¼ cup all purpose flour

4 cups milk

1 ½ cups heavy cream

3 medium potatoes, peeled and cubed

3 ears of corn, kernels removed and cobs reserved

salt and pepper, to taste

green onions, finely chopped, for garnish

In large stockpot, brown sausage, garlic and onion over medium heat; drain. Return to pan and add flour; mix well and cook for 2 minutes, stirring constantly.

Add milk, cream, potatoes and corn to sausage mixture and bring to a boil. Add corn cobs, reduce heat to low and simmer for 1 hour.

Remove cobs, season with salt and pepper to taste. Ladle into soup bowls, garnish with green onions and serve.

SHORT CUT

FRESH CORN SUBSTITUTIONS

When in season, substitute fresh corn for canned or frozen corn in recipes. One regular ear of corn will yield about ½ cup of kernels (possibly a little more or less depending on size). You will need four ears of corn for the equivalent of a 10-ounce package of frozen corn or 3 ears for equivalent of a 15 ½ oz can of corn.

CREAM OF TOMATO & PARMESAN SOUP

Serves 4

1 (28 ounce) can peeled tomatoes, including liquid

1 tablespoon sun-dried tomato paste

1 cup heavy cream

$\frac{1}{4}$ cup fresh basil, chopped

$\frac{1}{4}$ cup fresh parsley, chopped

$\frac{1}{4}$ teaspoon salt

1 teaspoon ground black pepper

$\frac{1}{2}$ cup Parmesan cheese, grated

In blender, add tomatoes, tomato paste, heavy cream, basil, parsley, salt and pepper; pulse no more than 20 seconds until mixture is smooth.

Pour mixture into medium saucepan and cook over medium heat until heated thoroughly. Add Parmesan cheese and heat until melted.

Serve with warm Parmesan Crostinis (recipe below).

DO IT YOURSELF

PARMESAN CROSTINI

1 French baguette, sliced thin

2 tablespoons olive oil

1 teaspoon paprika

salt and pepper, to taste,

$\frac{1}{2}$ cup Parmesan Reggiano, freshly grated

Preheat oven to 400°. Place bread slice on baking sheet and brush both sides with olive oil. Season with paprika, salt and pepper and top with Parmesan Reggiano. Bake for 8 to 10 minutes, or until cheese is fully melted and golden brown.

CREAMY TOMATO BASIL SOUP

. . . .

Serves 4 - 6

1 (14 ounce) can diced tomatoes
    seasoned with garlic, basil and
    oregano

salt and pepper, to taste

³/₄ cup olive oil, divided

2 garlic cloves, minced

1 yellow onion, diced

2 carrots, diced

2 celery stalks, diced

1 cup chicken broth

1 - 2 fresh bay leaves

¹/₄ cup fresh basil, chopped

¹/₂ cup heavy cream

Preheat oven to 450°. Strain tomatoes, reserve juices. Spread single layer of tomatoes on a baking sheet, sprinkle with salt and pepper and drizzle with ¹/₄ cup olive oil. Roast tomatoes until caramelized, about 15 minutes.

In medium sauté pan, heat remaining olive oil over medium heat. Add garlic, yellow onion, carrots and celery and cook until softened, about 8 minutes. Add roasted tomatoes, reserved tomato juice, chicken broth and bay leaves. Reduce heat and simmer for 15 to 20 minutes. Add basil and heavy cream, stirring to combine; remove bay leaves. In a food processor or using a hand blender, purée until smooth.

Serve with warm crusty bread.

FENNEL & CREAMY TOMATO SOUP

Serves 10

2 tablespoons olive oil

2 - 3 garlic cloves, minced

2 teaspoons fresh thyme, chopped

1 leek, chopped & soaked, with green parts removed

2 fennel bulbs, 1 chopped and 1 thinly sliced

¼ cup dry vermouth

⅛ cup red wine

2 (28 ounce) cans crushed tomatoes

2 sticks butter

1 pint heavy cream

5 - 6 fresh basil leaves

salt and pepper, to taste

Parmesan cheese, freshly grated

In a 2-quart stockpot over medium-high heat, heat olive oil. Sauté garlic and thyme for 1 minute. Add leeks and fennel and sauté for 8 to 10 minutes. Add dry vermouth and red wine; reduce heat to medium and cook for 3 to 5 minutes. Add tomatoes, cover, reduce heat to low and simmer for 20 minutes.

Remove from heat and place in food processor or blender; purée until smooth and creamy. Return to pot over medium-low heat; add butter, cream and basil; continue to cook for 15 minutes. Season with salt and pepper to taste; remove basil leaves.

Ladle into bowls and top with Parmesan cheese.

DID YOU KNOW?

HOW TO PREPARE A LEEK?

The leaves of leeks tend to trap dirt and sand, so it is very important to wash leeks thoroughly. To prepare and clean leeks: First, remove the fibrous root; remove any tough, dark green outer leaves and trim ends of remaining leaves. Slice leek in half lengthwise and chop according to recipe; place chopped leek in a bowl of warm water and stir, allowing dirt to fall to bottom of bowl. Transfer leeks to a colander and rinse until the leeks no longer feels gritty.

ITALIAN SAUSAGE &
HARVEST VEGETABLE SOUP

½ pound ground Italian sausage

2 tablespoons olive oil

2 onions, cut into wedges

1 garlic clove, minced

1 tablespoon fresh rosemary, chopped

1 tablespoon fresh thyme, chopped

6 carrots, chopped

3 baking potatoes, peeled and cubed

3 cups tomatoes, chopped

1 cup chicken broth

1 teaspoon salt

1 teaspoon pepper

1 tablespoon fresh Italian parsley,
   chopped

Roll Italian sausage into small meatballs. In a Dutch oven over medium heat, add olive oil. Add meatballs and onions; cook for about 10 minutes or until browned. Add garlic, rosemary, thyme, carrots, potatoes, tomatoes and chicken broth and allow to come to a slow boil. Cover and simmer over low heat for 45 minutes.

Season with salt and pepper and garnish with fresh parsley before serving.

ITALIAN TURKEY & SPINACH MEATBALL SOUP

Serves 12 - 14

1 pound ground turkey

1 (10 ounce) package frozen spinach, thawed and drained

1 cup Italian style dry breadcrumbs

3 tablespoons butter

3 tablespoons olive oil

2 cups carrots, diced

2 cups celery stalks, diced

1 cup sweet onion, diced

8 ounces mushrooms, sliced

2 tablespoons Italian herb blend seasoning

3 (32 ounce) cans chicken broth

2 bay leaves

8 ounces pasta shells

croutons, for garnish

Parmesan cheese, freshly grated, for garnish

In mixing bowl, combine turkey, spinach and breadcrumbs. Roll mixture into small meatballs, about 1-inch diameter and set aside.

In large Dutch oven, melt butter and olive oil over medium-high heat. Once melted, add carrots and cook for 5 minutes. Add celery, cook for an additional 5 minutes and add onions. Cook until onions are slightly tender and add mushrooms and Italian seasoning to vegetables. Once mushrooms have browned, add chicken broth and bay leaves. Allow soup to come to a simmer, add meatballs and cook over low heat for 2 hours.

Add pasta to soup and cook an additional 20 minutes, or until pasta has cooked to desired doneness. Remove bay leaves and top with croutons and cheese before serving.

PUMPKIN SOUP WITH GRUYÈRE

¼ cup butter

1 large onion, chopped

6 cups chicken broth

1 bay leaf

2 (14 ounce) cans pumpkin puree*

1 ½ cups heavy cream

2 tablespoons orange zest

2 tablespoons orange juice

⅛ teaspoon nutmeg, freshly grated

⅛ teaspoon ginger, ground

¾ pound Gruyère cheese

salt, to taste

white pepper, to taste

Gruyère cheese, for garnish

2 tablespoons chives, chopped, for garnish

toasted pumpkin seeds, for garnish

In large saucepan, melt butter over medium heat. Add onion and sauté until tender, about 5 to 6 minutes. Add chicken broth, bay leaf and pumpkin puree and bring to a boil. Reduce heat to low, cover and simmer for about 25 minutes.

Remove from heat and using a food processor or hand blender, purée until smooth. Return mixture to pan; add cream, orange zest, orange juice, nutmeg and ginger and cook over low heat. Gradually add cheese, stirring constantly until cheese has fully melted.

Season with salt and pepper and garnish with additional cheese, chives and toasted pumpkin seeds.

SEAFOOD CHOWDER

6 tablespoons butter

2 medium onions, chopped

1 cup crabmeat

30 (51 - 60 ct) shrimp, peeled and deveined

½ pint oysters, shucked

½ pint clams, shucked

½ pound haddock, cubed

½ cup crackers, crumbled

2 cups heavy cream

2 medium potatoes, cooked and diced

salt and pepper, to taste

In large stockpot, melt butter over medium heat. Add onions and cook until tender, about 5 to 6 minutes. Add crabmeat, shrimp, oysters, clams and haddock to onions and sprinkle with crackers. Bring to a boil, then reduce heat to low. Add cream, potatoes, salt and pepper and cook for 1 hour, stirring occasionally.

To serve, ladle into bowls or serve in hollowed out bread boules.

Spicy Shrimp & Coconut Soup

Serves 15

15 garlic cloves, peeled and smashed

3 ³/₄ teaspoons coriander seeds, roasted

2 tablespoons ginger, freshly grated

zest of 7 limes

4 (14 ounce) cans coconut milk

7 sprigs of lemongrass

3 cups chicken broth

12 peppers (serrano or jalapeño)

3 pounds (51 - 60 ct) shrimp, peeled & cut in half

1 French baguette, sliced

4 tablespoons fresh basil, chopped, for garnish

In large Dutch oven over medium heat, combine 10 garlic cloves, coriander seeds, ginger, lime zest, coconut milk, lemongrass and chicken broth. Roughly chop 5 peppers and add to pot. Bring mixture to a boil and reduce heat to medium-low for 6 to 8 minutes.

Strain mixture and return liquid to pot; discard contents in strainer. Add shrimp and poach, about 8 to 10 minutes, at medium-low heat. Remove pot from heat.

Meanwhile, finely slice remaining peppers; set aside. Grill bread, or place under broiler to lightly toast. Remove from heat and rub with remaining garlic and butter. Add peppers to soup and ladle into bowls; garnish with fresh basil and grilled slice of garlic bread.

Short Cut

Roasting Coriander Seeds
In a small saute pan over medium heat, add coriander seeds and saute until the seed gives off a fragrant citrus smell, about 10 mintues

THREE BEAN STEW

2 tablespoons vegetable oil

1 medium onion, diced

1 cup red or green bell pepper, diced

1 pound kielbasa or Italian sausage, thinly sliced

½ pound (21 - 25 ct) shrimp, peeled & deveined, butterflied

1 cup black-eyed peas, cooked

1 cup garbanzo beans, cooked

1 cup red kidney beans, cooked

1 (14 ounce) can crushed tomatoes

½ teaspoon paprika

½ teaspoon red pepper flakes

½ teaspoon garlic salt

1 cup banana peppers, diced

crusty bread or flat bread

In a large saucepot over medium heat, add vegetable oil and cook onions, bell pepper, sausage and shrimp until lightly browned. Add beans and crushed tomatoes; then season with paprika, red pepper and garlic salt and add banana peppers. Simmer over medium heat for 20 minutes, stirring occasionally.

Serve hot with warm crusty bread or flat bread.

SHORT CUT

FRESH BEAN EQUIVALENTS

If you prefer to cook with dry beans instead of using canned, here are some basic measurements to keep in mind: 1 cup of dried beans equals about 3 cups of cooked beans. There is about 1 ½ cups of cooked, drained beans in a 15-oz can. ½ cup dried beans is the equivalent of 1 15-oz can cooked, drained beans.

TORTILLA SOUP
WITH FRESH AVOCADO

Serves 8

2 tablespoons olive oil

½ cup sweet onions, finely chopped

2 tablespoons chili powder

2 tablespoons tomato paste

6 skinless chicken thighs

1 teaspoon salt

2 (32 ounce) cans chicken broth

12 fresh cilantro stems

1 ½ cups tomatoes, diced

1 cup fresh corn

1 (14 ounce) can black beans, rinsed
    and drained

3 tablespoons lime juice

½ cup fresh cilantro

2 avocados, chopped

sour cream (optional)

tortilla chips

Heat olive oil in a large sauté pan over medium-high heat. Add onions and sauté for about 5 minutes or until translucent. Meanwhile, combine chili powder and tomato paste in a small bowl. Add tomato paste mixture to pan and mix into onions. Cook 2 to 3 minutes, but do not let the chili powder scorch.

Season chicken thighs with salt, place into pan with onions and turn once so they are entirely coated. Add 2 cups broth to pan and lower heat down until mixture reaches a simmer. Cover and cook mixture 30 to 40 minutes (turning chicken once), until chicken is tender when pierced with a knife. Remove chicken from pan and allow to cool. Once cool, shred chicken, discarding any bones, fat and/or gristle. Set shredded meat aside.

Add remaining chicken broth and cilantro stems to pan, stir and simmer uncovered until broth has reduced by one third, about 20 to 30 minutes. Add chicken, diced tomatoes, corn, black beans and lime juice to broth mixture. Stir in fresh cilantro and avocado just before serving.

To serve, ladle into bowls and top with a dollop of sour cream and tortilla chips.

Turkey & Andouille Sausage Stew

Serve 8 - 10

2 cups dried great northern beans

9 cups water, divided

2 pounds raw turkey breast, cut into 2-inch pieces

8 ounces Andouille sausage

1 ½ cups onions, coarsely chopped

1 ½ cups carrots, cut into ½-inch pieces

3 garlic cloves, minced

1 tablespoon chicken bouillon

3 sprigs fresh thyme, chopped

1 tablespoon dried oregano

¼ cup dry red wine

⅓ cup tomato paste

¼ cup fresh Italian parsley, julienned

Rinse beans; drain. In a large stockpot over high heat, bring beans and 6 cups cold water to a boil. Remove from heat. Cover and let stand for 1 hour; drain.

Transfer beans to a 4 to 5 quart slow cooker. In a large skillet, sear turkey for 5 to 6 minutes or until golden; remove and place in slow cooker. Cook sausage over medium-high heat until no longer pink; break into pieces while cooking. Drain fat and transfer sausage to slow cooker. Add onions, carrots and garlic to slow cooker and top with 3 cups lukewarm water, bouillon, thyme, oregano, red wine and tomato paste. Cover and cook on low heat for 7 to 8 hours.

To serve, top with fresh parsley.

WHISKEY CHILI

1 pound ground beef

$\frac{1}{2}$ pound ground pork

1 medium red onion, diced

1 small red bell pepper, diced

1 small green bell pepper, diced

2 (14.5 ounce) cans petite diced
   tomatoes

1 (8 ounce) can tomato paste

4 tablespoons chili powder

1 tablespoon cumin

1 tablespoon paprika

4 garlic cloves, minced

1 tablespoon garlic powder

$\frac{1}{2}$ teaspoon cayenne pepper

$\frac{1}{2}$ cup water

4 slices bacon

1 tablespoon cocoa powder

$\frac{1}{4}$ cup whiskey

salt and pepper, to taste

$\frac{1}{4}$ cup Cheddar cheese, grated

1 teaspoon fresh cilantro, chopped

In a large skillet, brown beef, pork, onion and peppers until cooked thoroughly and vegetables are soft. Transfer to large stockpot and add tomatoes, tomato paste, chili powder, cumin, paprika, garlic, garlic powder, cayenne pepper and water. Cover and simmer over medium heat for 1 hour, stirring occasionally.

Meanwhile, render bacon until crispy; crumble bacon and set aside for garnish.

After one hour, stir cocoa, whiskey, salt and pepper to taste into chili. Cover and simmer for 10 additional minutes.

To serve, spoon into bowls and garnish with Cheddar cheese, bacon and cilantro.

pre

APPETIZERS

SOUPS

SALADS

APPLE CHICKEN SALAD WITH ROSEMARY PECANS

Makes 4 cups

ROSEMARY PECANS

2 tablespoons butter

1 ½ cups pecans

1 teaspoon seasoned salt

2 tablespoons fresh rosemary, chopped

APPLE CHICKEN SALAD

2 tablespoons olive oil

2 chicken breasts (approximately 1 pound)

4 - 6 fresh thyme sprigs, chopped

2 cups apple cider

2 apples, cored and chopped (do not peel)

1 cup celery, chopped

⅓ cup golden raisins

1 cup mayonnaise

1 tablespoon sugar

2 teaspoons rosemary, chopped

½ teaspoon seasoned salt

1 teaspoon salt

½ teaspoon pepper

Preheat oven to 350°. Place butter on a pizza pan in the oven and allow to melt while oven preheats. Remove pizza pan from oven when butter is melted and spread pecans on the pan; stir to coat pecans with butter then sprinkle seasoned salt and rosemary over pecans. Bake 7 to 10 minutes in preheated oven; remove from oven, stir and let cool.

Meanwhile, heat olive oil in a large sauté pan over medium heat. Place chicken breasts in pan and sear 5 to 6 minutes on each side until golden brown. Add thyme and sauté for 1 minute. Pour in apple cider, bring to a boil then reduce heat to low; poach chicken for 15 to 20 minutes until cooked through (liquid will barely bubble while poaching but should not be boiling).

Remove chicken from pan, increase heat to high and boil liquid about 10 minutes until reduced to ½ cup; strain into a bowl and allow liquid to cool. Shred chicken after it has cooled.

Mix shredded chicken, apples, celery, raisins, mayonnaise, strained apple cider mixture, sugar, rosemary, seasoned salt, salt and pepper until well blended. Fold in ½ cup Rosemary Pecans.

Sprinkle remaining pecans on top of salad before serving and serve on a croissant or over a bed of lettuce.

ASPARAGUS SALAD WITH ROASTED RED PEPPERS & ASIAGO CHEESE

Serves 8

2 pounds asparagus, tough ends removed

1 (12 ounce) jar roasted red peppers with garlic

1 ½ cups Asiago cheese, shaved for garnish

VINAIGRETTE

2 tablespoons white wine vinegar

12 caper berries, cut into quarters

2 teaspoons dill pickles, chopped

1 tablespoon Dijon mustard

1 garlic clove, minced

salt and pepper

¼ cup olive oil

Boil salted water in a large stockpot over high heat; add asparagus and cook 3 minutes. Remove asparagus from water, submerge in cold water, drain in colander, then pat dry and set aside.

In a medium bowl, whisk together vinegar, caper berries, pickles, mustard and garlic. Season with salt and pepper. Whisk in olive oil then store at room temperature.

Arrange asparagus on a serving platter and place roasted peppers on top. Drizzle with the vinaigrette and garnish with cheese shavings.

SERVING SUGGESTION

For a complete meal, create an Antipasta Platter. Add slices of fresh mozzarella, a selection of your favorite olives and cubes of soppresosota or salami.

AVOCADO TOMATO SALAD

2 avocados, pitted and cut into 1-inch cubes

2 medium heirloom tomatoes, cubed

1 small red onion, chopped

3 tablespoons olive oil

1 tablespoon Blackberry Balsamic Vinegar with Pears (or balsamic vinegar with $1/4$ teaspoon sugar)

hot sauce, to taste

6 slices of bacon, cooked and crumbled

In a serving bowl, gently toss avocados, tomatoes and onion.

In a small bowl, whisk together oil, vinegar and hot sauce; drizzle over vegetables and toss gently.

Refrigerate for at least 2 hours and sprinkle crumbled bacon on top just before serving

BBQ RANCH CHICKEN SALAD

BUTTERMILK RANCH DRESSING

1 cup sour cream

$\frac{1}{4}$ cup buttermilk

3 cloves garlic

$\frac{1}{4}$ cup mayonnaise

3 tablespoons cider vinegar

1 teaspoon Worcestershire sauce

$\frac{1}{8}$ cup fresh basil, chopped

2 tablespoons fresh parsley, chopped

$\frac{1}{8}$ cup fresh chives, chopped

$\frac{1}{4}$ cup Parmesan cheese, grated

1 teaspoon sugar

1 tablespoon salt

2 tablespoons black pepper

CHICKEN SALAD

4 boneless, skinless chicken breasts

$\frac{1}{2}$ cup barbeque sauce

1 head of romaine lettuce, cut into strips

6 slices of bacon, cooked, drained and crumbled

1 pint grape tomatoes, seeded and halved

3 ounces blue cheese, crumbled

1 red onion, diced

2 large eggs, hard-boiled and chopped

$\frac{1}{4}$ cup fresh chives, chopped

Whisk all dressing ingredients together in a bowl until well mixed. Set aside.

Grill chicken breasts over medium-high heat for about 10 minutes, flipping halfway through cooking time, until slightly charred on each side and cooked through (until meat thermometer inserted in center reaches 160° or juices run clear). Baste chicken with barbeque sauce during last couple of minutes on the grill. Transfer fully cooked chicken breasts to a cutting board and cool completely; cut into $\frac{1}{2}$-inch cubes and coat with extra barbeque sauce.

To serve, spread romaine lettuce over bottom of a 6 to 8 quart glass bowl and top with an even layer of chicken cubes. Sprinkle bacon over chicken and layer with tomatoes, cheese, onion, eggs and chives; serve with Buttermilk Ranch Dressing on the side.

CANDIED PECAN AND APPLE SALAD

BALSAMIC VINAIGRETTE

1 small shallot, minced

¼ cup balsamic vinegar

1 teaspoon Dijon mustard

3 teaspoons black sage honey

2 garlic cloves, minced

⅔ cup olive oil

salt and pepper, to taste

SALAD

1 (5 ounce) package mixed baby greens

1 apple, chopped

¼ cup celery, finely chopped

½ cup bourbon pecans

½ cup Blue cheese, crumbled

In a medium mixing bowl, combine shallots, vinegar and Dijon mustard; let stand for 20 minutes. Whisk in honey and garlic, then slowly drizzle in olive oil while rapidly whisking. Season with salt and pepper to taste. Reserve extra dressing in a tightly sealed container in the refrigerator.

In a large bowl, toss mixed baby greens, apples, celery, pecans and Blue cheese. Toss with Balsamic Vinaigrette just before serving.

CRUNCHY CHINESE CHICKEN SALAD

DRESSING

2 teaspoons fresh ginger, minced

1 small garlic clove

1 - 2 tablespoons sweet chili sauce, to taste

1 cup mayonnaise

¼ cup sour cream

3 - 4 tablespoons soy sauce

2 tablespoons brown sugar

SALAD

1 head of iceberg lettuce, chopped

3 boneless, skinless chicken breasts, cooked and shredded

¼ package white glass noodles, prepared

2 cups red cabbage, shredded

2 medium sized carrots, shredded

3 green onions, chopped

¼ cup honey roasted peanuts

⅛ cup fresh cilantro, chopped

Combine all dressing ingredients in a blender or food processor and process until smooth. Store in refrigerator until ready to serve.

In a large serving bowl, mix lettuce, shredded chicken, glass noodles, red cabbage, carrots and green onions. Pour prepared dressing over salad and toss to coat. Serve garnished with honey roasted peanuts and fresh cilantro.

CURRIED CHICKEN SALAD

Makes 3 ½ cups

1 pound boneless, skinless chicken breasts, cooked

salt and pepper, to taste

3 tablespoons curry powder

3 tablespoons honey

¼ cup walnuts, chopped

½ cup green seedless grapes, halved

¼ cup celery

¼ cup dried cranberries

2 tablespoons green onions, chopped

1 cup yogurt

1 tablespoon lime juice

Cut each chicken breast into 4 or 5 strips; season with salt and pepper to taste and grill over medium-high heat until cooked through. Let cool, cut into bite sized pieces and set aside.

In a large mixing bowl, combine curry powder and honey until well incorporated, then toss chicken cubes until evenly coated. Add walnuts, grapes, celery, cranberries and green onions; mix to combine with chicken. In a separate bowl, mix yogurt with lime juice. Gently fold yogurt dressing into salad mixture until all ingredients are evenly coated.

Serve salad tucked into whole wheat pitas or over a bed of mixed greens using any remaining dressing for garnish.

Fall Salad

DRESSING

1 cup olive oil

$^3/_4$ cup sugar

$^1/_2$ cup red wine

$^1/_2$ teaspoon salt

$^1/_2$ teaspoon paprika

$^1/_4$ teaspoon white pepper

2 garlic cloves, minced

SALAD

1 head of leaf lettuce

2 - 3 apples, sliced

1 $^1/_2$ cups cran-raisins

1 $^1/_2$ cups sliced almonds

8 ounces Blue cheese, crumbled

In a medium mixing bowl, whisk all dressing ingredients until well combined. Make dressing the night before you plan on serving the salad and refrigerate overnight to bring out its fullest flavor. Refrigerate until ready to use.

Combine lettuce, apples, cran-raisins, almonds and Blue cheese in large bowl. Toss with dressing just before serving.

FRESH DILL SALAD

1 cup Greek yogurt, strained

1 tablespoon fresh dill

2 teaspoons white sugar

1 large cucumber, peeled and diced

¼ cup onions, chopped

¼ cup bell peppers, chopped

In a large serving bowl, combine yogurt, dill and sugar. Add cucumber, onions and peppers, mixing until ingredients are evenly coated. Refrigerate at least 2 hours and serve chilled.

Excellent served with lamb or fatty fish.

? DID YOU KNOW?

WHAT IS GREEK YOGURT?

Greek yogurt differs from regular yogurt in that the watery whey is strained from the yogurt. This gives the yogurt a higher concentration of nutrients, a creamier, thicker texture and a higher heat tolerance, making it less likely to curdle and ideal for cooking. Due to the creaminess of Greek yogurt, it is great for recipes such as creamy dips, desserts and main dishes.

GAZPACHO SALAD

● ●

Makes 9 cups

DRESSING

3 garlic cloves, minced

¼ cup red wine vinegar

¼ cup olive oil

2 tablespoons fresh parsley

1 tablespoon fresh basil, chopped

1 teaspoon hot sauce

salt and pepper, to taste

SALAD

6 tomatoes, chopped

1 onion, chopped

2 cucumbers, peeled, seeded and chopped

½ cup black olives, sliced

2 green bell peppers, chopped

3 celery stalks, chopped

lettuce leaves, Boston or leaf

In a medium mixing bowl, whisk all dressing ingredients until well combined and refrigerate for several hours before using.

In a large serving bowl, combine tomatoes, onion, cucumber, black olives, green peppers and celery. Pour dressing over salad just before serving and toss well; serve over lettuce leaves.

GORGONZOLA PEAR SALAD

MERLOT SHALLOT DRESSING

1 large shallot, finely minced

2 cups Rose wine

$1/2$ cup red wine vinegar

1 tablespoon brown sugar

1 garlic clove, minced

2 teaspoon Dijon mustard

2 cups olive oil

salt and pepper, to taste

SALAD

1 (5 ounce) package baby lettuce salad

$1/2$ cup Gorgonzola cheese, crumbled

$1/2$ cup walnuts, toasted and chopped

3 slices applewood smoked bacon,
   cooked and crumbled

1 pear, peeled, cored and chopped

Combine shallots and Rose wine in a medium sauce pan over high heat. Bring liquid to a boil. Reduce heat to medium and simmer until reduced to $1/4$ cup, about 20 to 30 minutes.

Let mixture cool completely. Add vinegar, sugar, garlic and mustard. Slowly whisk in olive oil. Season with salt and pepper. Refrigerate dressing until ready to serve.

In a large bowl, mix baby lettuce, gorgonzola cheese, walnuts and bacon. Add pears and toss with Merlot Shallot Dressing just before serving.

GRAND CHICKEN SALAD DULAINE

Serves 8

1 rotisserie chicken, skin removed and shredded

3 celery stalks, chopped

2 Granny Smith apples, cored and diced

$\frac{1}{4}$ cup raisins

$\frac{1}{4}$ cup almonds, slivered

$\frac{1}{4}$ cup walnuts, chopped

2 tablespoons garlic paste

$\frac{1}{2}$ cup light mayonnaise

$\frac{1}{2}$ cup mayonnaise

3 tablespoons yellow mustard

2 teaspoons sea salt

1 teaspoon black pepper

1 cup seedless grapes, halved

3 tablespoons fresh cilantro, coarsely chopped

In a large serving bowl, combine chicken, celery, apples, raisins, almonds, walnuts, garlic paste, mayonnaise, mustard, salt and pepper; mix thoroughly. Garnish with grapes and cilantro and chill for at least 2 hours before serving.

GREEK STYLE PLUM TOMATOES

7 - 8 plum tomatoes, sliced

$^1/_4$ cup red onions

$^1/_4$ cup Feta cheese, crumbled

12 Kalamata olives, pitted and halved

2 tablespoons Kalamata olive brine

juice of 1 lemon

$^1/_2$ teaspoon red pepper flakes

$^1/_2$ cup olive oil

1 pack ($^3/_4$ ounce) fresh oregano leaves

On large serving platter, arrange sliced tomatoes. Sprinkle onion, cheese and sliced olives over tomatoes.

In a small mixing bowl, whisk together Kalamata olive brine, lemon juice, red pepper flakes and olive oil until well mixed. Drizzle mixture over platter and garnish with fresh oregano leaves.

GREEN BEAN SALAD WITH SOY GLAZED ALMONDS

1/4 cup almonds

4 teaspoons soy sauce

1 pound green beans, cut into 1-inch pieces

2 tablespoons rice vinegar

1 tablespoon vegetable oil

1 large garlic clove, pressed

1 teaspoon fresh ginger, peeled and minced

salt and pepper, to taste

2 tablespoons green onions, thinly sliced

1 cup fresh cilantro or parsley, julienned

Heat a small nonstick frying pan over medium heat; add almonds and stir until lightly toasted, about 5 minutes. Increase heat to medium-high and add 3 teaspoons soy sauce; stir for 1 minute or until soy sauce evaporates and almonds are coated. Remove from heat and allow almonds to cool, then chop almonds.

Bring a large pot of salted water to a boil; add green beans and cook for 5 minutes, or until tender crisp. Pour cooked beans into a colander, rinse well and allow to drain thoroughly.

In a large serving bowl, whisk vinegar, oil, garlic, ginger and remaining teaspoon of soy sauce until combined. Add beans and toss lightly; season to taste with salt and pepper. Sprinkle green onions, cilantro and almonds over salad before serving.

Honey Roasted Butternut Squash Salad with Pomegranate Vinaigrette

Serves 8

1 medium butternut squash, peeled and cubed

3 tablespoons olive oil, divided

2 tablespoons honey

2 ½ tablespoons unsalted butter

1 tablespoon sugar

½ teaspoon cumin

¼ teaspoon cinnamon

¼ teaspoon paprika

¼ teaspoon cayenne pepper

¼ teaspoon salt

½ cup pumpkin seeds

4 slices of pre-made polenta, sliced into ½ -inch medallions

2 (5 ounce) bags arugula

¾ cup Parmesan cheese, grated

Dressing

2 tablespoons pomegranate vinegar (or Champagne vinegar)

1 tablespoon shallots, minced

6 tablespoons olive oil

Preheat oven to 400°. Spray a cookie sheet with cooking spray and set aside. In a large mixing bowl, whisk together 1 tablespoon olive oil and honey until combined. Add butternut squash and toss to coat. Spread evenly on cookie sheet and bake 30 to 35 minutes, or until tender. Remove and set aside.

Meanwhile, melt butter in a saucepan over medium heat. Stir in sugar, cumin, cinnamon, paprika, cayenne and salt until combined. Allow spice mixture to cook, without stirring, until caramelized. Add pumpkin seeds and stir to coat, continue to cook until seeds are puffed and golden, about 3 to 4 minutes.

Heat 2 tablespoon olive oil in a skillet over medium heat. Add polenta slices and fry until golden brown and crispy, about 5 to 6 minutes. Remove from skillet and slice into quarters.

In a small mixing bowl, whisk together all dressing ingredients and set aside.

To serve, place arugula on salad dish, top with crispy polenta, hot butternut squash and Parmesan cheese; drizzle with salad dressing and serve.

ITALIAN TOMATO BREAD SALAD

½ loaf Ciabatta bread, cut into 1-inch
    pieces

6 tablespoons olive oil, divided

4 heirloom tomatoes, diced

1 red onion, peeled and cut into rings

4 fresh basil sprigs, leaves removed and
    stems discarded

3 tablespoons pear vinegar (or
    Champagne vinegar)

1 tablespoon honey

1 tablespoon Dijon mustard

1 garlic clove, minced

2 tablespoons vegetable broth

salt and pepper, to taste

1 (8 ounce) mozzarella ball, cubed

Preheat oven to 450°. In a large mixing bowl, toss bread with 2 tablespoons olive oil. Arrange on a baking sheet and place in oven for 10 minutes or until crusty.

Meanwhile, in a large mixing bowl, combine tomatoes, onion and basil.

In a smaller mixing bowl, whisk together vinegar, remaining olive oil, honey, mustard, garlic and vegetable broth. Season to taste with salt and pepper.

Pour vinaigrette over vegetables and toss to coat. Add toasted bread and mozzarella cubes and toss. Serve immediately.

MACHE & GOAT CHEESE SALAD

· ·

BACON HERB DRESSING

6 slices applewood smoked bacon

$1/2$ cup cider vinegar

2 teaspoons fresh thyme, chopped

1 teaspoon fresh basil, chopped

1 teaspoon fresh oregano, chopped

$1/2$ teaspoon fresh rosemary, chopped

$1/2$ cup olive oil

SALAD

1 (5 ounce) package arugula

1 (3 ounce) package mache

$1/4$ cup dried cherries

$1/2$ cup cashews, chopped

1 shallot, finely chopped

2 ounces goat cheese, crumbled

In a medium frying pan, cook bacon over medium-low heat until crispy. Remove bacon and drippings, crumbling the bacon and reserving the drippings; set aside. Add cider vinegar to pan and cook for about 2 minutes until reduced to $1/3$ cup. Stir in herbs, remove from heat and pour into a mixing bowl. Slowly drizzle in olive oil while whisking rapidly. After oil is incorporated, whisk in crumbled bacon and bacon drippings.

In a large bowl, mix salad greens, dried cherries, cashews and shallot. Sprinkle crumbled goat cheese over salad. Serve Bacon Herb Dressing warm over salad.

MARINATED MASHED POTATO SALAD

· ·

Serves 12 (6 cups)

3 pounds potatoes, peeled and cubed

1 ½ cups mayonnaise

¾ cup celery, chopped

¼ cup onions, chopped

¼ cup sweet relish

2 tablespoons Dijon mustard

1 teaspoon dried dill

2 eggs, hard-boiled and chopped

pinch of sugar

salt and pepper, to taste

Add potatoes to a large stockpot of cold, salted water. Bring to a boil, then reduce to medium-high heat for 20 to 25 minutes. Drain and place in a large mixing bowl.

Combine potatoes and mayonnaise then stir in remaining ingredients until well mixed. Chill for at least 3 hours before serving.

MARINATED POTATO SALAD

5 - 6 medium red potatoes

MARINADE

$\frac{1}{2}$ cup vegetable oil

$\frac{1}{3}$ cup cider vinegar

$\frac{3}{4}$ teaspoon kosher salt

2 teaspoons sugar

$\frac{1}{4}$ teaspoon black pepper, freshly ground

$\frac{1}{4}$ teaspoon dry mustard

$\frac{1}{4}$ teaspoon dried basil

1 tablespoon fresh parsley, finely chopped

2 tablespoons sweet onions, finely chopped

1 tablespoon pimentos, finely chopped

In large pot over high heat, bring potatoes to a boil; reduce heat to medium-high and gently boil for 30 to 35 minutes. Potatoes should be thoroughly cooked, but not mushy. Remove from heat and drain. Peel and slice potatoes while warm.

Meanwhile, whisk together all marinade ingredients in a large mixing bowl. Place potatoes in a 9x13-inch baking dish in 3 to 4 rows, overlapping each slice. Let stand for 10 minutes before adding marinade. Pour marinade evenly over potatoes and let stand at room temperature for 1 to 2 hours before serving.

POTATO ARTICHOKE SALAD
WITH HORSERADISH DRESSING

Serves 10 - 12

5 pounds russet potatoes, peeled and diced

2 (14 ounce) cans artichoke hearts, drained and quartered

3 celery stalks, diced

1 large red bell pepper, diced

1 small red onion, diced

DRESSING

1 (16 ounce) jar mayonnaise

¹/₂ cup Dijon mustard

¹/₂ cup horseradish

¹/₂ cup fresh parsley, chopped

salt and pepper, to taste

Place potatoes in large pot of salted water over high heat and bring to a boil. Lower heat and simmer for 25 to 30 minutes or until tender; drain and cool.

Combine cooled potatoes, artichoke hearts, celery, red bell pepper and onion in a large bowl.

In a separate bowl, mix all dressing ingredients until well combined. Pour dressing over vegetables and gently stir until completely coated. Garnish with additional parsley and freshly ground black pepper.

Sistafriend's Bean Salad

Marinade

1 cup sugar

¾ cup olive oil

¾ cup pear balsamic vinegar

salt and pepper, to taste

Bean Salad

1 pound French beans, stems removed

1 can shoepeg corn, drained

1 can mini butter beans or lima beans, drained

1 large Vidalia onion, finely chopped

1 cup celery, finely chopped

In a small mixing bowl, whisk together all marinade ingredients until full combined. Set aside.

Steam French beans for 4 to 5 minutes, remove from heat and rinse with cold water.

In a large bowl, combine marinade, French beans and remaining ingredients; toss to coat evenly. Refrigerate for 24 hours before serving.

Spicy Black-Eyed Pea Salad with Tomatoes, Cucumbers & Cilantro

1 ½ cups dried black-eyed peas

1 large cucumber, peeled, seeded and chopped

1 small red onion, chopped

4 medium tomatoes, seeded and chopped

1 jalapeño, minced

½ cup fresh cilantro, chopped

2 garlic cloves, minced

½ cup olive oil

¼ cup lemon juice

salt and pepper, to taste

fresh cilantro sprigs, for garnish

Bring a large pot of water to a boil then add black-eyed peas and a pinch of salt; cover and bring back to a boil. Reduce heat and simmer partially covered for 15 to 20 minutes. Drain, rinse and allow to cool.

In a serving bowl, combine cooled black-eyed peas, cucumber, onion, tomatoes, jalapeño, cilantro, garlic, oil, lemon juice, salt and pepper; toss to combine. Serve immediately or place in refrigerator for 30 minutes to allow flavor to develop. Garnish with fresh cilantro sprigs.

Excellent with quesadillas or fajitas.

SPICY PEAR SALAD

SWEET AND SOUR DRESSING

1 cup salad oil

$1/8$ cup pear vinegar

$1/2$ cup white wine vinegar

$1/4$ cup sugar

2 teaspoons dry mustard

1 teaspoon paprika

1 tablespoon shallots, minced

SALAD

1 head of iceberg lettuce, washed and
    dried

4 Bosc pears, quartered

4 tablespoons extra-sharp Cheddar
    cheese, freshly grated

1 cup pecans, chopped

$1/2$ teaspoon hot sauce

In a medium mixing bowl, whisk all dressing ingredients together. Refrigerate until ready to serve salad.

Divide lettuce equally between 4 individual plates. Add equal amount of pears to each plate followed by a sprinkle of cheese; refrigerate for 30 minutes. Place pecans and hot sauce in a food processor to coarsely chop. When ready to serve, remove plates from refrigerator and sprinkle pecan mix on top of each salad. Drizzle each salad with Sweet and Sour Dressing to taste, or serve dressing on the side.

SPINACH & GRILLED PEAR SALAD

SPICED PECANS

2 cups pecan halves

$\frac{1}{2}$ cup demerara sugar

1 teaspoon cinnamon

$\frac{1}{4}$ cup butter, melted

$\frac{1}{2}$ teaspoon vanilla extract

SALAD

1 pear, cored and halved

1 (8 ounce) bag spinach

$\frac{1}{3}$ cup Goat cheese, crumbled

1 red onion, chopped

DRESSING

$\frac{1}{2}$ cup vegetable oil

$\frac{1}{4}$ cup sugar

$\frac{1}{4}$ cup red wine vinegar

1 garlic clove, minced

$\frac{1}{4}$ teaspoon salt

$\frac{1}{4}$ teaspoon pepper

$\frac{1}{4}$ teaspoon paprika

Preheat oven to 300°. Mix pecan halves, demerara sugar, cinnamon, butter and vanilla extract in a medium mixing bowl. Pour onto baking sheet and bake for 10 minutes. Remove from oven, stir, then bake an additional 8 minutes. Remove from oven, pour onto a cold surface and allow to cool. Break pecans apart when cool to the touch and set aside.

Heat grill to high. Grill each pear half for approximately 30 seconds per side. Allow to cool then cut into bite-sized pieces. Set aside until ready to assemble salad.

In a large serving bowl, combine spinach, pear, cheese, onion and spiced pecans.

In a separate bowl, whisk together all dressing ingredients. Pour dressing over salad before serving.

Strawberry & Onion Salad with Cashew Lime Dressing

. . . .

Serves 4

$^1/_4$ cup lime juice, freshly squeezed

$^1/_4$ cup orange juice

$^1/_4$ cup black sage honey

1 tablespoon jalapeño, finely chopped

$^1/_2$ teaspoon salt

$^1/_4$ cup cilantro, chopped

$^2/_3$ cup vegetable oil

$^3/_4$ cup cashews, chopped

1 head of romaine lettuce, washed and dried

1 pint strawberries, sliced with tops removed

1 large red onion, thinly sliced

Combine lime juice, orange juice, honey, jalapeño, salt and cilantro in a blender or food processor. Blend while slowly adding vegetable oil in a steady stream. When oil is incorporated, turn off and add cashews; pulse until nuts are finely chopped.

Place lettuce in a large serving bowl and top with strawberry slices and onions. Pour dressing over lettuce and serve immediately.

TURKEY ALMOND SALAD WITH HERB DRESSING

Serves 4

1 pound raw turkey breast

salt and pepper, to taste

$1/2$ cup mayonnaise

$1/4$ teaspoon ground thyme

$1/8$ teaspoon garlic powder

$1/8$ teaspoon fresh oregano, chopped

$1/8$ teaspoon fresh rosemary, chopped

$1/8$ teaspoon fresh sage, chopped

2 ounces almonds, slivered

1 tart Granny Smith apples, cored and diced

1 tablespoon lemon juice

2 celery stalks, chopped

2 green onions, chopped

1 tablespoon fresh parsley, chopped

Preheat oven to 450°. Season turkey with salt and pepper and place on a baking dish. Bake 10 to 15 minutes, then reduce to 300° for 1 to 1 $1/2$ hours. Remove from oven, cool and shred.

Meanwhile, in a small bowl, combine mayonnaise, thyme, garlic powder, oregano, rosemary and sage. Mix thoroughly. Refrigerate until ready to serve.

In a shallow sauté pan, toast almonds over low heat until lightly brown; cool. In a large serving bowl, toss diced apple and lemon juice. Add herbed mayonnaise, turkey, almonds, celery, onion and parsley; stir to coat evenly.

Serve over a bed of lettuce or on a flaky croissant.

Watermelon Salad with Balsamic Vinaigrette

• •

¼ cup balsamic vinegar

¼ cup canola oil

¼ cup olive oil

1 tablespoon Dijon mustard

1 tablespoon honey

1 garlic clove, minced

salt and pepper, to taste

1 medium seedless watermelon, diced

1 red onion, thinly sliced

¾ cup fresh mint, chopped

8 ounces Feta cheese, crumbled

pepper, to taste

In a small mixing bowl, whisk together vinegar, canola oil, olive oil, mustard, honey and garlic. Season with salt and pepper and set aside. Refrigerate until ready to serve.

Spread ⅔ of watermelon on serving platter. Top with onion, mint and cheese and season with pepper.

Pour dressing over salad and garnish with remaining watermelon cubes.

Excellent with grilled shrimp or chicken.

WILD RICE SALAD WITH ARUGULA

3 cups water

1 cup wild rice

salt, to taste

³/₄ cup raisins

1 cup dry red wine

2 tablespoons sugar

1 small head of radicchio

1 cup arugula, stems included

1 cup Belgian endive, thinly sliced

1 head of romaine lettuce, chopped

5 tablespoons fresh basil, chopped

1 cup almonds, toasted

DRESSING

3 tablespoons peanut oil

1 ¹/₂ tablespoons sesame oil

1 ¹/₂ tablespoons balsamic vinegar

1 teaspoon soy sauce

black pepper, to taste

Bring 3 cups of water to a boil in a large pot over high heat; add wild rice and salt to taste. Reduce heat to low, cover and simmer for 50 minutes. Remove from heat and let stand for 10 minutes.

Meanwhile, combine raisins, red wine and sugar in a saucepan, bring to a boil, remove from heat and let stand for 10 minutes; drain. In a large serving bowl, toss radicchio, arugula, endive, romaine, basil, almonds, drained raisins and cooked rice.

In a separate bowl, whisk all dressing ingredients until well combined. Pour dressing over salad and toss to combine.

WINTER CHERRY SALAD WITH CRISPY PANCETTA

ROASTED SHALLOT BLACK SAGE HONEY VINAIGRETTE

2 medium sized shallots

1 cup vegetable oil

2 cups merlot

1/8 cup black sage honey

1/2 cup blackberry balsamic vinegar (or balsamic vinegar with 1 tablespoon sugar)

SALAD

1 tablespoon olive oil

5 ounces pancetta

1 (5 ounce) package baby salad greens

1/3 cup dried cherries

5 ounces Goat cheese, crumbled

Preheat oven to 350°. Place shallots and vegetable oil in a roasting pan and roast in oven for 45 minutes. While shallots are roasting, place merlot in a medium saucepan over medium heat and cook for about 30 minutes until reduced to 1 cup. Remove reduced merlot from heat and whisk in black sage honey and blackberry balsamic vinegar; set aside. Remove shallots from roasting pan, reserving the cooking oil, and place in a food processor; add wine mixture and blend, slowly drizzling in cooking oil from shallots. Refrigerate until ready to use.

Heat olive oil in a medium frying pan over medium-low heat; add pancetta and cook for approximately 6 minutes or until crispy. Drain on paper towels.

In a large serving bowl, combine salad greens, dried cherries and Goat cheese; crumble cooked pancetta and add to salad mixture. Toss salad with desired amount of Roasted Shallot Black Sage Honey Vinaigrette.

Beef Tenderloin with Fennel and Ancho, page 129

Pecan Chicken Roll-up with a Raspberry Currant Sauce, page 195

Duck Breast with a Warm Cherry-Pineapple Relish, page 238

Salmon with a Sesame & Orange-Ginger Relish, page 224

Crab Stuffed Eggplant, page 211

The Best Ever Macaroni and Cheese, page 279

Pacific Rim Meatballs with Spiced Glass Noodles, page 156

Pork Chops with Sweet Potato & Pear Crisps, page 174

Proscuitto Pasta, page 159

Sausage & Gorgonzola Stuffed Pork Chops, page 178

Roasted Root Vegetable Medley, page 269

Arroz con Camarones, page 203

Tequila Fajitas, page 144

Smoky Corn Risotto, page 271

Cranberry Pecan Turkey Roulade, page 189

main

Beef

Pasta

Pork

Poultry

Seafood

Veal, Lamb & Duck

Accompaniments

BEEF CASALINGA

⅓ cup sugar

⅓ cup + 2 teaspoons black fig or balsamic vinegar

1 cup red wine

2 cups beef broth

⅔ cup + ½ cup olive oil, divided

½ cup shallots, finely chopped

2 garlic cloves, minced

⅔ cup prosciutto, julienned

½ pound mushrooms, sliced

2 tablespoons unsalted butter

1 ⅓ cups Marsala wine

⅔ cup brown gravy

2 tablespoons tarragon flakes

⅓ cup all purpose flour

⅓ teaspoon salt

½ teaspoon ground black pepper

6 filet mignon steaks, ¾-inch thick

6 slices of mozzarella cheese, ¼-inch thick

In a saucepan over medium-high heat, heat sugar and 2 teaspoons vinegar until they form a 'cola' color, about 6 to 8 minutes. Add in ⅓ cup vinegar and reduce to a syrup, 5 to 6 minutes. Add 1 cup red wine and reduce to a thin syrup, about 8 to 10 minutes. Add beef broth, reduce heat to medium heat and simmer for 15 to 20 minutes. Remove from heat and set aside.

Heat ⅔ cup olive oil in a large sauté pan over medium heat; add shallots and garlic and cook for 5 minutes or until translucent. Add prosciutto and mushrooms; cook for 8 minutes, stirring occasionally. Remove mixture to a plate with paper towels.

Return empty sauté pan to medium heat. Melt butter and add mushroom-prosciutto mixture. Stir in vinegar reduction, Marsala wine, brown gravy and tarragon; bring to a simmer and cook 15 to 20 minutes.

Preheat oven to 500°. Meanwhile, place flour, salt and pepper in a plastic bag or shallow baking dish. Dredge each steak with flour and set aside. In a new frying pan, heat ½ cup olive oil over medium-high heat. Add floured steak and cook until golden on both sides, about 2 minutes each side. Remove meat to a plate with paper towels to drain.

Spoon half of prosciutto-mushroom sauce into a 9x13-inch baking dish, cover with steaks, top with remaining sauce and slices of mozzarella. Bake in oven for 10 minutes or until cheese is hot and bubbling.

BEEF FILETS WITH CHERRY ANCHO ESPRESSO SAUCE

Serves 4

1 ½ cups red wine

1 shallot, minced

3 fresh thyme sprigs, chopped

½ cup dried cherries

2 tablespoons beef bouillon dissolved in 1 ½ cups water

1 cup brewed coffee

½ cup Demerara sugar

1 tablespoon cumin

1 dried ancho chili, chopped

1 teaspoon cornstarch dissolved in ½ teaspoon water

2 tablespoons butter

4 (6 - 7 oz) filet mignon steaks, about 1-inch thick

2 teaspoons salt

1 teaspoon pepper

½ teaspoon fresh rosemary, minced

In a saucepan over medium heat, reduce red wine, shallot and thyme for 35 minutes.

Meanwhile, in a small saucepan, combine dried cherries and dissolved beef bouillon. Bring to a boil; remove from heat and steep for 10 minutes. To red wine reduction, add coffee, sugar, cumin, ancho chili and cherries in beef broth. Bring to a boil, then add cornstarch slurry. Reduce heat to low to keep sauce warm as you prepare steaks.

Melt butter in a large frying pan over medium heat. Sprinkle steaks with salt, pepper and rosemary and add to pan; cook to desired doneness, about 4 minutes per side. Place one steak on each plate and top each with ¼ cup sauce.

BEEF TENDERLOIN WITH FENNEL & ANCHO

Serves 12 - 14

1 teaspoon fennel seeds

1 star anise

1 small dried ancho chile, seeded and torn

2 garlic cloves, chopped

4 tablespoons olive oil, divided

1 beef tenderloin

salt and pepper, to taste

Preheat oven to 525°. In a saucepan over medium heat, toast fennel seeds, star anise and ancho chile for 6 to 8 minutes. Remove from heat and grind with a pestle and mortar or in a coffee grinder to form a paste; combine with garlic and set aside.

Preheat 2 tablespoons oil in large frying pan over medium heat. Drizzle 2 tablespoons oil over tenderloin, rub with salt and pepper then rub with garlic-spice mixture. Sear in pan for 5 to 6 minutes, place on a baking sheet and bake for 20 minutes. Reduce heat to 350° and bake an additional 15 minutes.

BEEF TIPS IN PEARL ONION PINOT NOIR SAUCE

2 tablespoons olive oil

1 ½ pounds stew beef

2 cups Pinot Noir

8 slices applewood smoked bacon, diced

5 - 6 garlic cloves, sliced

2 cups pearl onions, peeled and quartered (or 1 large sweet onion cut into 1-inch pieces)

2 tablespoons fresh thyme, divided

½ teaspoon red pepper flakes

2 tablespoons roux (1 tablespoon softened butter and 1 tablespoon flour combined)

3 - 4 cups beef broth

2 teaspoons Worcestershire sauce

½ teaspoon hot sauce

¼ cup fresh Italian parsley

1 tablespoon fresh rosemary

3 tablespoons chives

salt and pepper, to taste

Heat olive oil in a large frying pan over medium-high heat and sear beef in 3 to 4 batches for 5 to 6 minutes each; set aside.

Deglaze pan with wine by scraping the brown bits off the bottom. Pour into a bowl and reserve.

In a Dutch oven over medium-low heat, render bacon until crispy. Remove ½ of bacon drippings. Add garlic, onions, 1 tablespoon thyme and red pepper flakes to bacon drippings. Sauté for 5 to 6 minutes then add roux and coat evenly. Add reserved wine and reduce by half, about 6 to 8 minutes stirring often. Add beef broth and beef; simmer for 45 minutes on low. Season with Worcestershire and hot sauce; bring to a simmer and add remaining thyme, parsley, rosemary, chives, salt and pepper. Serve over rice or egg noodles.

BLACK FIG FILET WITH SWEET POTATO PANCAKES

BLACK FIG SAUCE

$1/3$ cup sugar

$1/3$ cup + 1 tablespoon black fig vinegar (may substitute balsamic vinegar)

$3/4$ cup Pinot Noir

2 teaspoons beef bouillon

2 cups beef broth

2 tablespoons cornstarch

1 tablespoon water

salt and pepper, to taste

FILETS

8 - 10 fresh basil leaves, torn

3 - 4 garlic cloves, chopped

2 fresh rosemary sprigs, chopped

4 - 5 tablespoons sea salt

2 tablespoons cracked pepper

8 tablespoons olive oil, divided

4 filet mignon steaks

SWEET POTATO PANCAKES

1 cup fresh Italian parsley, chopped

3 tablespoons all purpose flour

2 eggs

salt and pepper, to taste

1 sweet potato, shredded

1 russet potato, shredded

2 tablespoons olive oil

In a small saucepan, bring sugar and 1 tablespoon vinegar to boil and caramelize for 8 to 10 minutes. Remove from heat and add remaining vinegar; return to heat and reduce by $2/3$, about 8 to 10 minutes. Add wine and allow to reduce by $3/4$, approximately 8 to 10 minutes. Add boullion and beef broth and bring to a boil; reduce for 10 minutes.

In a small bowl, combine cornstarch and water; pour 1 tablespoon at a time into broth until a desired consistency is reached. Season with salt and pepper; set aside and keep warm.

To prepare beef, combine basil, garlic, rosemary, salt and pepper. Drizzle olive oil over filets, rub with spice mixture and set aside.

Preheat 2 tablespoons olive oil in a frying pan over medium-high heat. Place spice-rubbed steaks in pan and cook 4 to 5 minutes on each side. Remove from pan and allow to rest while cooking potato pancakes.

To prepare sweet potato pancakes, combine parsley, flour, eggs, salt and pepper in a large mixing bowl. Add shredded potatoes and stir to combine. Take $1/2$ cup potato mixture and flatten to form a cake. Repeat with remaining potatoes.

Heat 2 tablespoons olive oil in pan used to cook steaks, over medium-high heat. Add potato pancakes and cook 3 to 4 minute each side. Place one pancake on a plate, cover with a beef filet and drizzle with black fig sauce before serving.

CITRUS GINGER STRIP STEAKS

Serves 4

½ cup orange marmalade

¼ cup water

¼ cup soy sauce

⅛ cup balsamic vinegar

2 teaspoons dried thyme

1 teaspoon dried basil

1 teaspoon dried chives

½ cup olive oil

2 tablespoons orange juice

1 ½ teaspoons orange peel, freshly grated

1 teaspoon ground ginger

2 garlic cloves, minced

4 New York strip or filet mignon steaks

In a mixing bowl, whisk together all ingredients except steak until well combined. Combine 1 cup marinade and steaks in an airtight container and refrigerate 8 hours or overnight. Cover and refrigerate remaining marinade.

Preheat grill to medium. Remove beef from marinade and grill 10 to 12 minutes each side or until beef reaches desired doneness. Baste meat frequently with the reserved marinade for maximum flavor.

DAUBE DE BOEUF PROVENCALE

• •

Serves 6

1 ½ pounds bottom round, cut into cubes

1 cup red wine

2 tablespoons brandy

5 tablespoons olive oil, divided

2 slices bacon, diced

1 large onion, grated

1 garlic clove, minced

1 large carrot, grated

1 bay leaf

¼ teaspoon dried thyme

1 (32 ounce) can whole tomatoes, with juices

12 green olives, pitted

3 tablespoons butter, melted

3 tablespoons all purpose flour

¼ cup white mushrooms

¼ cup chanterelle mushrooms

¼ cup shiitake mushrooms

3 fresh parsley sprigs, chopped

½ teaspoon salt

1 teaspoon ground black pepper

Place beef, wine, brandy and 3 tablespoons oil in an airtight container and refrigerate at least 2 hours (overnight is best).

In a large frying pan, cook bacon over medium heat; remove bacon and set aside, reserving drippings in pan.

Remove beef from marinade, reserving marinade, and brown at medium heat in bacon drippings plus 2 tablespoons olive oil in 3 to 4 batches; remove and set aside. Sweat onions, garlic and carrots in pan for 5 to 6 minutes. Add browned beef, reserved beef marinade, bay leaf, thyme, tomatoes and olives. Bring to a boil.

In a mixing bowl, combine melted butter and flour. Add to beef mixture and simmer over low heat 2 to 2 ½ hours.

During the last 15 minutes of cooking, sear mushrooms in a separate frying pan over medium-high heat. When beef is complete, remove from heat, stir in mushrooms and parsley and season with salt and pepper.

GRILLED HALLOUMI & STEAK KABOBS

Serves 8

½ bunch cilantro

½ bunch fresh Italian parsley

1 garlic clove, chopped

½ tablespoon apple cider vinegar

¼ cup olive oil

1 teaspoon lemon zest, grated

1 pound sirloin meat, cut into 1-inch cubes

1 pound halloumi cheese, cut into 1-inch cubes

Combine cilantro, parsley, garlic, apple cider vinegar, olive oil and lemon rind in a food processor; pulse for 1 minute. In an airtight container, combine steak and marinade and refrigerate for 3 to 4 hours.

Preheat grill to high. Carefully skewer alternating meat and cheese. Grill 2 to 3 minutes then carefully turn, touching only the meat as you turn. Cook an additional 2 to 3 minutes, remove from heat and serve.

DID YOU KNOW?

WHAT IS HALLOUMI CHEESE?

Halloumi cheese originates in Cypress and is traditionally made from a combination of sheep and goats' milk. This versatile cheese is similar in texture to fresh mozzarella and features a higher melting temperature than most cheeses. Because of this higher melting temperature, Halloumi can be grilled or fried to golden brown perfection on the outside with a soft, never runny, texture on the inside.

Pacific Rim Flank Steak

Serves 4

¹/₃ cup soy sauce

¹/₄ cup rice vinegar

¹/₄ cup lime juice, freshly squeezed

2 tablespoons dark sesame oil

2 tablespoons fish sauce

¹/₂ small red onion, chopped

¹/₄ cup fresh basil, chopped

¹/₄ cup fresh mint, chopped

3 tablespoons fresh lemongrass, sliced

1 serrano pepper, chopped

3 tablespoons peanuts, crushed

3 tablespoons sweet chili sauce

1 tablespoon coriander

¹/₂ teaspoon garlic salt

2 pounds flank steak

In a large bowl, whisk together soy sauce, rice vinegar, lime juice, sesame oil and fish sauce. Stir in onion, basil, mint, lemongrass, serrano pepper and crushed peanuts. Season with chile sauce, coriander and garlic salt; stir to combine. Place flank steak and marinade in an airtight container for 6 hours or overnight.

Preheat grill to medium-high heat and lightly oil the grate. Drain liquid from marinated steak, reserving the steak and non-liquid ingredients. Spray a large sheet of aluminum foil with cooking spray; place flank steak and non-liquid marinade ingredients on top and fold to seal. Grill for 20 minutes or until beef reaches desired doneness.

Pear Balsamic Flank Steak
· ·

Serves 4

2 garlic cloves, minced

zest of 2 lemons

³/₄ cup white grape juice

¹/₂ cup black balsamic vinegar with
    pear (may substitute with balsamic
    vinegar and ¹/₂ teaspoon sugar)

1 ¹/₂ cups beef broth

¹/₄ cup turbinado sugar

¹/₂ cup raspberry melba sauce

3 tablespoons tomato paste

3 pounds flank steak

3 Bosc pears, peeled, cored and thinly
    sliced

1 red onion, sliced

In a saucepan over high heat, combine garlic, lemon zest, grape juice, vinegar, beef broth, sugar, raspberry melba sauce and tomato paste; bring to a boil. Remove from heat and cool for 20 minutes.   Combine flank steak and marinade in an airtight container and refrigerate for 6 to 8 hours.

Remove steak from marinade and strain into a saucepan over medium heat. Gently reduce marinade by ¹/₂ , about 10 minutes. Add pears and onion and continue to reduce over medium heat for 10 minutes.

Meanwhile, preheat grill to medium-high heat and lightly oil the grates. Grill flank steak for 8 minutes per side; remove from heat and let rest for 5 to 6 minutes. To serve, slice against the grain and drizzle with pear balsamic reduction.

PETITE FILETS WITH PORT SHALLOT SAUCE & ROQUEFORT PEPPERCORN CRUST

. . . .

Serves 4

1 large shallot, sliced

3 fresh thyme sprigs, chopped

4 tablespoons butter, divided

1 cup ruby port

1 tablespoon all purpose flour

1 ¼ cups beef broth

2 fresh rosemary sprigs, chopped

zest of 1 lemon

1 ½ tablespoons coarse ground green peppercorns

4 oz Roquefort cheese, crumbled

2 tablespoons olive oil

4 (5 - 6 ounce) filet mignon steaks, about 1-inch thick

In a saucepan over medium-high heat, combine shallot, thyme, 2 tablespoons butter and port wine. Reduce to a syrup, about 5 minutes. In a small mixing bowl, combine flour and 1 tablespoon melted butter; gradually add to the reduction. Add beef broth and reduce by ¼, approximately 8 to 10 minutes; set aside.

In a small bowl, combine rosemary, lemon zest and peppercorn. Mix in cheese until well combined. Divide mixture equally into 4 parts, wrap each separately in plastic wrap and refrigerate until ready to use.

Preheat grill to medium-high. Brush each steak with olive oil and place on the grill. Grill 6 to 8 minutes per side; basting frequently with remaining butter. When filets are done, remove from grill and place cheese on top. Allow the cheese to melt and the meat to rest for 5 to 10 minutes. To serve, drizzle with port shallot sauce.

? DID YOU KNOW?

WHAT IS ROQUEFORT CHEESE?

Roquefort cheese is a domestic blue cheese from southern France made from sheep's milk. It is one of the most famous French cheeses and features distinctive blue veins that come from the mold of local caves where the cheese is aged. Roquefort is crumbly and moist with a mild tangy flavor and salty finish. While Roquefort has a very unique flavor and is not easily substituted, you could replace it in most recipes with another blue cheese like Bresse Bleu or your favorite local blue cheese.

PICADILLO STYLE ENCHILADAS

Makes 12 enchiladas

1 pound skirt or flank steak

1 small onion, thinly sliced

½ green bell pepper, seeded and diced

1 chipotle chile, chopped

1 (8 ounce) can tomato sauce

2 tablespoons garlic, chopped

dash of salt

dash of pepper

½ cup white wine

¼ cup Worcestershire sauce

4 green olives, sliced

1 tablespoon olive oil

12 corn tortillas

1 ½ cups Cheddar or Monterey Jack cheese, shredded

Preheat oven to 350°. In a large sauté pan over medium-high heat, sear flank steak for 4 to 5 minutes each side. Remove steak from pan and add onions, peppers, chile, tomato sauce, garlic, salt and pepper to pan; sauté for 5 to 6 minutes. Deglaze pan with wine by scraping the brown bits off the bottom; allow to boil for 1 minute. Add Worcestershire sauce and green olives and return to a boil; add flank steak, cover loosely with foil and place in the oven for 1 to 1 ½ hours. Remove from oven and place in refrigerator until chilled.

Remove steak from sauce and purée sauce in a food processor or blender; set aside. Slice meat very thin and place in a bowl with 3 to 4 tablespoons of puréed sauce.

Heat 1 tablespoon oil in a non-stick frying pan over medium heat. Add tortilla and heat through for 10 seconds. Remove and place on a kitchen towel; add ¼ cup of sliced meat, roll tightly and place in a 9x13-inch baking dish. Repeat process with remaining tortillas and meat. Spoon sauce over the top, then sprinkle with shredded cheese and bake for 20 minutes.

POLYNESIAN MEATBALLS

POLYNESIAN SAUCE

¹/₂ jalapeño, chopped

¹/₃ cup cider vinegar

¹/₂ cup Demerara sugar

1 ¹/₄ cup pineapple juice

1 (8.25 ounce) can crushed pineapple
   with juice

1 tablespoon water

2 tablespoons cornstarch

1 tablespoon soy sauce

2 green onions, thinly sliced

¹/₂ red bell pepper, cut into 2-inch long
   thin strips

1 teaspoon fresh mint, chopped

1 tablespoon fresh cilantro, chopped

MEATBALLS

1 ¹/₂ pounds ground beef

²/₃ cup Panko breadcrumbs

¹/₄ onion, minced

1 egg

¹/₄ cup coconut milk

2 teaspoons fresh ginger, grated

¹/₂ teaspoon salt

1 tablespoon chili garlic sauce

Preheat oven to 450°. In a small saucepan over high heat, bring jalapeño and cider vinegar to a boil. Remove from heat, let stand 30 minutes, strain to remove jalapeños and set aside.

In a large saucepan over high heat, combine jalapeño vinegar, sugar, pineapple juice and crushed pineapple; bring to a boil until sugar has dissolved. In a mixing bowl, combine water and cornstarch until smooth; pour into sauce and bring to a boil. Remove from heat and add onions, bell peppers, mint and cilantro; set aside and keep warm.

In a medium bowl, gently fold together all meatball ingredients. Roll into 1-inch meatballs and place on a greased baking sheet. Bake 20 minutes.

Transfer meatballs to a shallow bowl. Pour sauce over top and toss to coat.

SPICED BEEF TENDERLOIN STEAKS WITH MANGO SALSA

MANGO SALSA

½ cup raspberry preserves

3 tablespoons lime juice, freshly squeezed

2 mangos, peeled, pitted and cubed

¼ cup coconut, shredded

zest and juice of 1 lime

1 jalapeño, minced

⅛ cup fresh cilantro, chopped

SPICED RUB

1 ½ tablespoons paprika

1 tablespoon coriander

2 teaspoons fresh thyme, chopped

2 teaspoons garlic, minced

1 teaspoon chili powder

2 teaspoons Demerara sugar

olive oil

1 beef tenderloin, cut into 1-inch thick slices

Whisk together raspberry preserves and lime juice in a large bowl. Add mangos, coconut, lime zest and juice, jalapeño and cilantro. Cover and chill up to 2 hours.

Preheat grill to medium-high. Combine all Spiced Rub ingredients except beef in a small bowl. Brush each steak with olive oil then sprinkle with Spiced Rub and gently massage into meat on both sides. Grill steaks to desired doneness, about 5 to 6 minutes per side for medium rare. Remove steaks from grill and allow meat to rest for 5 minutes. To serve, garnish with Mango Salsa.

SPICED HONEY PORTERHOUSE STEAKS

1 teaspoon ground ginger

1 teaspoon ground coriander

1 tablespoon paprika

1 teaspoon peppercorns

2 garlic cloves, chopped

2 tablespoons black sage honey

¼ cup butter

4 porterhouse steaks

8 teaspoons olive oil

salt and pepper, to taste

Combine ginger, coriander, paprika, peppercorns, garlic, honey and butter in a small saucepan over medium-low heat. Cook until butter is just melted; combine well, remove from heat and set aside.

Preheat grill to high heat. Drizzle each steak with 2 teaspoons of olive oil over both sides. Brush each with herb-butter glaze just before placing on the grill. Reduce grill heat to medium and cook steaks 3 to 4 minutes on each side (or until desired doneness). Baste frequently with butter mixture for maximum flavor.

Remove steaks from heat, brush with herb-butter mixture and sprinkle with salt and pepper to taste; allow the steaks to rest for 5 minutes before serving.

Sun-Dried Tomato
& Brazil Nut Wellington

Serves 6

½ cup Brazil nuts

1 large shallot, minced

6 tablespoons olive oil

1 (8 ounce) jar sun-dried tomatoes
   packed in oil, chopped

½ cup white wine

½ cup fresh Italian parsley, chopped

3 - 4 fresh basil leaves, chopped

2 tablespoons fresh chives, chopped

1 ½ cups breadcrumbs

5 garlic cloves, minced

¼ cup Asiago cheese, grated

4 sheets puff pastry, thawed

6 (5 - 6 ounce) beef filets

1 egg, beaten

Preheat oven to 350°. Toast Brazil nuts on a cookie sheet for 20 minutes. Remove from oven and set aside. Increase oven temperature to 425°.

In a small sauté pan, sweat shallots in olive oil over medium heat, about 3 to 4 minutes. Add sun-dried tomatoes and sauté 3 additional minutes. Pour in wine and reduce until liquid is almost gone, about 5 to 6 minutes. Add toasted Brazil nuts (reserving 6 nuts). Remove from heat and coarsely process in a blender or food processor until nuts are broken into pea-size pieces. Fold in parsley, basil, chives, breadcrumbs, garlic and Asiago cheese; set aside.

Once pastry shells are pliable, roll out dough to ½ the original thickness. Place 3 steaks on one sheet, allowing a 1 ½ gap between each. Place ¼ cup sun-dried tomato mixture over each steak and spread over top of steak. Brush egg wash around the steak, then lay the second sheet on top. Press layers together and cut around the steaks. Crimp the edge of each pastry with a fork, then brush with egg wash and top with a single brazil nut. Repeat with additional steaks and pastries. Place steaks on a lightly greased cookie sheet and bake for 15 minutes at 425°. Reduce heat to 350° and cook an additional 20 minutes or until the internal temperature reaches 145°. Remove from oven and let meat rest for 5 minutes before serving.

SWEET N' SPICY BRISKET

3 pounds beef brisket

1 (12 ounce) can beer

salt and pepper, to taste

1 medium onion, thinly sliced

$\frac{1}{2}$ teaspoon cayenne pepper

$\frac{3}{4}$ cup chili sauce

3 garlic cloves, minced

$\frac{1}{2}$ cup brown sugar, packed

1 pound bag of baby carrots

8 small Yukon Gold potatoes, cut into 1-inch cubes

Pierce brisket with a fork several times on both sides and marinate in beer overnight in an airtight container.

Reserve beer and remove brisket. In a frying pan over medium-high heat, sear brisket for 8 minutes per side. Remove from pan and place in a baking dish (fatty side up). Rub each side with salt and pepper and cover with thinly sliced onions.

Preheat oven to 300°. In a mixing bowl, combine reserved beer, cayenne, chili sauce, garlic and brown sugar. Pour over brisket and tightly cover with foil; bake for 1 $\frac{1}{2}$ hours. Remove foil, add carrots and potatoes, recover and bake an additional 1 $\frac{1}{2}$ hours. Remove foil and bake for 30 additional minutes. Remove from oven and allow meat to rest for 5 to 10 minutes before serving. Spoon sauce over meat to serve.

TEQUILA FAJITAS

TEQUILA MARINADE

1/2 cup fresh lime juice

1/2 cup peanut oil

3/4 cup tequila

1 tablespoon garlic, finely chopped

3 tablespoons fresh cilantro

2 teaspoons cumin

2 teaspoons oregano

1 tablespoon black pepper

2 teaspoons fajita seasoning

1 tablespoon sugar

1/2 red onion, quartered

1 tablespoon hot sauce

1 tablespoon Triple Sec

FAJITA STUFFING

1 (2 1/2 - 3 pound) top sirloin

2 - 3 poblano peppers, sliced

1 - 2 red onions, sliced

10 - 12 tortillas, warmed

8 ounces fresh guacamole

8 ounces sour cream

Place marinade ingredients in a blender or food processor and blend until smooth. Pierce sirloin several times on each side, then place in marinade in an airtight container. Refrigerate overnight.

Preheat grill to medium-high. Grill sirloin to desired doneness, reserving marinade, about 6 to 8 minutes per side for medium, then remove from heat and allow meat to rest 5 to 10 minutes.

Meanwhile, in a large saucepan over high heat, add remaining marinade and bring to a boil. Reduce heat to medium and add poblanos and onions. Cook until just tender, but still crunchy.

Slice steak across the grain and serve with warm tortillas, Tequila Marinade, fresh guacamole and sour cream.

main

BEEF

PASTA

PORK

POULTRY

SEAFOOD

VEAL, LAMB & DUCK

ACCOMPANIMENTS

ARTICHOKE HEARTS WITH SHIITAKE CREAM SAUCE OVER LINGUINE

1 (14 ounce) can artichoke hearts, drained and quartered

1 teaspoon olive oil

1 (8 ounce) package linguine

1 tablespoon butter

2 shallots, thinly sliced

1 cup shiitake mushroom caps, diced

1 garlic clove, minced

$\frac{1}{2}$ cup dry white wine

1 teaspoon black pepper

$\frac{1}{4}$ cup heavy cream

$\frac{1}{4}$ cup Morbier cheese

juice of $\frac{1}{2}$ lemon

Preheat oven to 400°. Place artichoke hearts on a lined baking sheet, drizzle with oil and roast for 10 to 15 minutes. Remove from oven and set aside.

Meanwhile, prepare linguine according to package directions, drain and set aside.

Heat butter in a saucepan over medium heat. Add shallots and mushrooms; cook 5 minutes. Stir in garlic and white wine and bring to a simmer. Add black pepper; reduce heat to low. After 5 minutes, slowly stir in cream, cheese and lemon juice until cheese is melted. Add artichokes and linguine and toss to coat.

ASIAN PASTA SALAD WITH BEEF, BROCCOLI & BEAN SPROUTS

• •

Serves 10 - 12

SOY GINGER DRESSING

3 garlic cloves, minced

6 tablespoons soy sauce

1 tablespoon rice wine vinegar

1 tablespoon turbinado sugar

1 tablespoon sesame oil

2 tablespoons fresh ginger, minced

$^1/_8$ cup sweet chili sauce

2 tablespoons mayonnaise

1 lemongrass stalk

$^1/_4$ cup vegetable oil

PASTA SALAD

2 pounds sirloin steak

1 (10 ounce) bottle teriyaki sauce or marinade

1 gallon water

2 tablespoons salt

1 (16 ounce) package rotini pasta

$^1/_2$ pound broccoli florets

3 medium carrots, julienned

1 medium red bell pepper, julienned

2 cups bean sprouts

3 green onions, thinly sliced diagonally

$^1/_2$ cup honey roasted peanuts, chopped

$^1/_4$ cup fresh cilantro, chopped

Combine all dressing ingredients except vegetable oil in a food processor or blender; blend into a paste. Then, while mixer is running, drizzle in vegetable oil in a slow steady stream until well mixed and vegetable oil has been incorporated. Store covered in refrigerator until ready to serve.

Marinate sirloin steaks in teriyaki sauce or marinade for 6 hours or overnight. Preheat grill to medium-high and oil the grates. Grill 5 to 6 minutes per side or until desired doneness. Remove and let stand 5 minutes, then slice into 2-inch long strips and set aside.

In a large pot, bring 1 gallon of water and 2 tablespoons of salt to a boil over high heat; add pasta and boil according to package directions, stirring frequently. Add broccoli during the last minute of cooking and remove from heat, drain and rinse with cold water; set aside.

In a large serving bowl, combine pasta and broccoli with beef, carrots, red pepper, bean sprouts, green onions, peanuts and cilantro; chill until ready to serve.

To serve, pour Soy Ginger Dressing over salad and toss to evenly coat.

FOUR CHEESE & SHRIMP ANGEL HAIR

Serves 12

1 (16 ounce) package angel hair pasta

2 eggs

1 cup half & half

1 cup plain yogurt

1 ½ pounds (21 - 25 count) shrimp, peeled and deveined

¾ cup Blue cheese, crumbled

8 ounces Feta cheese, crumbled

½ cup Swiss cheese, shredded

1 (18 ounce) jar chunky salsa

½ cup Monterey Jack cheese, shredded

¾ cup fresh parsley, chopped

1 ½ tablespoons fresh basil, chopped

1 ½ tablespoons fresh oregano, chopped

Preheat oven to 350°. Prepare angel hair pasta according to package directions, drain and set aside.

In a small mixing bowl, whisk together eggs, half & half and yogurt. Set aside.

In a greased 9x13-inch baking dish, layer ⅓ of pasta, shrimp, blue cheese, feta cheese, Swiss cheese and salsa. Repeat layers. Sprinkle Monterey Jack cheese, parsley, basil and oregano over top, then top with cream sauce. Bake uncovered for 25 to 30 minutes. Let stand 5 minutes before serving.

FOUR CHEESE RAVIOLI WITH TOMATO-BASIL CREAM SAUCE

. . . .

Serves 4

1 package frozen four cheese ravioli

2 tablespoons olive oil

2 links Italian sausage, casings removed and crumbled

1 medium shallot, chopped

1 garlic clove, minced

1 (28 ounce) can whole tomatoes

½ cup heavy cream

salt and pepper, to taste

Parmesan cheese, freshly grated

fresh basil, coarsely chopped

Cook ravioli as directed on package; drain and set aside.

Heat olive oil in a large sauté pan over medium heat and sauté sausage and shallots for 8 to 10 minutes or until browned. Add garlic and sauté an additional 2 minutes.

Meanwhile, pour tomatoes in a food processor or blender and purée until smooth. Add puréed tomatoes and heavy cream to saucepan with sausage, then simmer over low heat for 30 minutes.

Season sauce with salt and pepper to taste and add ravioli; toss to evenly coat. Divide ravioli among serving plates and garnish with Parmesan cheese and basil.

GNOCCHI WITH BACON & BRUSSELS SPROUTS

Serves 4

7 ounces bacon, cut into ½-inch pieces

1 teaspoon salt

½ teaspoon baking soda

1 pound Brussels sprouts, halved

2 tablespoons + 2 teaspoons butter

1 (16 ounce) package gnocchi

1 teaspoon olive oil

1 cup chicken broth

2 teaspoons garlic, minced

½ cup Asiago cheese

In a medium frying pan over medium-low heat, cook bacon until crisp but not fully cooked; drain and set aside.

Meanwhile, bring a large pot of water to a boil; add salt and baking soda. Add Brussels sprouts along with 2 tablespoons butter and cook for 3 to 4 minutes; drain and shock sprouts in ice cold water to stop the cooking process. Drain and set aside.

Prepare gnocchi according to directions on package. Once cooked and drained, immediately transfer gnocchi to a large frying pan over medium-high heat with remaining 2 teaspoons butter and olive oil. Sear for 2 to 3 minutes and add cooked Brussels sprouts, bacon, chicken broth and garlic. Cook for 1 minute, then remove from heat. To serve, sprinkle with cheese.

DID YOU KNOW?

WHAT IS GNOCCHI?
Generally considered a type of dumpling or pasta, Gnocchi is traditionally made from potatoes and flour. The basic dough for gnocchi consists of cooked potatoes that have been processed in a potato ricer or mashed by hand and a minimal amount of flour and salt; an egg is sometimes added to help the gnocchi hold together. These ingredients are combined to form a light, fluffy dough and then shaped into small nuggets with an indentation on one side and textured lines on the other; the textured side can be achieved by rolling each individual gnocchi against a fork or cheese grater.

GRILLED EGGPLANT RIGATONI WITH PEPPERED GOAT CHEESE

· ·

Serves 14 - 15

GRILLED EGGPLANT

4 - 6 Roma tomatoes, quartered

2 baby eggplants, cut into ¹/₂-inch slices

3 tablespoons olive oil, divided

salt and pepper, to taste

PASTA

1 (16 ounce) package rigatoni

1 tablespoon olive oil

1 red bell pepper, chopped

2 carrots, peeled and diced

2 sweet onions, chopped

6 garlic cloves, minced

2 tablespoons fresh oregano, chopped

1 tablespoon fresh basil, chopped

1 teaspoon dried marjoram

¹/₈ teaspoon fresh mint

¹/₂ teaspoon dried dill

¹/₂ teaspoon celery salt

¹/₈ teaspoon crushed red pepper flakes

¹/₄ teaspoon cinnamon

salt and pepper, to taste

¹/₄ cup Parmesan cheese, freshly grated

8 ounces peppered Goat cheese, crumbled

Preheat grill to medium-high heat and lightly oil grate. Rub roma tomatoes and eggplant with 2 tablespoons olive oil and sprinkle with salt and pepper to taste. Grill until each side has golden brown grill marks and is fragrant. Let cool, then cut into cubes and set aside.

Prepare pasta according to package directions, drain and set aside.

Preheat oven to 325°. Heat olive oil in a Dutch oven over medium heat; add bell pepper, carrots, onion and garlic and sauté until onions are translucent, about 5 to 6 minutes. Stir in eggplant and sauté until tender, about 2 to 3 minutes. Add grilled diced tomatoes, oregano, basil, marjoram, mint, dill, celery salt, crushed red pepper, cinnamon, salt and pepper. Stir in Parmesan cheese and transfer mixture to a large mixing bowl; add pasta and stir until well mixed.

Spoon mixture into a 9x13-inch baking dish and sprinkle Goat cheese evenly over top. Cover and bake for 15 minutes; remove cover and continue baking for 10 minutes. Remove from oven and serve immediately.

GRILLED SWEETS & GARDEN PEA RAVIOLI

1 large sweet potato, peeled and cut into ½-inch slices

3 tablespoons olive oil, divided

salt and pepper, to taste

1 package frozen cheese ravioli

2 tablespoons butter, divided

2 garlic cloves, minced

½ cup chicken broth

½ cup frozen peas

¼ cup Romano or Parmesan cheese

⅛ cup white wine (optional)

fresh parsley, chopped

ground black pepper

Preheat grill to medium-high heat. Drizzle sweet potato cubes with 1 ½ tablespoons olive oil and sprinkle with salt and pepper to taste. Grill 1 minute per side; remove from grill and cut into triangles. Set aside.

Cook ravioli according to directions on package; drain and set aside.

In a deep sauté pan over medium-high heat, add 1 tablespoon butter and 1 tablespoon olive oil and heat until butter is melted. Add garlic and cook until browned. Add broth, peas and Parmesan cheese and cook over medium-low heat for 1 minute; add cooked ravioli to pan. Increase heat to medium and add sweet potatoes, remaining butter, oil and wine; toss to coat ravioli thoroughly. To serve, transfer to a serving dish and garnish with parsley and pepper.

Lobster Lasagna

Alfredo Sauce

4 tablespoons butter

2 garlic cloves, minced

1 large shallot, minced

4 tablespoons all purpose flour

$\frac{1}{8}$ cup white wine

1 cup milk

$\frac{1}{2}$ cup heavy cream

$\frac{1}{2}$ cup Parmesan cheese, grated

Lasagna

1 (16 ounce) package lasagna noodles

3 tablespoons butter

1 small sweet onion, chopped

3 garlic cloves, minced

1 cup fresh corn

2 pounds lobster, cut into 1-inch
   pieces

2 eggs, beaten

8 ounces Mascarpone cheese

1 cup Mozzarella cheese, shredded

2 cups Parmesan cheese, grated and
   divided

1 cup fresh basil, chopped

Melt butter in a small sauté pan over medium heat. Add garlic and shallots and cook for 5 to 6 minutes. Add flour and stir to combine. Cook for another 2 minutes being sure not to let flour turn brown, stirring occasionally. Add wine and scrape bottom of pan, cook for about 3 to 4 minutes. Add milk and reduce heat to medium-low. Simmer for another 15 minutes. Remove from heat and stir in cream and Parmesan cheese; set aside

Cook pasta according to package directions; drain and set aside.

Meanwhile, in a large sauté pan over medium heat melt butter until it rapidly bubbles. Add onion and garlic and sauté 5 to 6 minutes. Add corn and cook 2 additional minutes before adding lobster. Cook 3 to 4 minutes and remove from heat; set aside.

In a mixing bowl, combine eggs, Mascarpone cheese, Mozzarella cheese and 1 cup Parmesan cheese; mix well.

In a 9x13-inch baking dish, spread $\frac{1}{2}$ cup Alfredo Sauce on bottom. Lay down 4 pieces of pasta, $\frac{3}{4}$ cup Mascarpone cheese mixture and $\frac{1}{2}$ lobster mix. Top with $\frac{1}{4}$ cup Alfredo sauce and repeat procedure with remaining ingredients. Top with basil and remaining 1 cup of Parmesan cheese.

Bake for 35 to 40 minutes covered. Uncover and bake an additional 12 to 15 minutes.

MEDITERRANEAN PASTA

Serves 8

1 (16 ounce) box pasta

1 pound chorizo, crumbled

½ cup pine nuts

2 garlic cloves, minced

1 red bell pepper, roasted and diced

¼ cup green or Kalamata olives, packed in oil and pitted

1 cup tomatoes, diced

¼ cup fresh basil, cut into thin strips

¼ cup Feta cheese, crumbled

½ cup Parmesan cheese, freshly grated

1 teaspoon lemon juice, freshly squeezed

1 tablespoon olive oil

salt and pepper, to taste

Cook pasta according to package directions; drain and set aside.

While pasta is cooking, cook chorizo in a sauté pan over medium heat for 5 minutes or until browned. Add pine nuts and cook until toasted, about 5 minutes. Add garlic and remove from heat.

In a large serving bowl, toss together pasta, chorizo mixture, red bell pepper, olives, tomatoes, basil, Feta, Parmesan, lemon juice and olive oil. Season with salt and pepper and serve immediately.

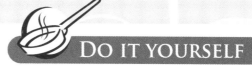

DO IT YOURSELF

HOW TO ROAST PEPPERS
Place whole peppers on grill and turn frequently until skins are blistered and blackened. Once roasted, immediately remove peppers from grill and place in a covered container; allow them to steam for 15-20 minutes to help loosen the skin. Once peppers have steamed and cooled, the skins will slide right off. After skins are removed, slice the peppers in half, remove seeds and core and slice into strips (or slice according to recipe).

Pacific Rim Meatballs with Spiced Glass Noodles

Serves 5 - 6

4 tablespoons shallots, chopped

1 tablespoon hoisin sauce

1 tablespoon soy sauce

2 tablespoons + 1 3/4 teaspoons lime juice, divided

5 garlic cloves, smashed and divided

1 slice bacon, finely chopped

1/4 pound ground pork

1/4 pound ground beef

2 tablespoons fresh ginger, grated

1/4 cup sweet chili sauce

juice of 1 lime

2 teaspoons fish sauce

1/2 teaspoon sesame oil

2 fresh basil leaves, chopped

2 fresh mint leaves, chopped

2 tablespoons fresh cilantro, chopped

1 tablespoon tea oil

1 (8 ounce) package glass noodles

fresh cilantro, chopped (for garnish)

Preheat oven to 325°. Chill a large metal bowl in refrigerator for at least 30 minutes before combining shallots, hoisin sauce, soy sauce, 1 3/4 teaspoons lime juice, 4 garlic cloves and bacon. Add ground pork and ground beef and fold ingredients gently to combine. Roll into 1/2-inch balls, yielding about 30; place meatballs on wax paper and set aside while preparing remaining ingredients.

In a food processor or blender, combine ginger, 1 garlic clove, chili sauce, lime juice, fish sauce, sesame oil, basil, mint and cilantro. Process until smooth and set aside.

In a large frying pan over medium-high heat, heat about 1/4 inch of tea oil and sear meatballs until golden brown. Transfer to a shallow baking dish and bake for 8 minutes or until a meat thermometer reads 155°. Remove from oven and keep warm until ready to serve.

Meanwhile, cook glass noodles according to package directions; drain and transfer to a large mixing bowl. Add chili sauce mixture and toss to coat noodles evenly.

To serve, place noodles on individual plates, top with meatballs and garnish with fresh cilantro.

156

Pasta Corona

2 tablespoons olive oil

6 garlic cloves, minced

1 large sweet onion, chopped

1 (24 ounce) package mushrooms, cleaned and sliced

1 (6 ounce) jar artichokes, drained and chopped

1 (3.8 ounce) can olives, drained and sliced

1 (7.5 ounce) jar sun-dried tomatoes in oil, drained and sliced with oil reserved

2 teaspoons balsamic vinegar

$\frac{1}{4}$ cup white wine

1 (16 ounce) package thin spaghetti

3 ounces pine nuts

Heat olive oil in a large sauté pan over medium heat; add garlic and onion and sauté until soft and slightly browned, about 6 to 8 minutes. Add mushrooms; cook until slightly browned and juice from mushrooms is cooked away, about 8 minutes. Add artichokes, olives and tomatoes and pour reserved sun-dried tomato oil into pan; add balsamic vinegar and white wine. Cover and simmer on low heat for about 15 minutes.

Meanwhile, cook pasta according to package directions; drain and transfer to a large serving bowl. Pour mixture from pan over pasta, add pine nuts and toss to coat pasta evenly.

PENNE PASTA WITH ITALIAN SAUSAGE IN A GARLIC TOMATO CREAM SAUCE

Serves 8 - 10

3 garlic bulbs

2 tablespoons olive oil, divided

1 (16 ounce) package whole wheat penne pasta

1 ½ pounds ground Italian sausage

½ large white onion, diced

8 baby bella mushrooms, sliced

1 (28 ounce) can diced tomatoes

1 (¾ ounce) package fresh basil, chopped

1 cup half & half

salt and pepper, to taste

4 ounces Parmesan cheese, freshly grated and divided

Preheat oven to 375°. Cut tips off garlic bulbs, place in a roasting pan and drizzle with 1 tablespoon olive oil. Cover with foil and roast in oven until garlic bulbs are soft and golden in color, about 1 hour. Remove roasting pan from oven and squeeze garlic cloves from bulbs into a small bowl; set aside.

Cook pasta according to directions on package; drain and return to pot. Drizzle remaining olive oil over pasta and toss to evenly coat.

In a large frying pan over medium-high heat, brown sausage for 8 to 10 minutes; drain excess fat. Add onion to sausage in pan and cook until tender, about 5 to 6 minutes. Stir in roasted garlic cloves, mushrooms and diced tomatoes; reduce heat to low and simmer 10 minutes. Add basil and heat through. Stir in cream, salt, pepper and 2 oz Parmesan cheese. Heat for 5 additional minutes, add pasta and stir making sure that pasta is evenly coated with sauce.

Garnish with remaining Parmesan cheese before serving.

PROSCIUTTO PASTA

Serves 6

3 tablespoons unsalted butter

2 tablespoons vegetable oil

1 (4 ounce) package sliced prosciutto, diced

1 small sweet onion, finely chopped

4 large tomatoes, seeded and cubed (or 2 cups seeded chopped Italian plum tomatoes)

¼ tablespoon red pepper flakes

½ pound garden peas, sliced on the bias

1 (16 ounce) package penne pasta

salt and pepper, to taste

Parmesan cheese, grated

1 tablespoon fresh parsley, chopped

Heat butter and oil in a large sauté pan over medium heat; add prosciutto and sauté for about 4 minutes. Add onion and reduce to medium-low heat, cook 4 additional minutes or until onions are opaque and pale yellow. Stir in tomatoes and red pepper flakes; gently simmer uncovered for 20 minutes. Remove from heat and set aside.

Steam garden peas for 3 to 4 minutes; remove from steamer and set aside.

Meanwhile, cook penne pasta according to package directions; drain and transfer back to pot in which they were cooked. Add garden peas and half prosciutto mixture; toss to coat evenly.

To serve, transfer pasta to a large serving plate; top with remaining prosciutto mixture and garnish with Parmesan cheese and parsley.

ROASTED TOMATO PASTA WITH GRILLED FENNEL RAGOUT

1 large fennel bulb, halved

4 tablespoons olive oil, divided

1 tablespoon fennel seeds

3 garlic cloves, chopped

2 teaspoons fresh thyme, chopped

$1/2$ teaspoon red pepper flakes

1 small sweet onion, diced

salt and pepper, to taste

1 (28 ounce) can roasted diced tomatoes, drained

$1/2$ cup vegetable broth

1 (8 ounce) package orecchiette pasta

3 teaspoons fresh oregano, chopped

Asiago cheese, freshly grated

Preheat grill to medium-high. Drizzle fennel bulb halves with 2 tablespoons olive oil and grill for 5 to 6 minutes. Remove from grill and let cool. Once cooled, cut halves in half again and then thinly slice; set aside.

Prepare fennel seeds by placing on cutting board and rolling over once or twice with a rolling pin to coarsely break; set aside.

Heat remaining 2 tablespoons olive oil in a large sauté pan over medium-high heat; add garlic, thyme and red pepper flakes and sauté for 30 seconds. Add onion, crushed fennel seeds and salt and pepper to taste; cook for 5 minutes. Stir in tomatoes, vegetable broth and grilled, sliced fennel; simmer for 15 minutes.

Meanwhile, cook pasta according to package directions; drain. Add oregano to sauce and gradually stir in cooked pasta. To serve, garnish with freshly grated Asiago cheese

ROASTED VEGETABLE & FOUR CHEESE LASAGNA

Serves 12

12 lasagna noodles

2 cups butternut squash, peeled and diced

1 eggplant, sliced in ½-inch slices

5 tomatoes, halved

1 (1 pint) container Ricotta cheese

8 ounces Feta cheese, crumbled

⅔ cup basil pesto

2 eggs, beaten

½ teaspoon salt

½ teaspoon black pepper

1 (15 ounce) can tomato sauce

2 cups Mozzarella cheese, shredded

1 cup Parmesan cheese, freshly grated

Preheat oven to 350°. Prepare lasagna noodles according to package directions; drain and set aside.

Place diced squash on a baking sheet and roast in preheated oven until browned and tender, about 30 minutes.

In a sauté pan over medium-high heat, sauté eggplant slices, turning once, until browned on each side and tender, approximately 10 to 12 minutes; set aside.

Meanwhile, place tomatoes skin side up on a separate baking sheet; place in oven with squash during last 15 minutes of cooking time. Cook tomatoes until tender and wrinkly. Remove both tomatoes and squash from oven when done; set aside and let cool.

In a medium mixing bowl, stir together Ricotta, Feta, pesto, eggs, salt and pepper until well combined; gently fold roasted squash into mixture.

To assemble lasagna, spoon half the tomato sauce into the bottom of a 9x13-inch baking dish; place 4 lasagna noodles over sauce. Arrange a single layer of eggplant slices over noodles and top with half Ricotta mixture. Cover ricotta mixture with another layer of 4 lasagna noodles; arrange roasted tomatoes evenly over the noodles and spoon remaining ricotta mixture over tomatoes. Sprinkle with 1 cup Mozzarella and cover with remaining 4 lasagna noodles. Pour remaining tomato sauce evenly over noodles and sprinkle with remaining 1 cup Mozzarella and 1 cup Parmesan.

Bake uncovered lasagna in preheated 350° oven for 30 to 40 minutes, until cheese is golden and bubbly.

161

SUN-DRIED TOMATO PASTA

1 (8 ounce) package orzo

chicken broth, substitute for water
   amount per orzo package

2 tablespoons olive oil

1 jar sun-dried tomatoes, packed in oil

1 jar Kalamata olives, drained, pitted
   and coarsely chopped

1 medium purple onion, thinly sliced

8 ounces Feta cheese crumbled

1 ($^3/_4$ ounce) package fresh basil,
   chopped

Cook orzo according to directions on package, replacing water with chicken broth. Drain, place in a large serving bowl and drizzle with olive oil; toss to coat pasta evenly.

Add sun-dried tomatoes, olives and onion; toss to combine. Refrigerate for at least 2 hours. Before serving, sprinkle with Feta cheese and basil; serve warm or chilled.

THAI STYLE PEANUT SHRIMP WITH NOODLES

SAUCE

$1/2$ cup peanut butter

2 teaspoons vegetable oil

$1/4$ teaspoon sesame oil

3 garlic cloves, finely minced

1 tablespoon fresh ginger, chopped

1 small chili pepper (serrano or Thai), finely minced

1 cup water

$1/4$ cup soy sauce

$1/8$ cup rice wine vinegar

1 teaspoon brown sugar, packed

PASTA

1 (8 ounce) package spaghetti

1 pound (21 - 25 ct) shrimp, peeled and deveined

3 celery stalks, chopped

4 green onions, chopped

peanuts, for garnish (optional)

For sauce, whisk all ingredients together in a medium mixing bowl until well combined; set aside.

Cook pasta according to package directions; drain and set aside.

Meanwhile, in a large sauté pan over medium-high heat, cook shrimp for 3 to 4 minutes on each side until pink. Add celery and green onions to pan and sear for 1 to 2 minutes. Pour prepared sauce into pan and stir to mix well with shrimp; add pasta and toss until pasta is evenly coated. Garnish with chopped peanuts, if desired.

main

BEEF

PASTA

PORK

POULTRY

SEAFOOD

VEAL, LAMB & DUCK

ACCOMPANIMENTS

BOURBON & HONEY SMOKED PORK CHOPS

1 cup olive oil

$\frac{1}{2}$ cup bourbon

3 tablespoons honey

$\frac{1}{2}$ cup lemon juice

1 tablespoon garlic, minced

1 $\frac{1}{2}$ tablespoons fresh ginger, grated

$\frac{1}{4}$ cup soy sauce

$\frac{1}{2}$ cup onions, thinly sliced

1 tablespoon fresh sage, chopped

1 tablespoon fresh thyme, chopped

2 tablespoons pepper

1 tablespoon salt

4 center cut pork chops

3 - 4 handfuls hickory wood chips

In a large mixing bowl, combine all ingredients except pork chops and wood chips; mix well and pour into a sealable bag. Add pork and refrigerate for 12 to 24 hours, turning periodically.

Soak wood chips in water for 15 to 20 minutes before starting grill. Drain and add to coals; then heat grill to high heat and grill pork chops for 8 to 10 minutes per side, or until meat has reached an internal temperature of 165°. Remove from grill and let rest for 10 minutes before serving.

BALSAMIC VINEGAR & SAGE PORK

Serves 4 - 6

1 ½ pounds pork tenderloin

2 tablespoons all purpose flour

salt and pepper, to taste

1 tablespoon butter

1 tablespoon olive oil

⅔ cup balsamic vinegar

¼ cup chicken broth

1 tablespoon fresh sage, chopped

Cut tenderloin at a slight angle into 8 medallions; lightly flatten (for ease, place each medallion between two pieces of plastic wrap and gently flatten with a kitchen mallet).

Combine flour, salt and pepper on a plate; coat medallions in flour mixture, shaking off excess. Heat butter and oil in a large sauté pan over medium heat until butter is melted; add medallions and cook 2 to 3 minutes on each side until brown. Transfer medallions to a serving dish and cover with aluminum foil to keep warm; set aside.

Drain drippings from pan and reserve. Add balsamic vinegar to same pan and deglaze by scraping the brown bits off of the bottom; continue to cook over medium heat until reduced by half. Add chicken broth and reserved pan drippings; simmer 1 minute until sauce is dark and shiny. Add sage and adjust seasoning if needed; pour sauce over medallions before serving.

SERVING SUGGESTION

Excellent served with Herbed Asparagus
Saute, page 260

CARIBBEAN SPICE PORK TENDERLOIN

½ cup white wine

2 tablespoons salt

¼ teaspoon allspice

¼ teaspoon nutmeg

¼ teaspoon cinnamon

¼ teaspoon onion, grated

1 garlic clove, minced

¼ teaspoon cayenne pepper

1 tablespoon paprika

1 ½ pounds pork tenderloin

Preheat oven to 325°. In a mixing bowl, whisk together all ingredients except pork. Once fully incorporated, place tenderloin and marinade in an airtight container and place in the refrigerator for 3 to 4 hours.

Remove tenderloin from marinade and place in a baking dish. Bake for 35 to 45 minutes, until pork is no longer pink; remove from oven and let rest for 5 minutes before slicing into ½-inch medallions.

SERVING SUGGESTION

Excellent served with Saffron Rice with Asparagus and Raisins, page 270

GARLIC STUDDED DIJON PORK TENDERLOIN

Serves 4 - 6

1 ½ tablespoons white wine vinegar

2 teaspoons Dijon mustard

2 tablespoons olive oil

1 teaspoon dried oregano

⅛ teaspoon black pepper

salt, to taste

1 ½ pounds pork tenderloin

4 garlic cloves, halved lengthwise

Preheat oven to 400°. In a small mixing bowl, whisk together vinegar, mustard, oil and spices. Place tenderloin in an airtight container and pour marinade over pork, coating evenly; let sit for at least 30 minutes in the refrigerator.

Grease a 9x13-inch baking dish; remove pork from marinade and place in dish. Cut 8 slits along top of pork and stuff a garlic clove half into each slit. Pour reserved marinade over pork and bake for 45 minutes. Remove from oven and let rest for 5 minutes before slicing.

SERVING SUGGESTION

Excellent served with Potatoes & Leeks
with Gruyere, page 266

Grilled Lime Center Cut Pork Chops

Serves 2

4 garlic cloves, minced

1 ½ tablespoons soy sauce

1 jalapeño, chopped

½ tablespoon Dijon mustard

⅓ cup lime juice

½ cup olive oil

salt and pepper, to taste

2 thick-cut pork chops

tomatillo salsa

cilantro, chopped, for garnish

In a small mixing bowl, whisk together all ingredients except pork and cilantro; pour into a large sealable bag. Add pork and marinate for several hours at room temperature or in the refrigerator for 1 or 2 days.

Preheat grill to medium-high and brush grates with oil. Remove pork from marinade and grill, turning frequently, for 15 to 20 minutes. Remove from grill and let stand for 5 minutes before slicing. Top with tomatillo salsa and garnish with fresh cilantro.

TOMATILLO SALSA

3 (11 oz) cans tomatillos

½ cup onion, chopped

juice of 1 lime

1 garlic clove, minced

½ cup fresh cilantro, chopped

2 peppers, seeded and chopped (serrano or jalapeño)

1 teaspoon sugar

salt to taste

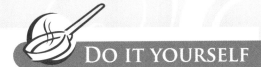
DO IT YOURSELF

In a mixing bowl, combine all ingredients. Transfer to food processor or blender and puree. Place salsa back in mixing bowl and allow to cool in refrigerator for 1 to 2 hours before serving.

Macadamia Crusted Jerk Pork with Apricot Relish

· ·

Serves 4 - 5

Apricot Relish

2 apricots, diced

1 tablespoon apricot preserves

2 teaspoons fresh ginger, grated

1 small papaya, diced

2 mint leaves, chopped

$1/4$ cup cilantro, chopped

$1/2$ red bell pepper, finely diced

Glaze

$1/4$ cup crushed pineapple

1 tablespoon hoisin

2 tablespoons soy sauce

$1/2$ cup pineapple juice

2 teaspoons cornstarch dissolved in 1
  tablespoon water

Pork

$3/4$ cup macadamia nuts, finely chopped

$1/4$ teaspoon jerk spice blend

3 tablespoons tea oil

1 pound pork loin, cut into $1/2$-inch
  wide slices

bibb lettuce leaves, for plating

In a medium mixing bowl, combine all relish ingredients; stir until well mixed and set aside.

In a small bowl, combine crushed pineapple, hoisin, soy sauce and pineapple juice until fully incorporated. Whisk in cornstarch until well combined; set aside.

In a shallow bowl, combine macadamia nuts and jerk spice blend.

Heat tea oil in a large frying pan over medium heat; add pork and cook until golden brown, about 5 to 6 minutes. Add glaze and cook an additional 2 to 3 minutes. Remove pork and dip into macadamia nut crust.

To serve, place lettuce on each plate, top with crusted pork and top with Apricot Relish.

Pork Chops with a Cranberry Port Sauce

3 tablespoons olive oil

4 thin-cut pork chops

1 ½ tablespoons herbes de Provence seasoning blend

salt and pepper, to taste

¼ stick of butter, cut into pieces

¾ cup chicken broth

⅔ cup Tawny port

1 cup cranberry relish

¼ cup dried cranberries

rosemary sprigs, for garnish

Heat olive oil in a large sauté pan over medium-high heat; sprinkle pork chops with herbes de Provence, salt and pepper to taste. Place pork chops in pan and sear on both sides for 8 to 10 minutes until golden brown. Place pats of butter on each pork chop; reduce heat to low and cook 4 to 5 minutes or until pork chops are cooked through. Transfer pork chops to a serving platter and keep warm.

Add broth and port to the same sauté pan that was used for cooking the pork chops and reduce by half over medium-high heat. Stir in cranberry relish and dried cranberries and reduce to medium heat for about 5 minutes or until sauce is thickened.

To serve, spoon sauce over warm pork chops and garnish with rosemary sprigs.

 DO IT YOURSELF

FRESH CRANBERRY RELISH
2 lbs fresh cranberries
¾ cup sugar
1 teaspoon lemon juice
zest of 1 orange

Place all ingredients in a food processor or blender and pulse until contents are well incorporated and finely chopped. For best flavor, allow the relish to sit at room temperature before serving.

PORK CHOPS WITH
SWEET POTATO & PEAR CRISPS

4 large sweet potatoes, peeled

3 large pears, peeled, cored and chopped

1/3 cup pecans, toasted

1/3 cup brown sugar, packed

1/2 cup + 2 tablespoons all purpose flour, divided

3 tablespoons butter, melted

2 tablespoons oil

2 eggs, beaten

1 cup seasoned breadcrumbs

4 thick-cut pork chops

Preheat oven to 350°. In a large stockpot, bring water to a boil; add whole sweet potatoes and boil for 6 to 8 minutes. Drain potatoes, cut into wedges and set aside.

In an 8x8-inch baking dish, alternately place potatoes and pears. In a small mixing bowl, combine pecans, sugar, 2 tablespoons flour and butter; crumble mixture over sweet potatoes and pears; set aside.

Heat oil in a large sauté pan over medium-high heat. Place eggs in a wide shallow bowl; place remaining 1/2 cup flour on a plate and place breadcrumbs on a separate plate. Coat each pork chop first in flour, then in eggs and finally in breadcrumbs. Place chops in sauté pan, reduce heat to medium and sear for 3 to 4 minutes or until golden brown.

Place seared pork chops in a greased 9x13-inch baking dish. Transfer both sweet potato and pear crisps and pork chops to oven; bake for 20 minutes then remove from oven and allow both dishes to rest 5 minutes before serving. To serve, place sweet potato and pear crisps over pork chops.

PORK CHOPS WITH BASIL CREAM SAUCE

Serves 4

1 tablespoon olive oil

1 tablespoon butter

4 thin-cut pork chops

salt, to taste

white pepper, to taste

⅓ cup onions, thinly sliced

¼ cup capers, drained

½ cup heavy cream

¼ cup fresh basil, chopped

Heat oil and butter in a medium sauté pan over medium-high heat until butter is melted; add pork and sauté for 10 to 12 minutes on each side until juices run clear. Transfer pork to a plate lined with paper towels, season with salt and pepper and set aside.

In same sauté pan, add onions and capers and cook over medium-high heat, stirring continuously until golden brown, about 3 minutes. Add cream and basil; bring to a boil. Reduce heat to low and cook about 3 minutes until cream thickens slightly; return pork to skillet and coat evenly with sauce.

Excellent served over Zucchini Cakes, page ___.

SERVING SUGGESTION

Excellent served with Zucchin Patties with Feta, page 284

PORK TENDERLOIN WITH CHERRY PECAN STUFFING

1 ½ cups water

1 ½ cups dried cherries

⅛ cup pecans, toasted

2 teaspoons ground cinnamon

pinch of ground cloves

2 tablespoons fresh cilantro, chopped

2 tablespoons olive oil

1 ½ pounds pork tenderloin

salt and pepper, to taste

butcher's twine

Preheat oven to 400°. In a medium saucepan over high heat, bring water to a boil. Add cherries and immediately remove from heat; let rest for 1 hour then drain. Transfer cherries to a food processor and add pecans, cinnamon and cloves; pulse until coarsely chopped. Transfer to a bowl and stir in cilantro.

Preheat olive oil in a large sauté pan over medium high heat. Cut tenderloin in half lengthwise ¾ of the way through and unfold like a book in front of you. Place a sheet of plastic wrap over the top and, using a mallet, flatten slightly. Remove plastic, season with salt and pepper to taste. Spread cherry stuffing over tenderloin and fold back together; secure with butcher's twine. Sear tenderloin in sauté pan for 5 to 6 minutes then transfer to a baking dish and bake for 15 to 20 minutes.

Remove from oven and let rest 5 minutes before slicing into medallions to serve.

PORK MEDALLIONS WITH BLACK PEPPER CREAM SAUCE

Serves 4 -6

5 tablespoons olive oil, divided

1 ½ pounds pork tenderloin

2 medium red onions, chopped

1 teaspoon sugar

¼ cup brandy

½ cup heavy cream

2 tablespoons black pepper

1 teaspoon garlic powder

3 tablespoons fresh parsley, chopped

salt and pepper, to taste

sprigs of fresh rosemary, for garnish

Preheat oven to 375°. Heat 2 tablespoons olive oil in a shallow ovenproof sauté pan over medium-high heat; add tenderloin and sear until browned on all sides. Transfer to preheated oven and roast 30 minutes until meat thermometer reads 165°. Remove from oven and cover with aluminum foil; set aside.

Heat remaining olive oil in a medium sauté pan over medium heat; add onions and cook until slightly translucent. Add sugar and stir continuously for 3 to 4 minutes or until onions are caramelized; add brandy and reduce mixture by half. Mix in cream, pepper and garlic powder; simmer for 8 to 10 minutes or until sauce thickens. Remove from heat, season with parsley and salt and pepper to taste.

To serve, slice tenderloin into ½-inch medallions and fan out on a serving platter; spoon sauce over medallions and garnish with rosemary sprigs.

Sausage & Gorgonzola Stuffed Pork Chops

4 bone-in pork chops

1 pound ground hot Italian sausage, crumbled

$1/4$ cup pine nuts, toasted

4 ounces Gorgonzola cheese, crumbled

$1/4$ cup sun-dried tomatoes packed in oil, drained and chopped

1 quart water

$1/4$ cup salt

$1/8$ cup brown sugar

2 teaspoons red pepper flakes

$1/2$ cup apple cider vinegar

2 tablespoons olive oil

salt and pepper, to taste

Preheat oven to 350°. Pierce pork chops several times with a fork; carefully cut a $1/2$-inch slit in the side of each pork chop and place in a large baking dish.

Meanwhile, heat a small sauté pan over medium heat; add sausage and cook until browned. In a medium mixing bowl, combine crumbled cooked sausage, toasted pine nuts, cheese and tomatoes; mix well. Chill for at least 1 hour in refrigerator.

In a large mixing bowl, combine water, salt, brown sugar, red pepper flakes and apple cider vinegar and mix well; pour over pork chops. Cover and let brine in refrigerator for 45 minutes.

Heat oil in a large sauté pan over medium-high heat. Remove pork chops from brine, discard birne and pat pork chops dry with a paper towel; season with salt and pepper to taste. Sear chops for 4 minutes per side.

Using a spoon, scoop sausage mixture into pork chop slits and secure with a toothpick if necessary; return to baking dish and bake for 30 minutes. Remove from oven and let rest for 5 minutes before serving.

TANGY BABY BACK RIBS

2 racks baby back ribs

2 tablespoons olive oil

salt and pepper, to taste

BARBEQUE SAUCE

2 tablespoons olive oil

$\frac{1}{2}$ cup onions, chopped

1 cup ketchup

$\frac{1}{2}$ cup apple cider vinegar

2 tablespoons Worcestershire sauce

2 tablespoons sugar

1 teaspoon pepper

2 teaspoons chili powder

$\frac{1}{4}$ teaspoon paprika

1 teaspoon salt

1 cup water

Preheat oven to 450°. Drizzle ribs with 2 tablespoons olive oil and season with salt and pepper; place on a baking sheet and bake 20 minutes or until browned.

Meanwhile, heat remaining oil in a sauté pan over medium heat and sauté onions until translucent, about 5 to 6 minutes. Add remaining barbeque sauce ingredients, reduce heat to medium-low and simmer for 20 minutes. Remove ribs from oven and reduce heat to 350°. Pour half of barbeque sauce mixture evenly over top and return ribs to oven. Bake for about 2 $\frac{1}{2}$ hours until meat pulls away from the bones. Remove from oven and baste with remaining sauce before serving.

main

BEEF

PASTA

PORK

POULTRY

SEAFOOD

VEAL, LAMB & DUCK

ACCOMPANIMENTS

Apricot Chicken with Mushroom Cream Sauce

Mushroom Cream

1 (8 ounce) container white mushrooms, cleaned and sliced

1 quart heavy cream

1 large shallot, minced

1 teaspoon fresh thyme, chopped

Chicken

³/₄ cup chicken broth

4 ounces dried apricots

1 cup sour cream

¹/₄ cup sherry (optional)

12 portabella mushrooms, chopped

6 boneless, skinless chicken breasts

¹/₂ cup fresh parsley, chopped

salt and pepper, to taste

Preheat oven to 350°. Combine all Mushroom Cream ingredients in a saucepan over high heat; bring to a boil. Reduce heat to medium-low and simmer 15 minutes. Remove from heat and remove ¹/₂ mushrooms and 1 cup cream to a food processor or blender, purée until smooth. Add puree back to saucepan, stir to combine and set aside.

In a medium saucepan, bring chicken broth to a simmer over medium-low heat. Remove from heat and add dried apricots; cover with plastic wrap and set aside for 20 to 30 minutes. Remove from heat and purée in a blender or food processor until smooth.

In a mixing bowl, combine apricot puree, sour cream, sherry and mushroom cream. Stir in portabella mushrooms and season with salt and pepper to taste.

Meanwhile, pound chicken to flatten and sprinkle with salt, pepper and parsley. Roll each chicken breast and secure with a toothpick; place in a baking dish. Pour mixture over chicken, cover with foil and bake 45 minutes. Remove foil and bake an additional 20 minutes.

BAKED CHICKEN WITH CINNAMON BRAISED APPLES

· ·

Serves 10 - 12

6 Fuji apples, peeled, cored and sliced

½ teaspoon cinnamon

⅛ cup Demerara sugar

3 tablespoons butter, softened

2 tablespoons dried parsley

1 tablespoon fresh rosemary, chopped

1 tablespoon fresh thyme, chopped

1 tablespoon fresh sage, chopped

salt and pepper, to taste

1 (5 - 6 pound) whole roasting chicken, cut into quarters (or 6 split chicken breasts)

Sear apples in a 4 quart saucepan over medium-high heat until you hear a sizzle on the bottom. Add cinnamon and sugar and stir after 5 minutes. Once apples begin to steam, about 10 minutes, reduce heat to low and simmer for 2 hours, stirring every 30 minutes. Remove from pan and place in a 9x13-inch baking dish.

Preheat oven to 375°. In a small bowl, combine butter, parsley, rosemary, thyme, sage, salt and pepper. Gently separate skin from chicken and spread butter mixture under skin. Place chicken on top of apples, cover dish tightly with foil and bake 1 hour. Remove foil and continue baking for 30 minutes.

BIG BANG CHICKEN

Serves 6

3 tablespoons olive oil

6 boneless, skinless chicken breasts

all purpose flour

4 garlic cloves, minced

1 medium green bell pepper, sliced

2 (6 ounce) jars marinated artichoke hearts, with juices

2 (15 ounce) cans stewed tomatoes, with juices

8 ounces fresh mushrooms, sliced

1/2 cup sherry

1 teaspoon fresh rosemary, chopped

1 teaspoon fresh oregano, chopped

1 teaspoon fresh basil, chopped

1 teaspoon paprika

1 teaspoon salt

1/2 teaspoon black pepper

Preheat oven to 350°. Heat oil in a large frying pan over medium heat. Dredge chicken in flour then place in pan and brown for 10 minutes. Add garlic and bell pepper and cook until soft, about 5 to 6 minutes. Add artichoke hearts, stewed tomatoes and mushrooms; remove from heat and place in a 9x13-inch baking dish.

Cover and bake 30 minutes. Remove from oven, add sherry, fresh herbs and spices then bake an additional 30 minutes uncovered.

CHICKEN MARRAKECH WITH JEWELED COUSCOUS

Serves 4

CHICKEN

1 stick butter, softened

4 scallions, minced

2 garlic cloves, minced

1 tablespoon paprika

1 tablespoon cumin

1 teaspoon coriander

$1/2$ teaspoon cayenne pepper

2 tablespoons fresh parsley, chopped

2 tablespoons fresh cilantro, chopped

$1/2$ teaspoon salt

4 large split chicken breasts, skin-on

COUSCOUS

2 tablespoons vegetable oil

1 medium carrot, finely chopped

1 small red bell pepper, finely chopped

4 scallions, sliced

1 small zucchini, diced

2 garlic cloves, minced

1 tablespoon coriander

1 teaspoon turmeric

$1/4$ teaspoon cayenne pepper

3 cups chicken broth

salt and pepper, to taste

$1 1/2$ cups Israeli couscous

$1/2$ cup golden raisins

$1/2$ cup almonds, sliced

$1/4$ cup fresh parsley, chopped

Preheat oven to 425°. In a small bowl, combine butter, scallions, garlic, paprika, cumin, coriander, cayenne pepper, parsley, cilantro and salt. Gently separate, but do not remove, skin from chicken. Stuff $1/4$ of butter mixture under skin of each chicken breast and place on a baking dish. Bake for 30 to 40 minutes. Baste with any pan juices at least once halfway through roasting process.

Meanwhile, heat oil in a Dutch oven over medium heat. Add carrot and pepper; cook for 3 to 4 minutes. Add scallions and zucchini and cook an additional 3 to 4 minutes. Add garlic, coriander, turmeric and cayenne pepper; sauté briefly. Pour in chicken broth and bring to a boil. Season with salt and pepper, then add couscous. Remove from heat, stir briefly, cover and let stand while chicken finishes, about 5 to 6 minutes. Just before serving add raisins, almonds and parsley to couscous and fluff with a fork.

To serve, spread couscous on a platter, top with chicken and drizzle any leftover juices from the pan over chicken.

CHICKEN WITH MUSHROOMS AND HERBS

Serves 6

6 boneless, skinless chicken breasts

salt and pepper, to taste

3 tablespoons butter

3 tablespoons olive oil

2 garlic cloves, minced

2 tablespoons shallots, finely minced

4 ounces mushrooms, sliced

2 tablespoons all purpose flour

$\frac{1}{2}$ cups vermouth

1 $\frac{1}{4}$ cup chicken broth

1 bay leaf

$\frac{1}{4}$ teaspoon thyme

$\frac{1}{8}$ teaspoon marjoram

2 tablespoons fresh parsley, chopped

$\frac{1}{2}$ cup heavy cream

Season chicken with salt and pepper and set aside. Melt butter and oil in a large sauté pan over medium-high heat. Add chicken and brown on both sides, about 8 minutes. Remove chicken; cover with foil to keep warm and set aside.

To same sauté pan over medium-high heat, add garlic, shallots and mushrooms and cook 3 minutes, until slightly tender. Sprinkle with flour and cook 2 additional minutes, stirring constantly. Slowly add vermouth and broth and stir until fully incorporated. Add herbs and bring to a boil; reduce heat to low and simmer for 5 minutes. Return chicken to pan and cook another 8 minutes. Add cream, simmering 3 additional minutes. Remove bay leaf and adjust seasoning to taste.

Excellent with rice pilaf or over pasta.

CHICKEN WITH TOMATILLOS AND POBLANOS

Serves 3 - 4

8 boneless chicken thighs

1 teaspoon salt

1/2 teaspoon black pepper

3 poblano peppers

3 Anaheim peppers

1 tablespoon olive oil

2 cups chicken broth

1 (12 ounce) jar tomatillo salsa

2/3 cup fresh cilantro, chopped

blue corn tortilla chips

Preheat grill to high heat. Season chicken with salt and pepper. Rub peppers with olive oil. Place chicken and peppers on grill. Sear chicken for 3 to 4 minutes per side and roast peppers until all sides are blistered.

When chicken is seared, place in a 4 quart saucepan with chicken broth and tomatillo salsa. Bring to a simmer then turn heat down to just below a simmer for 25 to 30 minutes.

Meanwhile, place roasted peppers in a metal bowl and seal tightly for 10 to 15 minutes. Then, carefully peel and seed peppers. Cut poblanos into strips and Anaheims into cubes. When chicken is cooked, add peppers and combine. To serve, remove chicken from pan and place on a platter. Add cilantro to remaining sauce in pan then pour over chicken.

Garnish with blue corn tortilla chips and serve with Spanish rice or roasted potatoes.

CRANBERRY PECAN TURKEY ROULADE

Serves 4 - 6

CRANBERRY STUFFING

1 cup sourdough bread, diced into $\frac{1}{4}$ -inch pieces

1 cup rye bread, torn into bite-sized pieces

4 tablespoons butter, divided

1 medium shallot, chopped

2 garlic cloves

3 teaspoons fresh thyme

2 teaspoons fresh chives, chopped

1 teaspoon fresh sage, chopped

$\frac{1}{2}$ pound dried cranberries

1 cup chicken broth

TURKEY

8 turkey cutlets (or $\frac{1}{2}$ pound turkey breast cut into 8 cutlets)

butcher's twine

salt and pepper, to taste

1 cup pecans, chopped

$\frac{1}{4}$ cup pecan halves

Preheat oven 350°. Toast bread for 20 to 25 minutes. Remove from oven and set aside. Melt 1 tablespoon butter in a sauté pan over medium heat; sweat shallot, garlic, herbs and cranberries in butter, about 5 to 6 minutes. Fold toasted bread into cranberry mixture and add chicken broth; stir to combine. Let stand 10 to 15 minutes.

Increase oven temperature to 500°. Grease a baking wire rack and place on a sheet pan. Melt 3 tablespoons of butter; set aside. Pound turkey meat to half the thickness (for ease, place each cutlet between two pieces of plastic wrap and gently flatten with a kitchen mallet). Lay turkey cutlets side by side, slightly overlapping each other. Add 2 $\frac{1}{2}$ cups stuffing on the bottom $\frac{1}{4}$ of the cutlets. Using the plastic wrap, tightly roll the turkey, being sure to keep the stuffing inside. Pull the plastic wrap back and gently roll the roulade back towards you so that the seam is facing up. Tie 3 to 4 pieces of twine with a double knot around the roulade, but not too tightly. Place on the prepared baking pan and brush with melted butter. Season with salt and pepper and place on the highest shelf in your oven for 10 minutes. Then broil for 5 minutes. Remove from oven; allow to rest for 5 minutes then slice into medallions, garnish with pecans and serve.

FETA CHICKEN ROLLS

FETA STUFFING

16 ounces Feta cheese, crumbled

3 tablespoons Italian breadcrumbs

2 garlic cloves, minced

3 fresh basil leaves, finely chopped

2 tablespoons fresh chives, finely chopped

1 egg white

1 ½ teaspoons olive oil

CARAMELIZED ONIONS

2 tablespoons olive oil

2 large onions, thinly sliced

salt and pepper, to taste

CHICKEN

6 boneless, skinless chicken breasts

1 tablespoon olive oil

Using a fork, mix crumbled Feta cheese and breadcrumbs in a large bowl; breaking up any very large chunks of cheese. Add garlic, basil and chives, stir to combine. Add egg white and 1 ½ teaspoons olive oil; lightly toss mixture until all ingredients are evenly distributed; set aside.

Meanwhile, heat 2 tablespoons olive oil in a large sauté pan over medium heat. Add onions, salt and pepper and sauté, stirring frequently. Cook until golden brown, about 20 minutes.

Pound chicken breasts to ½ of their thickness (for ease, place each cutlet between two pieces of plastic wrap and gently flatten with a kitchen mallet). Place ⅓ cup of Feta stuffing on each, roll and secure with a toothpick.

Heat 1 tablespoon oil in a large pan over medium heat. Add chicken rolls and cook 5 to 6 minutes per side.

Remove from pan and top with caramelized onions to serve.

GARLIC CHICKEN WITH SHERRY BUTTER

Serves 4 - 6

1 cup French bread, coarsely grated into breadcrumbs

½ cup Parmesan cheese, grated

½ teaspoon salt

1 egg, beaten

3 boneless, skinless chicken breasts, cut in half

2 garlic cloves, minced

¼ cup butter

¼ cup water

⅓ cup sherry

1 teaspoon Worcestershire sauce

1 teaspoon Dijon mustard

Preheat oven to 500°. In a bowl, combine breadcrumbs, cheese and salt. Dip chicken pieces in egg and coat with cheese-bread mixture. Arrange in a 9x13-inch baking dish; set aside.

In a small sauté pan over medium heat, sauté garlic in melted butter for 5 minutes. Add water, sherry, Worcestershire sauce and mustard. Heat until ingredients are fully incorporated then pour over chicken. Bake for 20 to 30 minutes, or until juices run clear.

SERVING SUGGESTION

Excellent Served with Herbed Asparagus Sauté, page 260.

GREEK CHICKEN ON FLATBREAD WITH FETA-YOGURT SAUCE

Serves 4 - 6

GREEK CHICKEN

2 pounds boneless, skinless chicken breasts (about 2 - 3 chicken breasts)

3 tablespoons olive oil

1 teaspoon black fig vinegar (may substitute with red wine vinegar)

juice of 2 lemons

$\frac{1}{2}$ teaspoon salt

4 teaspoons black pepper

4 garlic cloves, minced

4 teaspoons dried oregano

$\frac{1}{2}$ cup fresh parsley, chopped

FETA-YOGURT SAUCE

6 ounces Feta cheese

$\frac{1}{2}$ cup fresh parsley, chopped

2 garlic cloves, minced

1 (32 ounce) container Greek strained yogurt

2 teaspoons pepper

1 tomato, seeded and chopped

1 cucumber, seeded and diced

4 slices of flatbread or pitas

Place chicken in a 9x13-inch baking dish. In a mixing bowl, whisk together oil, vinegar and lemon juice; drizzle over chicken. Season with salt and pepper and spread garlic, oregano and parsley evenly over chicken. Cover tightly and refrigerate overnight.

Preheat oven to 350°. Bake chicken for 30 minutes or until juices run clear.

Meanwhile, prepare Feta-Yogurt Sauce by combining Feta, parsley and garlic in a food processor. Pulse until well blended. Add yogurt and pepper and pulse to combine. Transfer sauce to a bowl and fold in diced vegetables.

To assemble, warm flatbread in oven for 2 to 3 minutes. Slice chicken into thin strips and place on top of warmed flatbread. Top with Feta-Yogurt Sauce.

Grilled Chicken Quarters with a Grilled Fennel Slaw

1 fennel bulb, quartered

1 head of radicchio, quartered

3 tablespoons olive oil, divided

salt and pepper, to taste

2 teaspoons thyme

2 garlic cloves, minced

4 boneless, skinless chicken breasts, cut into 4 tenders

¼ cup Italian parsley, julienned

1 Vidalia onion, thinly sliced

2 tablespoons blackberry balsamic vinegar (may substitute with balsamic vinegar and ¼ teaspoon sugar)

zest of 1 lemon

Preheat grill to high heat. Turn fennel and radicchio cut side up and drizzle with 1 tablespoon olive oil and season with salt and pepper. Grill fennel for 5 to 6 minutes per side and radicchio for 3 minutes per side; remove from grill and set aside. Reduce grill heat to medium.

Meanwhile, rub thyme, garlic, salt and pepper over chicken breasts and place on grill for 12 to 15 minutes or until internal temperature reaches 165° and juices run clear.

While chicken is grilling, slice radicchio and fennel into thin strips, place in bowl and add parsley, onion vinegar, lemon zest and 2 tablespoons olive oil. Toss to coat, then serve over chicken breasts.

LEMON HERB CHICKEN WITH GRUYERE & PANCETTA

HERB LEMON RUB

1 tablespoons fresh parsley, chopped

1 teaspoons fresh rosemary, chopped

2 tablespoon fresh thyme, chopped

2 tablespoons fresh chives, chopped

zest of 2 lemons

CHICKEN

4 boneless, skinless chicken breasts, halved

ground black pepper, to taste

4 slices Gruyere cheese

12 slices pancetta

In a small mixing bowl, combine all Herb Lemon Rub ingredients; set aside.

Preheat oven to 400°. Lightly grease a 9x9-inch baking dish and set aside. Slice each chicken breast in half horizontally to butterfly. Open up and sprinkle with herb lemon rub and pepper, add a slice of Gruyere and sprinkle with chives. Fold chicken breasts back together firmly. Place 3 slices of pancetta side by side, overlapping by one third.

Place stuffed chicken breast upside down on the bottom edge of the pancetta. Begin to roll, folding in the sides then rolling to the end of the pancetta. Place chicken seam-side down on baking dish.

Bake for 40 minutes or until internal temperature reaches 160°. Allow to rest for 5 minutes before serving.

PECAN CHICKEN ROLL-UPS WITH RASPBERRY CURRANT SAUCE

Serves 4

1 pint fresh raspberries

$^1/_4$ cup sugar

$^1/_2$ cup water, divided

$^1/_3$ cup currants

1 teaspoon cracked black pepper

12 ounces Camembert or Brie cheese, diced

$^3/_4$ cup green onions, chopped

2 garlic cloves, crushed

4 boneless, skinless chicken breasts

1 egg, beaten

1 cup all purpose flour

1 teaspoon salt

$^1/_2$ teaspoon pepper

2 cups pecans, toasted and chopped into rice-size pieces

1 cup Panko breadcrumbs

3 tablespoons olive oil

4 shallots, sliced

fresh parsley, chopped, for garnish

Preheat oven to 375°. Bring raspberries, sugar and water to a boil in a small stockpot over high heat. Turn burner off and let stand for 10 minutes. Pour into blender and pulse until smooth. Strain through a mesh strainer over a stockpot to remove seeds. Add currants and black pepper to pot and heat over medium. Bring to a boil, turn heat off and set aside.

In a mixing bowl, fold together cheese, green onions and garlic. Pound each chicken breast to flatten then place $^1/_4$ cup of cheese mixture onto each. Roll and secure with toothpicks.

In a small bowl, combine egg and $^1/_4$ cup water to make an egg wash. In another small bowl, combine flour, salt and pepper. Next, combine toasted pecans and breadcrumbs in separate shallow dish or bowl. Dip each chicken roll-up into flour, then egg wash, then into pecan-breadcrumbs; use your hands to press pecans and breadcrumbs around the roll-up.

Meanwhile, in a large pan over medium-high heat, cook chicken roll-ups for 15 minutes, turning to brown each side. When browned, transfer to an 8x8-inch baking dish and bake an additional 15 minutes or until cooked through and juices run clear.

Meanwhile, heat olive oil in a sauté pan over medium heat. Caramelize shallots for 12 to 15 minutes, stirring every 2 to 3 minutes.

Transfer chicken to a serving plate, drizzle with raspberry sauce and garnish with caramelized shallots and parsley.

REGAL CURRIED CHICKEN

4 tablespoons butter

3 ½ pounds boneless, skinless chicken breasts, cut into bite-sized pieces (about 4 chicken breasts)

4 tablespoons all purpose flour

1 cup onions, finely chopped

½ garlic clove, minced

1 ½ tablespoons curry powder

½ teaspoon ground ginger

½ teaspoon salt

1 ½ cups chicken broth

2 tablespoons mango chutney

¼ cup golden raisins

1 cucumber, peeled and diced

Preheat oven to 350°. Melt butter in a large sauté pan over medium heat. Dredge chicken breasts in flour and brown in melted butter, about 6 to 8 minutes. Transfer chicken to a 1 ½-quart casserole dish.

In same pan, brown onions and garlic about 5 to 6 minutes. Add curry powder, ginger and salt until evenly distributed. Deglaze the pan by adding chicken broth, scraping brown bits off the bottom of the pan. Add chutney, raisins and cucumber. Immediately pour over chicken and bake for 45 minutes.

Serve with Israeli couscous or your favorite rice.

ROASTED POBLANO CHICKEN

ANCHO CHILE SPICE

1 small dried ancho pepper, ground

3 tablespoons coffee grounds

2 teaspoons cumin

1 teaspoon garlic powder

2 tablespoons paprika

2 teaspoons salt

CHICKEN

8 boneless, skinless chicken breasts

8 ounces Monterey Jack cheese, sliced
   into 8 slices

2 poblano peppers, roasted and cut into
   4 slices each

1 cup plain dry breadcrumbs

$\frac{1}{2}$ cup butter, melted

Preheat oven to 400°. In a small bowl, combine all Ancho Chile Spice ingredients with a fork until evenly distributed; set aside.

Flatten chicken breasts to $\frac{1}{4}$-inch thickness (for ease, place each breast between two pieces of plastic wrap and gently flatten with a kitchen mallet).

In a shallow dish, combine Ancho chile spice with breadcrumbs. Wrap 1 slice of cheese cheese around each poblano pepper slice, then wrap flattened chicken breast around that and secure with a toothpick. Repeat with remaining cheese, peppers and chicken. Dredge chicken roll-ups in seasoned breadcrumbs, then roll through butter and dredge in breadcrumbs again. Place in a 9x13-inch baking dish. Drizzle remaining butter over chicken and refrigerate 1 hour (or overnight) before cooking.

Bake chicken for 25 to 30 minutes or until chicken juices run clear. To serve, let stand 5 minutes and then slice into medallions.

SURINAM CHICKEN CURRY

Serves 4

2 onions, chopped

2 garlic cloves

1 celery stalk, chopped

salt and pepper, to taste

1 whole roasting chicken, skin removed and cut into quarters

2 tablespoons olive oil

2 tomatoes, chopped

1 tablespoon brown sugar

¼ cup curry powder

½ teaspoon cumin

4 Yukon Gold potatoes, chopped

3 cups water

4 tortillas

mango chutney, to taste

⅛ teaspoon red pepper flakes (optional)

In a food processor, pulse onions, garlic, celery, salt and pepper until smooth. Rub over chicken and set aside.

Heat oil in a Dutch oven and add chicken, tomatoes, brown sugar, curry powder and cumin. Cook over medium-high heat until chicken is brown, about 10 to 15 minutes. Add potatoes and water. Reduce heat to low and simmer, about 1 hour.

Remove chicken from pot and thinly slice, reserving sauce. To serve, place tortilla on a plate and spread with chutney. Add sliced chicken and top with sauce and roll. For added heat, sprinkle with red pepper flakes.

DO IT YOURSELF

RED PEPPER CHUTNEY
1 jar roasted red peppers, chopped,
2 green onions chopped
¼ cup blood orange vinegar, or champagne vinegar
2 garlic cloves, roasted and minced
½ teaspoon brown sugar
½ teaspoon hot sauce
1 tablespoon fresh parsley, chopped

Combine peppers, white parts of green onions, vinegar, roasted garlic and brown sugar in a small sauce pot over medium high heat. Bring to a boil, reduce heat to medium low and simmer for about 12 to 15 minutes or until liquid is reduced to a syrup. Add in green parts of green onions, hot sauce and parsley.

TENDER YOGURT CHICKEN

Serves 6

6 boneless, skinless chicken breasts

2 teaspoons fresh lemon juice

salt and pepper, to taste

½ cup plain yogurt

¼ cup mayonnaise

¼ cup green onions, sliced

2 tablespoons Dijon mustard

1 tablespoon Worcestershire sauce

1 teaspoon fresh thyme, coarsely chopped

¼ cup Parmesan cheese, freshly grated

1 teaspoon fresh rosemary, coarsely chopped

Preheat oven to 350°. Arrange chicken in a single layer in a 9x13-inch baking dish. In a mixing bowl, combine lemon juice, salt and pepper; drizzle generously over chicken and set aside.

In a separate mixing bowl, combine yogurt, mayonnaise, green onions, mustard, Worcestershire sauce, thyme and cheese; mix well. Pour over chicken and sprinkle with rosemary. Bake for 50 minutes or until chicken is no longer pink and juices run clear. If desired, broil chicken 3 to 4 minutes longer to brown.

TROPICAL CURRIED CHICKEN

Serves 6-8

2 ½ pounds chicken legs and thighs

2 tablespoons curry powder

salt and pepper, to taste

5 tablespoons olive oil

1 large white onion, thinly sliced

2 red bell peppers, seeded and julienned

2 cups spicy tomato chutney

3 green onions, chopped

½ cup honey roasted peanuts

1 lime, cut into wedges

Sprinkle chicken with curry powder, salt and pepper; set aside.

Heat oil in a large sauté pan over medium-high heat and add white onions; sauté for 2 to 3 minutes. Add chicken and peppers; sauté until chicken is golden, about 3 to 5 minutes each side. Add chutney, reduce heat to low and simmer for 20 to 25 minutes.

Sprinkle with green onions and peanuts and place lime wedges on the side.

Serve over basmati rice.

main

BEEF

PASTA

PORK

POULTRY

SEAFOOD

VEAL, LAMB & DUCK

ACCOMPANIMENTS

ARROZ CON CAMARONES

3 tablespoons olive oil, divided

$1/2$ pound andouille sausage, sliced into $1/2$-inch pieces

1 yellow onion, diced

$1/2$ cup green bell pepper, diced

$2 1/2$ cups water

$1/2$ cup Chardonnay

2 cups white rice

1 chicken bouillon cube

1 teaspoon salt

1 pound (21 - 25 ct) shrimp, peeled & deveined

$1 1/2$ teaspoon garlic salt

$1/2$ cup sugar peas, sliced on bias

1 (12 ounce) jar roasted red peppers, sliced

In a deep frying pan or Dutch oven, heat $1 1/2$ tablespoons oil over medium-high heat for 1 minute. Add sausage, onion and bell pepper and cook for 4 minutes. Turn heat to high and add water, wine, rice, bouillon cube and salt, stirring to mix well; bring to a boil and boil for 3 minutes. Reduce heat to medium-low; cover and simmer for 15 minutes. Remove from heat and transfer to a serving platter; set aside and keep warm.

Return pan or Dutch oven to stovetop over medium-high heat; season shrimp with garlic salt and cook in $1 1/2$ tablespoons oil for 6 to 8 minutes, until pink.

Meanwhile, steam sugar peas for 5 to 6 minutes or until tender. To serve, place sliced roasted red peppers and cooked peas on rice and top with cooked shrimp.

BAKED BLUE CHEESE
& LIME SHRIMP

· ·

Serves 4 - 6

2 pounds (21 - 25 ct) shrimp, peeled & deveined

juice of 2 limes

1 stick unsalted butter

¼ cup heavy cream

1 (8 ounce) package cream cheese

2 ounces Blue cheese, crumbled

½ tablespoon hot sauce

1 (14 ounce) box brown rice

paprika, to taste

fresh parsley, to taste

Preheat oven to 350°. Place shrimp in a single layer in a 9x13-inch baking dish; drizzle lime juice evenly over shrimp and set aside.

In a 4-quart pot over high heat, melt butter; add cream and bring to a boil. Add cream cheese, blue cheese and hot sauce, whisking until smooth. Pour cheese mixture over shrimp and bake for 20 minutes in preheated oven.

Meanwhile, cook rice according to directions on package; set aside and keep warm.

Serve shrimp and cheese sauce over cooked rice; garnish with paprika and parsley.

BAKED TILAPIA WITH TOMATO FENNEL SAUCE

2 tablespoons olive oil

1 medium onion, finely chopped

1 fennel bulb, finely chopped

1 garlic clove, thinly sliced

1 pound tomatoes, chopped

¼ cup dry white wine

2 tablespoons capers, drained

⅛ teaspoon black pepper

4 (5 - 6 ounce) tilapia fillets

Preheat oven to 425°. Heat oil in a cast iron skillet over medium heat until hot. Add onion and fennel; sauté until golden brown, about 8 minutes. Add garlic and sauté for 30 seconds before adding tomatoes and wine, stirring to combine.

Reduce heat to low and simmer for 5 minutes. Add capers and black pepper. Place tilapia in pan, covering in sauce. Turn off heat and transfer skillet to oven; bake uncovered for 20 to 25 minutes or until fish flakes easily with a fork.

BRANDIED SHRIMP & LOBSTER

2 tablespoons olive oil

1 garlic clove

2 medium tomatoes, diced

3 tablespoons brandy

½ cup heavy cream

4 lobster tails, meat removed and cut into chunks, tails reserved

16 (21 - 25 count) shrimp, peeled, deveined and cut into quarters

1 ½ cups Parmesan cheese

Preheat oven to 350°. Heat oil in a large sauté pan over medium heat; add garlic and cook about 4 minutes or until translucent. Add tomatoes and stir; cook for 8 to 10 minutes.

Remove pan from heat and add brandy while shaking the skillet in order to coat; return pan to heat (for gas stoves, make sure to hold pan away from burner so that it does not catch fire). Cook for 2 minutes, constantly shaking the pan. Add cream, stirring constantly, and cook 2 to 3 minutes or until thickened; remove from heat and stir in lobster and shrimp. Stuff mixture into lobster shells, sprinkle with Parmesan cheese and bake in preheated oven for 12 to 15 minutes.

DO IT YOURSELF

PREPARING LOBSTER TAIL

To remove raw meat from a lobster tail, first, using heavy duty kitchen sheers, cut the bottom of the tail along the 2 edges where the hard shell meets the somewhat softer under-part of the tail being very careful not to cut into the meat. It's best to slide one blade into the tail between the shell and meat, then cut only with the top blade using your hand to guide the bottom blade through the tail. Then cut the shell from the top side, down the middle to the tail fin. Last, very carefully place your index finger between the shell and meat and loosen the meat from the shell. This should not tear the meat if you are careful as the tail meat is fairly durable.

BREAD PUDDING WITH SHRIMP & SAUSAGE

3 eggs

2 ½ quarts cream

1 sourdough baguette, cut into 1-inch chunks

2 tablespoons olive oil

1 pound andouille sausage, cut into ½-inch pieces

2 medium onions, diced

4 - 5 garlic cloves, chopped

1 pound (21 - 25 ct) shrimp, peeled & deveined and cut into thirds

1 tablespoon thyme, chopped

Preheat oven to 400°. In a large mixing bowl, whisk together eggs and cream. Fold in sourdough bread cubes until evenly coated, and let soak for 45 minutes. Press bread down occasionally to ensure a more even texture.

Meanwhile, heat olive oil in a sauté pan over medium-high heat; add sausage and sear 4 to 5 minutes. Sweat onions and garlic in pan for 2 to 3 minutes, or until onions are translucent.

Add sausage and vegetables to bread and stir to combine. Gently fold in shrimp and thyme, trying not to over mix.

Place mixture in a 9x13-inch baking dish and bake for 35 to 45 minutes.

BUCATINI & GRILLED SCALLOPS WITH A ROSEMARY & LEMON SAUCE

• •

Serves 4

12 large sea scallops

1 ½ cups dry white wine

4 sprigs of fresh rosemary, leaves
   removed

1 pound bucatini pasta

2 garlic cloves, thinly sliced

1 ½ cups olive oil

2 tablespoons fresh rosemary, chopped

1 teaspoon salt

½ teaspoon black pepper

juice of 3 lemons

½ cup Parmesan cheese, freshly grated

⅔ cup pine nuts, toasted

¼ cup Italian style breadcrumbs

Marinate scallops in wine for 30 minutes. Remove and pat dry and skewer 3 scallops on each rosemary sprig; set aside.

Meanwhile, cook pasta according to directions on package; drain, reserving ½ cup pasta water, and set aside.

Place garlic in a sauté pan with oil over medium heat; cook for 5 minutes. Mix in rosemary, salt, pepper and lemon juice; stir in cheese, pinenuts and breadcrumbs, coating evenly. Add pasta and ½ cup pasta water; toss gently to combine. Set aside and keep warm.

Preheat grill to medium heat. Grill scallops until firm, about 3 to 4 minutes per side.

Serve grilled scallops over pasta.

CHIPOTLE FISH WRAPS

2 cups water

2 tablespoons salt

2 (1 pound) cod fillets

2 tablespoons chipotle sauce

juice of 1 lime

dash of smoked paprika

$\frac{1}{2}$ head of lettuce, chopped

2 large tomatoes, chopped

2 green bell peppers, diced

1 - 2 jalapeño peppers, chopped

8 large flour tortillas

8 ounces cheddar cheese, shredded

$\frac{1}{2}$ cup fresh cilantro, chopped

In a large pot over medium-low heat, bring water to a boil; add salt and cod and cook for 3 to 5 minutes until cod is flaky. Place cod in a large mixing bowl and add chipotle sauce, lime juice and desired amount of smoked paprika. Stir until well mixed and set aside. In a separate mixing bowl, combine lettuce, tomatoes, bell pepper and jalapeño.

To assemble, lay tortilla out flat; fill with vegetable mixture, cod and cheese. Garnish with cilantro and fold tortilla like a burrito.

COCONUT-PANKO CRUSTED TILAPIA WITH MANGO CHUTNEY

Serves 4

CHUTNEY

2 tablespoons olive oil

1 small red onion, thinly sliced

¼ cup lime juice

2 mangos, peeled and chopped

chili powder, to taste

salt, to taste

¼ cup cilantro, to taste

FISH

¼ cup all purpose flour

2 eggs

3 tablespoons milk

⅓ cup unsweetened coconut flakes

⅓ cup Panko breadcrumbs

1 teaspoon salt

2 tablespoons olive oil

4 (4 - 5 ounce) tilapia fillets

To make chutney, heat olive oil in a large frying pan over medium heat; add red onion and cook for 5 minutes, stirring frequently. Add lime juice, mangos, chili powder and salt; reduce heat to low and cook until mangos are soft. Remove from heat and transfer to a serving bowl; allow to cool slightly (about 3 minutes) then stir in cilantro. Set aside.

Place flour in a shallow bowl or dish. In a small mixing bowl, whisk eggs and milk until combined. On a plate, mix coconut, Panko breadcrumbs and salt with a fork.

Heat oil in a medium saucepan over low heat. Dip tilapia first into flour, then into egg mixture and lastly into coconut-Panko mixture; place in pan, increase heat to medium and cook on first side for 3 to 5 minutes. Flip fillets and cook on other side until fish is cooked through and flakes easily with a fork, about 5 more minutes.

To serve, place fish on plate and top with chutney. Serve with couscous or mashed potatoes.

CRAB STUFFED EGGPLANT

1 eggplant, halved lengthwise

$1/2$ cup olive oil, divided

salt and pepper, to taste

1 shallot, finely chopped

4 garlic cloves, minced

$1/8$ cup fresh basil, chopped

2 teaspoons fresh thyme, chopped

8 ounces jumbo lump crab meat

$1/2$ cup white wine

$1/2$ cup Italian style breadcrumbs

$1/2$ cup Parmesan cheese, grated and divided

Preheat oven to 350°. Scoop out flesh of eggplant, chop into $1/4$-inch pieces and reserve. Coat shells with $1/4$ cup olive oil and season with salt and pepper; place in a baking dish and set aside.

Heat remaining $1/4$ cup olive oil in large sauté pan over medium-high heat; add shallots, garlic and basil and sauté for about 1 minute. Stir in reserved chopped eggplant, fresh thyme and crabmeat; season with salt and pepper to taste. Add wine and cook 5 minutes; remove from heat and transfer to a large mixing bowl. Add breadcrumbs and $1/4$ cup Parmesan and stir to mix well. If mixture is too dry, stir in more oil.

Add stuffing to eggplant shells and sprinkle remaining Parmesan over top. Bake for 30 to 40 minutes, until eggplant is tender and cheese is melted.

CRAB STUFFED WHITE FISH

4 fillets of white fish (halibut or tilapia)

$1/4$ cup olive oil

$1/2$ cup breadcrumbs

2 garlic cloves, minced

1 tablespoon fresh thyme, chopped

$1/2$ cup jumbo lump crab meat

$1/4$ cup onions, diced

$1/4$ pound (21 - 25 ct) shrimp, peeled & deveined

$1/2$ teaspoon Old Bay Seasoning, to taste

Preheat oven to 350°. Cut a 1-inch slit in the middle of each white fish fillet, going almost completely through; set fish aside in a baking dish.

In a medium mixing bowl, combine oil, breadcrumbs, garlic, thyme, crabmeat and onions. Place $1/4$ of mixture on top of each fillet; butterfly shrimp and apply decoratively to fish. Sprinkle Old Bay Seasoning over top and bake for 30 minutes

CREAMY LEMON GARLIC SCALLOPS

Serves 4

1 (8 ounce) package angel hair pasta

2 tablespoons olive oil

1 tablespoon pesto

¾ teaspoon roasted garlic, minced

1 pound sea scallops

1 ½ cups Alfredo sauce

salt and pepper, to taste

juice of ½ lemon

½ red bell pepper, diced

½ green bell pepper, diced

4 - 5 slices bacon, cooked & crumbled

Prepare pasta according to package directions; drain and set aside.

Heat olive oil in a sauté pan over medium heat; add pesto and garlic and sauté 2 minutes. Stir in scallops and cook for 3 to 5 minutes or until firm. Add Alfredo sauce to pan and season with salt and pepper to taste; reduce heat to medium-low and simmer 2 minutes. Add lemon juice and stir to combine.

Serve scallops and sauce over prepared pasta and top with diced peppers and crumbled bacon.

DO IT YOURSELF

ROASTING GARLIC

Remove as much of the outer layers of skin from each head of garlic as you can without peeling the individual cloves and making sure that the head stays in tact. Slice about ¼ to ½ inch off the top of the head so that each clove is exposed. Drizzle 1 teaspoon olive oil over each head of garlic; cover with foil and roast in a preheated 425° oven for approximately 45 minutes until garlic is tender and lightly browned.

FLOUNDER WITH A CANDIED GINGER BUTTER SAUCE

. . . .

Serves 4

4 (6 ounce) flounder fillets

³/₄ cup vegetable broth

¹/₄ cup teriyaki sauce

¹/₄ cup rice vinegar

¹/₄ cup crystallized ginger, finely chopped

2 garlic cloves, minced

3 green onions, sliced

2 tablespoons sugar

juice and zest of 1 lime

¹/₄ cup heavy cream

2 tablespoons butter, cut into pieces

8 ounces baby spinach

Preheat oven to 450°. Pierce flounder fillets several times with a fork and place skin side down in a 9x13 inch baking dish; set aside.

In a medium mixing bowl, combine broth, teriyaki sauce, rice vinegar, ginger, garlic, green onions, sugar, lime juice and lime zest; whisk until well blended and then pour over flounder.

Bake flounder for 12 minutes or until fillets flake easily with a fork. Remove from oven and transfer to a serving dish, reserving marinade.

In a small saucepan over medium heat, add marinade and cream; stir to combine. Bring to a boil for 2 minutes. Add butter, stirring until melted.

Serve flounder over spinach leaves and drizzle with sauce.

GRILLED BLACKENED RED SNAPPER

2 teaspoons paprika

2 teaspoons onion powder

2 teaspoons garlic powder

¾ teaspoon ground coriander

¾ teaspoon kosher salt

¼ teaspoon cayenne pepper

¼ teaspoon black pepper

¼ teaspoon white pepper

3 tablespoons unsalted butter

4 (6 - 8 ounce) red snapper fillets, scored

olive oil, to brush on grill

Combine paprika, onion powder, garlic powder, coriander, salt and peppers in a small bowl.

In a small sauté pan over medium heat, melt butter. Add spices and cook, stirring constantly, until spices are dark rust in color. Remove from heat; set aside and let cool.

Heat grill to medium-high heat. Coat each fillet with cooled spice mixture. Brush cooking grate with olive oil to prevent sticking and place fish on grill. Grill until fish is cooked through and flakes easily with a fork.

SERVING SUGGESTION

Excellent served with Grilled Garlic Baby Artichokes, page 259.

MUSSELS EXTRAORDINAIRE

Serves 8

2 tablespoons olive oil

¹/₂ stick butter

1 medium shallot, finely chopped

3 garlic cloves, minced

1 teaspoon crushed red pepper

1 small tomato, diced

¹/₂ (750 mL) bottle white wine (may substitute with champagne or seafood stock)

2 pounds mussels

¹/₄ cup cilantro, chopped

In a large Dutch oven over medium heat, add oil and butter and allow butter to melt. Add shallots, garlic and red pepper; sauté for about 3 minutes, making sure that garlic does not burn. Add diced tomato and wine (champagne or stock); stir together, increase heat to medium-high and add mussels. Cover and bring to a boil for 5 minutes.

Remove from heat and carefully remove lid; check to make sure that mussels are opened. Using a slotted spoon, transfer mussels to a serving platter deep enough to hold liquid; check each mussel and discard any that are not opened. Carefully pour liquid from pot over mussels making sure to transfer all ingredients from the pot to the serving platter.

Sprinkle chopped cilantro over mussels and serve.

SERVING SUGGESTION

Serve with a glass of wine or Champagne, warm crusty French bread and Saffron Rice with Fresh Asparagus and Raisins, page 270.

PAN SEARED TUNA STEAKS WITH WASABI BUTTER SAUCE

• •

Serves 4

2 tablespoons rice vinegar

1 ¼ cups white wine

¼ cup shallots, minced

¼ cup heavy cream

4 tablespoons wasabi paste

2 tablespoons soy sauce

½ cup unsalted butter, cubed

4 tuna steaks

1 tablespoon olive oil

salt and pepper, to taste

In a small saucepan over medium heat, simmer vinegar, wine and shallots until liquid has reduced to 2 tablespoons, about 10 minutes. Add cream and reduce by ¾, about 5 minutes. Strain out shallots and discard; return liquid to pan and stir in wasabi paste and soy sauce. Reduce heat to low and gradually whisk in butter one cube at a time, allowing mixture to emulsify; be careful not to allow mixture to boil. When all butter is incorporated, remove sauce from heat. Pour into a small serving bowl and set aside; keep warm.

Heat a large frying pan over high heat. Brush tuna steaks with olive oil and season with salt and pepper. Place tuna into pan and sear for 2 minutes on each side, being careful not to overcook; center of tuna steaks should still be pink. Transfer fish to a serving platter when cooked and serve with Wasabi Butter Sauce drizzled over top with extra on the side.

PANKO MAHI-MAHI WITH HAWAIIAN SOY BUTTER SAUCE

Serves 6

1 cup buttermilk

2 tablespoons hot sauce

3 garlic cloves, minced

2 teaspoons chili garlic sambal

6 mahi-mahi fillets

2 tablespoons olive oil

pineapple rings, for garnish

SOY BUTTER SAUCE

4 cups soy sauce

1 cup pineapple, chopped

1 star anise

2 cups sugar

1 cup heavy cream

$1/4$ cup butter, cut into pieces

PANKO BREADING

$1/8$ cup fresh cilantro

1 tablespoon fresh mint, chopped

1 cup Panko breadcrumbs

$1/2$ teaspoon paprika

$1/2$ teaspoon salt

In an airtight container, combine buttermilk, hot sauce, garlic, chili garlic and mahi-mahi fillets; refrigerate at least 30 minutes.

Meanwhile, in a medium pot over medium-high heat, combine soy sauce, pineapple and star anise; bring to a boil. Stir in sugar, then reduce heat to low and simmer for 20 to 25 minutes. Add cream and reduce for 5 to 6 minutes. Whisk in butter until melted, then remove from heat and set aside.

In a small mixing bowl, mix cilantro, mint, Panko breadcrumbs, paprika and salt. Remove marinated mahi-mahi from refrigerator and coat in Panko mixture. Heat a large frying pan with olive oil over medium heat and pan sear fillets for 6 to 8 minutes on each side until fully cooked.

Serve mahi-mahi over jasmine rice, drizzle with Soy Butter Sauce and garnish with fresh pineapple slices.

PARMESAN BAKED HALIBUT

1 ½ pounds halibut (about 4 - 5 fillets)

salt and pepper, to taste

juice of ½ lemon

2 tablespoons olive oil

¼ cup butter

2 tablespoons garlic

1 tablespoon fresh thyme

½ teaspoon crushed red pepper flakes

½ cup Parmesan cheese, grated

3 tablespoons mayonnaise

3 green onions, chopped

¼ teaspoon salt

¼ teaspoon black pepper

1 teaspoon hot sauce

½ teaspoon paprika

Preheat oven to 400°. Line a roasting pan with aluminum foil; place halibut fillets on foil and season with salt and pepper to taste. Drizzle fillets with lemon juice and oil and cover with aluminum foil cutting several slits in foil. Bake fillets for 25 to 30 minutes. Remove from oven and remove foil covering fish. Leave fish in roasting pan; set aside.

Preheat broiler to 500°. In a small sauté pan over medium heat, melt butter and sauté garlic, thyme and red pepper flakes; cook for 2 to 3 minutes and remove from heat.

In a small mixing bowl, combine sautéed herbs, Parmesan, mayonnaise, onions, salt, pepper, hot sauce and paprika; stir to mix well and spread evenly over baked fish. Place pan 6 inches from broiler and broil for about 90 seconds or until lightly browned and bubbly.

PROSCIUTTO WRAPPED HALIBUT

4 slices prosciutto, thinly sliced

4 halibut fillets

2 tablespoons olive oil

salt and pepper, to taste

4 teaspoons fresh sage, chopped

toothpicks

Preheat oven to 375°. Place prosciutto slices flat on a baking sheet; top each slice with a halibut fillet. Drizzle with olive oil and season to taste with salt and pepper. Top each fillet with sage leaves. Roll fillets with prosciutto on the outside and secure with toothpicks.

Bake for 12 to 14 minutes or until fish is flaky.

Serve with a rice pilaf and green vegetables or a fresh salad.

ROASTED SHRIMP WITH TOMATOES & FETA

Serve 4

1 (8 ounce) package cherry tomatoes, cut in half

1 tablespoon olive oil

1 tablespoon garlic, minced

¼ teaspoon salt

½ teaspoon black pepper

3 cups water

2 tablespoons Old Bay Seasoning

1 ½ pounds (21 - 25 ct) shrimp, peeled & deveined

¼ cup fresh parsley, chopped

1 tablespoon lemon juice

1 cup Feta cheese, crumbled

Preheat oven to 450°. Place tomatoes in a single layer in a 9x13-inch baking dish. Sprinkle with oil, garlic, salt and pepper; toss to coat. Roast for 20 minutes; remove from oven and set aside.

Bring water to a boil in a stockpot; add Old Bay Seasoning and shrimp. Cook until shrimp are pink; drain.

In a large serving dish, toss shrimp, parsley, lemon juice and Feta cheese with roasted tomatoes. If desired, place in oven for another 5 minutes to melt cheese completely.

SALMON STEAKS VERACRUZ-STYLE

Serves 4

2 tablespoons + 2 teaspoons olive oil, divided

1 small onion, finely chopped

2 garlic cloves, minced

1 teaspoon chili powder

1 (14.5 ounce) can diced tomatoes with juices

1 pickled jalapeño, finely chopped

$\frac{1}{4}$ fresh jalapeño pepper, finely chopped

$\frac{1}{4}$ cup pitted green olives, coarsely chopped

1 $\frac{1}{2}$ teaspoons capers, rinsed and drained

$\frac{1}{4}$ teaspoon dried oregano

$\frac{1}{4}$ teaspoon dried thyme

$\frac{1}{8}$ teaspoon cinnamon

$\frac{1}{8}$ teaspoon salt

$\frac{1}{4}$ cup water

4 (8 ounce) salmon fillets

salt and pepper to taste

2 tablespoons lime juice

1 avocado, pit removed and sliced, for garnish

Preheat oven to 350°. Heat 2 teaspoons oil in a sauté pan over medium heat; add onion and garlic and sauté 5 minutes or until tender. Add chili powder, stirring to coat. Stir in tomatoes, jalapeños, olives, capers, oregano, thyme, cinnamon, salt and water; bring to a boil. Reduce heat to low, cover and simmer 30 minutes.

Meanwhile, heat 2 tablespoons oil in a frying pan over medium-high heat. Season salmon fillets with salt and pepper to taste and sear for 6 minutes or until browned.

Transfer salmon to a 9x13-inch baking dish; sprinkle with lime juice and bake 15 to 20 minutes or until fish flakes easily with a fork.

Remove from oven and pour finished sauce over fillets before serving. For garnish, top with sliced avocado.

Salmon with Heirloom Tomato Crab Salsa

Salmon Marinade

¼ cup lime juice

¼ cup olive oil

2 tablespoons soy sauce

3 tablespoons shallots, minced

1 teaspoon sugar

2 large tomatoes, diced

¼ cup fresh basil

salt and pepper, to taste

4 (6 ounce) salmon fillets

Salsa

½ cup olive oil

2 cups corn kernels

8 ounces crab meat

2 - 3 tomatoes, diced

salt and pepper, to taste

Preheat oven to 400°. In a small mixing bowl, whisk together all salmon marinade ingredients, except fish. Place fish in a 9x13-inch baking dish and pour marinade over the top; refrigerate for 30 minutes.

Meanwhile, heat olive oil in a large saucepan over high heat until oil sizzles when a drop of water is added; place corn in a container and pour into saucepan, standing back until pan settles. (Do not add corn with your hands and be very careful as oil will splatter when corn is added!)

After pan has settled, reduce heat to medium; add crabmeat and tomatoes. Season to taste with salt and pepper; reduce heat to medium-low. Cook for 10 to 12 minutes then remove from heat; set aside until ready to serve.

Bake salmon for 30 to 40 minutes or until fish flakes easily with a fork. Serve with salsa on the side.

SALMON WITH SESAME & ORANGE-GINGER RELISH

Serves 4

1/3 cup dry white wine

1/3 cup orange juice

2 1/2 tablespoons soy sauce

4 (4 - 5 ounce) salmon fillets

ORANGE-GINGER RELISH

1/2 cup red bell peppers, julienned

1/2 cup red onions, thinly sliced

2 1/2 tablespoons fresh cilantro, chopped

2 teaspoons fresh ginger, minced

2 teaspoons orange zest, freshly grated

3 large naval oranges, peeled and divided into segments, juice reserved

1 teaspoon sesame oil

1/2 teaspoon kosher salt

1/4 teaspoon crushed red pepper flakes

2 tablespoons vegetable oil

sesame seeds, for garnish

In a small mixing bowl, whisk wine, orange juice and soy sauce until well combined. Pour mixture into a 9x13-inch baking dish; place salmon in orange juice mixture, skin side up. Cover and marinate in refrigerator at least 2 hours; remove from refrigerator 30 minutes before cooking and bring to room temperature.

To make relish, combine red bell pepper, onion, cilantro, ginger, orange zest, reserved orange juice, sesame oil, salt and red pepper flakes in a medium mixing bowl; fold in orange segments and set aside.

Preheat oven to 450°. Heat a nonstick frying pan over medium-high heat; add marinated salmon and sear until browned. Line a rimmed baking sheet with foil; generously brush with vegetable oil. Place browned salmon skin side down onto prepared baking sheet; sprinkle with salt and pepper to taste. Bake the salmon for 25 to 30 minutes or until fish flakes easily with a fork. Remove from oven and, using a large spatula, gently loosen salmon from foil; transfer salmon to a serving platter. Mound prepared relish down center of fillets, sprinkle with sesame seeds and serve.

SEARED SCALLOPS WITH MUSHROOM TRUFFLE OIL

Serves 4

3 ½ teaspoons olive oil, divided

12 sea scallops

salt and pepper, to taste

1 teaspoon shallots, minced

1 teaspoon garlic, minced

2 small white mushrooms, minced

2 baby Portabella mushrooms, minced

4 tablespoons unsalted butter

½ teaspoon white truffle oil

1 teaspoon fresh parsley

Heat 1 teaspoon olive oil in a large frying pan over medium-high heat; season scallops with salt and pepper to taste and add to pan. Sear scallops for 3 minutes on one side and 2 minutes on the other; remove from pan and cover with aluminum foil to keep warm and set aside.

Heat remaining olive oil in a separate frying pan over medium-high heat; add shallots and cook for 2 minutes or until tender and translucent. Add garlic and cook another minute; add mushrooms and cook for 3 to 5 minutes or until mushrooms are tender. Add butter, truffle oil and parsley; heat until butter is melted. Drizzle mixture over cooked scallops before serving.

Shrimp, Crab & Artichoke Casserole

. . . .

Serves 8 - 10

6 tablespoons butter

2 cups milk

2 garlic cloves, minced

1 cup heavy cream

$1/4$ cup all purpose flour

$1/2$ teaspoon salt

$1/2$ teaspoon onion powder

1 tablespoon Worcestershire sauce

$1/4$ cup dry sherry

1 $1/2$ tablespoons lemon juice

$1/4$ teaspoon cayenne pepper

3 tablespoons ketchup

1 cup sharp Cheddar cheese, shredded

1 pound jumbo lump crab meat

1 (14 ounce) can artichoke hearts,
   drained and sliced

2 pounds (26 - 30 ct) cooked shrimp,
   cut in half

1 cup breadcrumbs

Preheat oven to 350°. In medium saucepan over medium heat, whisk together butter, milk, garlic, cream and flour until butter has melted. Allow to thicken, then add salt, onion powder, Worcestershire sauce, sherry, lemon juice, cayenne pepper, ketchup and cheese. Remove from heat.

Grease a 3-quart casserole dish and place alternating layers of cheese mixture, crab meat, artichokes and shrimp ending with cheese mixture on top; sprinkle breadcrumbs evenly over top. Bake for 20 minutes or until golden brown.

SHRIMP ÉTOUFFÉE

Serves 8 - 10

1 stick butter

4 tablespoons all purpose flour

1 onion, chopped

4 shallots, chopped

1 bell pepper, seeded and chopped

1 quart chicken broth

2 cups diced tomatoes

1 tablespoon parsley

2 tablespoons garlic, minced

1 pound (21 - 25 ct) shrimp, peeled & deveined (or crawfish, if available)

salt and pepper, to taste

Creole seasoning, to taste

In large sauté pan over medium heat, melt butter; add flour and cook for 5 minutes, stirring constantly to create a roux. Cook for an additional 6 to 8 minutes until roux is browned. Add onions, shallots and bell pepper; sauté until tender and translucent, about 5 to 6 minutes. Add chicken broth and tomatoes; reduce heat to low and simmer for 30 minutes.

To complete, add parsley, garlic and shrimp (or crawfish); season to taste with salt, pepper and Creole seasoning. Cook an additional 15 minutes. Serve over white rice.

? DID YOU KNOW?

WHAT DOES ÉTOUFFÉE MEAN?

The French word étouffée literally translates to "smothered" and is applied to this dish because it must be cooked tightly covered in a small amount of liquid over extremely low heat, essentially "smothering" the dish. Using a dark brown roux base, this spicy Cajun stew is typically made with crawfish and hot spices and features a deep red color and thick consistency.

SHRIMP WITH TOMATO RICE

Serves 8

2 ½ cups basmati rice

2 large tomatoes, diced

salt, to taste

juice of 2 key limes

1 cup water

2 tablespoons olive oil

1 pound (26 - 30 ct) cooked shrimp

COCKTAIL SAUCE

1 small jar chili sauce

½ cup ketchup

⅛ - ¼ cup horseradish (adjust to your taste)

2 teaspoons brandy

black pepper, to taste

In a large stockpot over high heat, combine rice, tomatoes, salt to taste, key lime juice and water; bring to a boil. Boil for 2 minutes, stirring constantly; reduce heat to low, cover and cook for 1 hour.

Heat olive oil in a medium sauté pan over medium heat. Add shrimp and sauté until hot, about 4 to 5 minutes.

Meanwhile, in a small mixing bowl, whisk together all cocktail sauce ingredients until fully incorporated.

To serve, top rice with shrimp and serve with cocktail sauce.

DID YOU KNOW?

WHAT IS THE DIFFERENCE BETWEEN A LIME AND A KEY LIME?

Key limes are smaller and feature a stronger flavor and aroma than regular limes, making them ideal for cooking. When selecting ripe key limes, look for a yellowish green skin color and select a fruit that feels heavy for its size.

SMOKED FISH WITH TEQUILA CILANTRO SAUCE

Serves 4

SMOKED FISH

1 alderwood grilling plank

4 (4 ounce) halibut fillets

TEQUILA CILANTRO SAUCE

1 tablespoon olive oil

9 tablespoons butter, divided

2 small shallots, minced

juice of 2 limes

$\frac{1}{4}$ cup tequila

$\frac{1}{2}$ cup heavy cream

$\frac{1}{2}$ teaspoon salt

$\frac{1}{4}$ cup fresh cilantro

Soak alderwood plank in water for 1 hour.

Preheat grill to medium. Place fish on plank and grill for 20 minutes.

Meanwhile, heat oil in a medium saucepan over medium-high heat; add 1 tablespoon butter and allow it to melt. Add shallots and stir 3 to 4 minutes until they are tender. Pour in lime juice and cook until reduced, about 2 minutes. Add tequila and cook until liquid is reduced by half; add heavy cream and season with salt. Allow sauce to thicken, stirring constantly; add remaining butter and stir until melted. Just before serving, add cilantro to sauce.

To serve, drizzle warm sauce over smoked fish.

SWEET SALMON WITH A KICK

1 teaspoon cayenne pepper

½ teaspoon kosher salt

½ teaspoon 5 spice powder

4 (6 ounce) salmon fillets

¼ cup rice vinegar

2 tablespoons honey

1 tablespoon soy sauce

¼ cup green onions, sliced

Preheat broiler to low and spray broiler pan with cooking spray.

In a small mixing bowl, combine cayenne pepper, salt and 5 spice powder to create a rub; rub evenly over salmon fillets. Place salmon, skin side down, on broiler pan; broil for 16 minutes or until fish flakes easily with a fork. Transfer to a serving dish, cover with foil and let rest for 15 minutes.

While fish is resting, whisk together vinegar, honey and soy sauce in a small microwavable mixing bowl until well combined; microwave on high for 45 seconds. Drizzle mixture over fish just before serving and garnish with green onions.

TUNA IN LEMON BUTTER DILL SAUCE WITH ALMONDS & CAPERS

Serves 4

½ cup white wine

1 shallot, minced

¾ cup heavy cream

¾ cup butter, cut into pieces

2 teaspoons fresh dill

juice of ½ lemon

¼ cup capers

2 tablespoons olive oil

4 (8 ounce) yellowfin tuna fillets

⅔ cup almonds, sliced

In a 2-quart saucepan over high heat, bring wine and shallots to a boil. Reduce heat to medium-high and reduce sauce to ⅛ cup, about 8 to 10 minutes. Add cream, reduce for 6 minutes. Fold in butter until melted. Add dill, lemon juice and capers. Set aside and keep warm.

Heat oil in a medium sauté pan over medium-high heat. Sear tuna steaks until golden, about 3 to 4 minutes per side.

To serve, drizzle tuna with sauce and garnish with almonds.

main

BEEF

PASTA

PORK

POULTRY

SEAFOOD

VEAL, LAMB & DUCK

ACCOMPANIMENTS

ASIAGO STUFFED VEAL CHOPS

4 bone-in veal chops

3 tablespoons olive oil, divided

1 slice pancetta, sandwich thin and chopped

4 tablespoons shallots, minced

4 tablespoons butter

2 tablespoons breadcrumbs

¼ cup Asiago cheese

1 garlic clove, minced

1 tablespoon fresh Italian parsley, chopped

1 tablespoon fresh thyme, chopped

Preheat oven to 450°. Prepare veal chops for stuffing by making a cut 1 ½-inches long in the side of each veal chop about ¾ the way through.

Heat 1 tablespoon olive oil in a sauté pan over medium-low heat. Add pancetta and cook 8 minutes, stirring occasionally. Add shallots and cook until tender, about 5 minutes. Add butter, allow to melt, then remove pan from heat. Scrape mixture into a small mixing bowl; add breadcrumbs, cheese, garlic, parsley and thyme, stirring to form a paste. Stuff equal amounts of Asiago mixture into each veal chop.

Heat 2 tablespoons oil in an ovenproof frying pan over medium-high heat; sear stuffed veal chops for 2 minutes on each side. Place pan in oven and bake for 4 to 5 minutes; remove from oven and let chops rest 2 minutes before serving.

CITRUS PEPPERCORN VEAL CHOPS

Serves 4

juice and zest of 2 lemons

juice and zest of 1 orange

5 tablespoons green peppercorns

1/2 cup olive oil

4 veal chops

salt and pepper, to taste

In a blender or food processor, combine lemon and orange juice and zest, peppercorns and oil; process until peppercorns are broken up. Pour over veal and marinate in refrigerator 3 hours, turning once every hour.

Preheat grill to high heat. Remove veal from marinade, season with salt and pepper to taste and grill 6 to 8 minutes per side for medium or 12 to 15 minutes per side for well done.

DILL VEAL

4 tablespoons butter, divided

4 veal shanks

1 cup chicken broth

½ (.75 ounce) package fresh dill, stems separated and leaves chopped

2 tablespoons all purpose flour

2 tablespoons sugar

2 tablespoons black fig vinegar (or balsamic vinegar)

salt and pepper, to taste

Melt 2 tablespoons butter in a large sauté pan over medium heat; add veal and sauté until lightly browned, about 8 to 10 minutes. Add chicken broth and dill stems; cover and let simmer over medium-low heat 2 hours until veal is tender. Transfer veal to a platter and remove bones and gristle; reserve cooking liquid.

In a separate saucepan over medium heat, make a roux by combining 2 tablespoons butter and flour, being careful not to brown; add reserved cooking liquid and let simmer 10 minutes. Add sugar and vinegar, stirring to combine.

Add veal and chopped dill to pan and season with salt and pepper just before serving; serve with new potatoes or mashed potatoes.

DUCK BREAST WITH A WARM CHERRY-PINEAPPLE RELISH

Serves 4

CHERRY-PINEAPPLE RELISH

3 tablespoons blackberry balsamic vinegar (or balsamic vinegar)

3 tablespoons turbinado sugar

½ cup dried cherries

1 ½ tablespoons fresh ginger

2 ¼ cups pineapple, cubed

2 garlic cloves, minced

2 tablespoons shallots, minced

DUCK BREAST

2 tablespoons oil

2 pounds duck breast

2 teaspoons 5 spice powder

In a saucepan over high heat, bring vinegar, sugar, cherries, ginger, pineapple, garlic and shallots to a boil; reduce heat to medium and let simmer 10 minutes or until thickened. Remove from heat and set aside.

Heat oil in a large frying pan over medium-low heat. Rub duck with 5 spice powder and place skin side down in pan; cook 12 to 15 minutes (drain fat every 2 to 3 minutes) until skin is crispy. Flip duck over and cook for another 3 minutes; remove from heat and let rest 5 minutes. To serve, slice duck thinly and spoon relish over top.

FRENCH VEAL SAUTÉ

1 tablespoon olive oil

1 ½ pounds lean veal meat, cut into
    1-inch pieces

½ cup mushrooms, sliced

½ cup yellow onions, chopped

½ garlic clove, minced

¼ cup green bell peppers, seeded and
    sliced

1 cup canned diced tomatoes, with
    liquid

½ cup Burgundy wine

½ teaspoon salt

¼ teaspoon black pepper

1 cup fresh parsley, coarsely chopped
    and for garnish

Heat oil in a large sauté pan over medium heat; add veal and sauté until brown on all sides, about 8 to 10 minutes. Remove veal and set aside.

In same sauté pan over medium heat, add mushrooms, onions and garlic; cook until tender, about 5 to 6 minutes. Add green peppers, tomatoes, wine and veal, reduce heat to low; cover and simmer 1 ½ hours until meat is tender. To serve, season with salt and pepper and garnish with fresh parsley.

Excellent served over rice or fusilli pasta.

MARINATED SMOKED LEG OF LAMB

5 - 6 pound leg of lamb

2 bunches green onions, coarsely chopped

1 small onion, chopped

8 garlic cloves, minced

$\frac{1}{2}$ cup fresh cilantro, chopped

1 tablespoon fresh thyme, chopped

2 - 3 tablespoons fresh ginger, grated

2 tablespoons brown sugar, packed

$\frac{1}{4}$ cup paprika

2 tablespoons cumin

1 tablespoon coriander

$\frac{1}{8}$ cup olive oil

3 cups hickory smoked wood chips

Make 6 to 8 ($\frac{1}{2}$-inch) cuts over surface of lamb. Place in a non-aluminum pan and set aside. In a mixing bowl, combine green onions, onion, garlic, cilantro, thyme, ginger, brown sugar, paprika, cumin and coriander; mash until a paste forms. Slowly add in olive oil, stirring to combine. Rub over lamb, cover and refrigerate overnight.

Soak hickory chips in water for 30 minutes; drain. In a smoker, spread hickory chips over hot coals. Set water pan over coals and fill with water. Oil grill rack, then place lamb on rack. Cover and smoke until internal temperature reaches 145°, about 3 hours (see tip below). Be sure to turn lamb and add more water and wood chips as necessary. Slice lamb and serve hot.

SHORT CUT

If using a gas grill to smoke, first preheat the grill to medium-low. Add a cast iron box to one side of the grill. Fill with hot coals, then top with hickory chips. Place lamb on the other side of the grill and turn every 30 minutes.

PERFECT RACK OF LAMB

Serves 4

2 racks of lamb, frenched

1 tablespoon salt

3 tablespoons fresh rosemary, minced

4 garlic cloves, minced

¼ cup Dijon mustard

2 tablespoons balsamic vinegar

2 tablespoons olive pesto

Preheat oven to 450° and grease a roasting pan with cooking spray. Place lamb, rib side down, in pan.

In a food processor or blender, process salt, rosemary and garlic into a smooth paste; with processor running, add mustard, vinegar and pesto until all ingredients are well combined. Massage mixture onto lamb, coating evenly.

Roast lamb in preheated oven 20 to 30 minutes until meat reaches desired tenderness; remove from oven, cover with foil and let rest 15 minutes. Cut into chops and serve.

DO IT YOURSELF

OLIVE PESTO

1 cup black oil packed olives, pits removed

1 ½ cups green olives, pits removed

3 garlic cloves, smashed

⅛ cup capers, drained

2 tablespoons fresh oregano, chopped

3 tablespoons fresh basil, chopped

3 tablespoons pine nuts, toasted

⅓ cup olive oil

½ teaspoon black pepper

Place all ingredients except olive oil and pepper in food processor. Turn processor on and slowly add in olive oil. When oil has been added, add in pepper and let processor run about 30 more seconds.

Praline Pecan Lamb Chops

Praline Glaze

1 cup Demerara sugar

½ cup heavy cream

¼ cup Dijon mustard

Lamb Chops

4 - 6 lamb chops

salt and pepper, to taste

3 cups pecans, chopped

Preheat oven to 375°. In a medium saucepan over medium heat, combine sugar, cream and mustard. Bring to a boil, reduce heat to low and simmer 5 minutes. Remove from heat and set aside.

Season lamb chops with salt and pepper to taste; coat evenly with glaze, reserving ½ glaze.   Roll chops in pecans to evenly coat; place in baking dish and bake 20 to 25 minutes until desired doneness. Remove from oven, let cool and drizzle with remaining glaze before serving.

Veal Osso Bucco

• •

2 tablespoons sea salt

2 tablespoons black pepper

4 veal shanks

$\frac{1}{2}$ cup all purpose flour

3 tablespoons olive oil

3 garlic cloves, minced and divided

$\frac{3}{4}$ cup dry white wine

2 tablespoons tomato paste

4 roma tomatoes, quartered

3 carrots, peeled and chopped

2 celery stalks, chopped

2 cups chicken broth

4 sprigs of fresh thyme

1 - 2 tablespoons fresh parsley, chopped

2 tablespoons lemon juice, freshly
  squeezed

Preheat oven to 300°. Rub sea salt and pepper onto shanks and dredge in flour; set aside.

Heat oil in a large frying pan over medium heat; add shanks and brown on all sides, about 8 to 10 minutes. Transfer shanks to a baking dish and add $\frac{2}{3}$ minced garlic, wine, tomato paste, tomatoes, carrots, celery, broth and thyme; cover loosely with foil and bake for 60 to 70 minutes until fork tender. Remove shanks from oven and place on a serving platter.

In a small mixing bowl, combine parsley, lemon juice and remaining $\frac{1}{3}$ minced garlic. To serve, drizzle mixture over shanks and serve warm.

main

- Beef
- Pasta
- Pork
- Poultry
- Seafood
- Veal, Lamb & Duck
- Accompaniments

Asparagus in a Fig Balsamic Vinaigrette

● ●

Serves 10

½ pound green asparagus, trimmed

½ pound white asparagus, trimmed

¼ cup white wine

¼ cup fig balsamic vinegar (or red wine vinegar)

½ tablespoon fresh tarragon, chopped

¼ tablespoon dry mustard

¾ cup olive oil

½ teaspoon sesame oil

walnuts, chopped, for garnish

¼ pound Bleu cheese, crumbled, for garnish

To cook asparagus, steam in white wine for 5 minutes. Remove from pot and immediately plunge into ice water and drain. Place asparagus in a glass baking dish; set aside.

To prepare vinaigrette, whisk together vinegar, tarragon and dry mustard. Slowly add oils to emulsify.

Pour vinaigrette over asparagus and refrigerate for at least 2 hours. Prior to serving, garnish with chopped walnuts and Bleu cheese.

BABY ARTICHOKE RAGOÛT

Serves 4

2 cups water

4 baby artichokes, cut into ½-inch
   pieces

1 pound ground Italian sausage

2 tablespoons olive oil

1 medium onion, cut into wedges

1 shallot, minced

6 garlic cloves, minced

1 (16 ounce) can fire roasted tomatoes,
   chopped and with liquid

½ cup chicken broth

In a large sauté pan, bring 2 cups of water to a boil; add artichokes and simmer for 4 minutes. Drain artichokes and set aside.

In the same pan, brown sausage over medium-high heat for 10 minutes. Remove from pan and set aside. Add oil and sauté onions until lightly browned, about 6 to 8 minutes. Reduce heat to medium, add shallots and garlic and sauté for 3 minutes. Add tomatoes (with liquid), sausage and enough chicken broth to almost cover ingredients. Cover and simmer 20 minutes. After 20 minutes, add artichokes and simmer an additional 5 minutes.

Serve over stone-ground grits or with your favorite grilled beef, lamb or veal dish.

BAKED POTATOES
STUFFED WITH CRABMEAT

6 baking potatoes

6 ounces crabmeat

1/2 cup half & half

2 tablespoons butter, melted

salt, to taste

cayenne pepper, to taste

1 onion, grated

8 ounces Cheddar cheese, freshly
   grated

Preheat oven to 375°. Pierce each potato several times with a fork and bake for 45 to 60 minutes. Remove potatoes from oven and cool slightly. Cut each in half and scoop out insides, leaving skins intact. Place potato filling in a medium mixing bowl; set potato shells aside.

Reduce oven to 350°. To the potato filling, add crabmeat, half & half, butter, salt, cayenne pepper and onion and whip until smooth. Return potato mixture to potato shells and top with cheese. Bake for 30 minutes or until cheese is bubbly.

BARLEY STUFFED PORTABELLA MUSHROOMS

Serves 6

3 tablespoons olive oil, divided

1 small onion, chopped

2 garlic cloves, minced

1 cup barley

3 cups chicken broth

1 cup beef broth

2 tablespoons tomato paste

1 small zucchini, cut into ½-inch cubes

6 ounces baby bella mushrooms, sliced

1 teaspoon dried basil

1 teaspoon dried oregano

⅓ cup Parmesan cheese

2 tablespoons fresh parsley, chopped

6 large portabella caps

salt and pepper, to taste

Parmesan cheese, grated and for garnish

fresh parsley, for garnish

Preheat oven to 350°. Heat 1 tablespoon oil in large sauté pan over medium heat and sauté onions until slightly tender, about 5 to 6 minutes. Add garlic and barley, stirring to coat. Add chicken broth and bring to a boil. Reduce heat and simmer until most of broth has been absorbed, about 10 to 12 minutes.

Add beef broth, tomato paste, zucchini, baby bella mushrooms and herbs and reduce heat to simmer until all broth has been absorbed, about 6 to 8 minutes. Remove from heat, add cheese and parsley.

Meanwhile, brush remaining olive oil over portabella mushroom caps, season with salt and pepper and place on a baking sheet. Roast mushrooms for 10 minutes, remove from oven and transfer to a serving platter.

Top each mushroom cap with barley stuffing and sprinkle with parmesan cheese and parsley before serving.

SHORT CUT

The trick to preparing mushroom caps is to make sure that they are well-coated with oil. Mushrooms tend to be very dry, so you want to make sure they stay moist while cooking. First, wash your mushrooms well and dry them with a clean paper towel. There is no need to peel or "skin" your mushrooms, just brush clean dry mushrooms with oil and seasonings and they're ready for the grill or oven!

BRAISED LEEKS

Serves 4

3 tablespoons butter

4 - 6 leeks, soaked, green parts removed and cut lengthwise

$\frac{1}{2}$ cup chicken broth

2 teaspoons fresh thyme, chopped

$\frac{1}{4}$ teaspoon salt

$\frac{1}{8}$ teaspoon pepper

Melt butter in sauté pan over medium heat. Add leeks and sauté for 5 minutes. Add chicken broth, thyme, salt and pepper. Cover and reduce heat to low; cook about 10 minutes.

Serve immediately with grilled beef, lamb or veal.

DID YOU KNOW?

HOW TO PREPARE A LEEK?

See page 67 for more.

251

COCONUT MASHED SWEET POTATOES

· ·

Serves 4

1 tablespoon sugar

2 pounds sweet potatoes, peeled and sliced

½ tablespoon salt

pinch of pepper

½ can coconut milk

½ cup coconut flakes, toasted

In a medium saucepan over low heat, combine sugar and sweet potatoes and cook for 35 to 45 minutes. Stir occasionally and saute until potatoes fall apart when pierced with fork.

Remove potatoes from heat, add salt and pepper and mash with electric mixer. Fold in coconut milk and garnish with toasted coconut before serving.

DO IT YOURSELF

TOASTED COCONUT
Toasted coconut can add a burst of flavor to a number of dishes. Simply place on a baking sheet in 300° oven for 15 - 20 minutes until golden brown.

CORN PUDDING

Serves 8 - 10

¼ cup sugar

3 tablespoons all purpose flour

2 teaspoons baking powder

2 teaspoons salt

6 large eggs

2 cups heavy cream

½ cup butter, melted

6 cups corn kernels

paprika (optional)

Preheat oven to 350° and lightly grease a 9x13-inch baking dish. In a mixing bowl, sift together sugar, flour, baking powder and salt; set aside.

In a separate bowl, beat eggs; stir in cream and butter until smooth.

Carefully add dry ingredients to egg mixture. Fold in corn. Pour into baking dish and sprinkle with paprika, if desired.

Bake for 45 minutes or until golden brown and set.

SHORT CUT

FRESH CORN SUBSTITUTIONS

See page 64 for more

Costa Rican Tostada

2 tablespoons olive oil

1 garlic clove

¼ cup red onions, diced

1 cup black beans

½ red bell pepper, chopped

¼ cup green onions, chopped

1 tablespoon chili powder

1 tablespoon hot sauce

4 (6-inch) tortillas

1 egg

½ cup rice, cooked

1 tomato, diced

Cheddar cheese, shredded (optional)

Heat olive oil in a large skillet over medium heat. Sauté garlic and onions until tender, about 5 minutes. Add beans and stir. Add red peppers, green onions, chili powder and hot sauce; cook for 5 to 6 minutes.

Meanwhile, place tortillas in oven until crispy, about 6 to 8 minutes.

In a small skillet, scramble the egg. Add egg, rice and tomatoes to black bean mixture and stir to combine.

To serve, distribute rice and bean mixture over crispy tortillas and top with Cheddar cheese (optional); slice into quarters for ease.

Couscous with Mint, Pinenuts & Cranberries

2 cups couscous

2 tablespoons curry paste

2 cups water

$1/4$ cup olive oil

1 medium red bell pepper, diced

1 medium orange bell pepper, diced

1 jalepeño or serrano pepper, diced

$1/2$ cup pine nuts, toasted

$1/2$ cup dried cranberries

$1/4$ cup fresh mint, chopped

2 tablespoons fresh thyme, chopped

sea salt, to taste

In medium saucepan, bring couscous, curry paste and water to a boil, stirring well. Remove from heat; cover and set aside for 5 minutes until couscous is cooked.

In a large frying pan, combine oil and peppers and sauté over medium heat until tender, about 5 to 6 minutes. Add pine nuts and cranberries to peppers and cook until pine nuts are lightly toasted. Remove from heat, add mint, thyme and salt, to taste. Combine with couscous and serve.

For an easy meal, serve with grilled chicken overtop.

CURRIED CHICKPEAS & BLACK BEANS

Serves 4 - 6

2 tablespoons vegetable oil

1 cup onions, chopped

1 garlic clove, minced

1 tablespoon fresh ginger, minced

2 tablespoons curry paste

$\frac{1}{8}$ teaspoon salt

3 tablespoons cider vinegar

1 (14.5 ounce) can diced tomatoes

1 (15 ounce) can chickpeas, drained
   and rinsed

1 (15 ounce) can black beans

1 tablespoon lemon juice

$\frac{1}{3}$ cup fresh parsley, chopped

green onions, chopped, for garnish

Heat oil in a large sauté pan over medium heat and sauté onions, garlic and ginger until onions are tender, about 5 to 6 minutes. Mix in curry paste, salt, vinegar, tomatoes and chickpeas. Cover and reduce heat. Allow to simmer for 30 to 40 minutes.

Add black beans, lemon juice and parsley and simmer for an additional 10 minutes.

Garnish with green onions and serve over rice.

SHORT CUT

If canned chickpeas are not available or to use dry chickpeas rather than canned, simply soak 1 $\frac{1}{2}$ cups raw chickpeas in water overnight or for a few hours which will yield 2 cups soaked peas.

FILLED ROASTED TOMATOES

3 teaspoons chicken bouillon

1 ½ cups water

1 cup Israeli couscous

1 tablespoon butter

2 tablespoons fresh parsley

4 fresh mint leaves

2 fresh basil leaves

¾ cup Parmesan cheese, divided

½ cup breadcrumbs, toasted

½ tablespoon + 3 teaspoons garlic

6 medium tomatoes, cut in half, cored with flesh removed and reserved

1 tablespoon olive oil

½ cup vermouth

½ cup cream

Preheat oven to 350°. In a saucepan over high heat, dissolve chicken bouillon in water and bring to a boil. Add couscous; remove from heat, cover and let stand until all liquid is absorbed, about 5 minutes. Add butter, parsley, mint, basil and ½ cup Parmesan.

In mixing bowl, combine cooked couscous, breadcrumbs and ½ tablespoon garlic. Place cored tomato halves in muffin tin to hold in place and fill with couscous stuffing. Top with remaining Parmesan cheese and bake until browned, about 30 to 35 minutes.

Meanwhile, in a saucepan over medium heat, sauté 3 teaspoons garlic in olive oil. Add reserved innards from tomatoes and cook down, about 12 minutes. Add vermouth and simmer 5 minutes. Add cream and bring to a boil; simmer 5 minutes. Purée in a blender until smooth, then serve over roasted tomatoes.

GREEN BEANS WITH PEPPERED GOAT CHEESE & TOASTED WALNUTS

³/₄ cup walnuts

2 pounds fresh French or green beans, stems removed

1 teaspoon baking soda

3 tablespoons lemon juice

zest of 1 lemon

3 tablespoons olive oil

6 ounces peppered goat cheese (or tangy cheese like Feta or Gorgonzola), crumbled

Preheat oven to 350°. Spread walnuts on baking sheet and place in oven for 20 to 25 minutes. Remove from oven and set aside to cool.

Steam beans over water with baking soda until crisp tender, about 5 to 7 minutes. Remove from steamer and allow to cool to room temperature.

In a large mixing bowl, combine lemon juice, zest and olive oil. Add cooled beans and toss until fully coated. Add cheese and walnuts; toss lightly. Serve at room temperature.

DID YOU KNOW?

Why should you put baking soda in the water? Because baking soda is an alkaline, adding a small amount to your pot of boiling water will help your green vegetables to stay green as they are cooked. Great for cooking green beans, the same can be applied when cooking any green vegetable.

GRILLED GARLIC BABY ARTICHOKES

Serves 6 - 8

6 baby artichokes, halved

1 teaspoon salt

2 garlic cloves, minced and divded

1 shallot, chopped and divided

$\frac{1}{2}$ cup butter

Bring a large stockpot of water to a boil. Place artichokes into boiling water and season with salt. Add 1 clove garlic and $\frac{1}{2}$ shallots. Boil for 30 minutes or until a fork is easily inserted into the stem of the artichokes. Drain and set aside.

Preheat grill to low heat.

Melt butter in a small saucepan over medium heat. Stir in remaining garlic and shallots; set aside.

Place artichoke halves on grill for 5 to 10 minutes, turning once. Brush with garlic/shallot butter during grilling, reserving some sauce for dipping later. Serve with remaining butter as a dipping sauce.

HERBED ASPARAGUS SAUTÉ

Serves 6 - 8

3 tablespoons butter

3 garlic cloves, minced

1 teaspoon lemon juice

1 teaspoon fresh rosemary, crushed

$\frac{1}{2}$ teaspoon fresh oregano

$\frac{1}{2}$ teaspoon fresh basil

$\frac{1}{4}$ teaspoon salt

$\frac{1}{4}$ teaspoon white pepper

$\frac{1}{4}$ teaspoon garlic powder

1 pound asparagus, trimmed

$\frac{1}{4}$ cup Parmesan cheese, grated

Preheat oven to 350°. In large sauté pan over medium heat, melt butter and sauté garlic for 2 minutes. Add lemon juice, rosemary, oregano, basil, salt, pepper and garlic powder and sauté for 1 minute.

Add asparagus to sauté pan, toss well and sauté for about 10 minutes. Remove from heat, place asparagus in baking dish and sprinkle with Parmesan cheese; bake 10 minutes.

Indian Style curry potatoes, Cauliflower & Chickpeas

Serves 4 - 6

4 tablespoons vegetable oil, divided

2 medium onions, chopped

³/₄ pound red skin potatoes, scrubbed and cut into ¹/₂-inch pieces

1 tablespoon fresh ginger, grated

3 medium garlic cloves, minced

1 tablespoon tomato paste

2 tablespoons curry paste

2 teaspoons fresh cilantro, chopped

1 teaspoon fresh mint, chopped

¹/₂ head of cauliflower, cut into florets

1 (14 ounce) can diced tomatoes

¹/₄ cup water

1 (15 ounce) can chickpeas

¹/₂ teaspoon salt

¹/₄ cup coconut milk

In a Dutch oven, heat 3 tablespoons oil over medium-high heat and sauté onions and potatoes until browned, about 10 minutes. Reduce heat to medium and add remaining oil, ginger, garlic, tomato paste, curry paste and herbs, cook for 1 minute. Add cauliflower, stir to coat, then add tomatoes, water, chickpeas and salt and simmer for 15 minutes. Remove from heat, add coconut milk and serve.

SERVING SUGGESTION

Excellent served with Marinated Leg of Lamb, page 240, or as a vegetarian entrée.

LOBSTER TRUFFLE RISOTTO

1 tablespoon butter

2 teaspoons white truffle oil

1 tablespoon fresh thyme, chopped

$^1/_3$ cup shallots, minced

1 cup brown Arborio rice

$^1/_2$ cup dry white wine

$^3/_4$ teaspoon salt

6 cups lobster stock

2 lobster tails, meat removed

1 tablespoon fresh Italian parsley, chopped

2 teaspoons lemon juice

$^1/_4$ cup heavy cream

fresh chives, for garnish (optional)

In medium saucepan, melt butter over medium heat. Add oil, thyme and shallots and cook for 2 minutes, stirring constantly. Add rice and cook 1 additional minute, stirring constantly. Add wine and salt, cook 2 minutes or until almost absorbed, stirring constantly. Add broth, $^1/_2$ cup at a time, stirring frequently until each portion is absorbed before adding the next, about 30 minutes total. Add lobster meat and cook for 2 minutes or until lobster is cooked thoroughly; stir frequently. Stir in parsley and lemon juice. Before serving add cream and garnish with chives (optional).

DO IT YOURSELF

HOW TO MAKE LOBSTER STOCK

Remove meat from lobster tails and cut into small pieces, set aside. To sautepan over medium, add $^1/_2$ small onion, 1 celery stalk, chopped, 1 carrot, chopped and garlic and saute 6 to 8 minutes. Add 6 cups vegetable broth along with lobster and bring to a boil. Add 1 cup brandy and simmer to reduce, about 2 - 3 minutes. Skim foam off of top of stock and discard, strain stock and set aside until ready to be used.

MASHED CAULIFLOWER

2 cups cauliflower, finely chopped

1 tablespoon sour cream

1 tablespoon butter

1 teaspoon fresh thyme

salt and pepper, to taste

1 cup Cheddar cheese, freshly grated

1/2 cup green onions, chopped

Preheat oven to 350°. In large saucepan, steam cauliflower until very soft. Remove cauliflower from heat, drain and place in blender or food processor. Add sour cream and butter and blend until smooth. Season with thyme and salt and pepper, to taste.

Transfer cauliflower mixture to 9x9-inch baking dish, coat with shredded cheese and bake until golden brown and bubbly, about 10 to 12 minutes. Garnish with green onions just before serving.

POBLANO CRÈME FRAÎCHE MASHED POTATOES

6 poblano chiles

1 tablespoon olive oil

2 cups crème fraîche, divided

2 ½ pounds potatoes, peeled and cut into medium-sized chunks

½ cup butter

salt and pepper, to taste

Optional Toppings
1 ½ cups Cheddar cheese, shredded

1 can fried onions

¼ bunch cilantro, chopped

Preheat oven to 350°. Meanwhile, coat poblano chiles with oil and roast in pan 15 to 20 minutes over medium-high heat, turning every 3 to 5 minutes (skins should begin to look blistered). Remove peel and seeds from chiles and purée with 1 cup crème fraîche in food processor or with hand blender until smooth, set aside.

In a large stockpot of salted water, add potatoes and boil. Cook for 35 to 40 minutes or until easily pierced with a fork. Drain and then dry for 3 to 4 minutes before mashing.

Add poblano mixture and remaining crème fraîche to mashed potatoes and mix to incorporate. Add butter and mix again. Season with salt and pepper, to taste.

Prior to serving, garnish with cheddar cheese, fried onions or cilantro (optional).

Polenta & Spinach Casserole

4 tablespoons butter

1 cup dry polenta

4 cups chicken broth

$\frac{1}{2}$ cup sour cream

2 (10 ounce) packages frozen spinach, thawed

1 tablespoon butter, melted

1 tablespoon all purpose flour

$\frac{1}{2}$ cup milk

salt and pepper, to taste

1 teaspoon nutmeg

2 teaspoons onion powder

6 ounces white Cheddar cheese, freshly grated

Preheat oven to 400°. In medium saucepan, melt butter and sauté dry polenta over medium heat until golden brown. Add chicken broth slowly until polenta thickens and bubbles. Stir in sour cream; set aside.

Meanwhile, in a mixing bowl, combine thawed spinach, butter, flour, milk, salt, pepper, nutmeg and onion powder.

Butter a 9x13-inch baking dish and place $\frac{1}{3}$ polenta over bottom of dish. Top with $\frac{1}{3}$ of spinach mixture and top with $\frac{1}{3}$ cheese. Repeat layers, ending with cheese. Bake for 30 to 35 minutes, until bubbly and golden brown.

POTATOES & LEEKS WITH GRUYERE

2 tablespoons butter

1 pound leeks, thinly sliced

1 (8 ounce) package cream cheese, room temperature

1 teaspoon salt

$\frac{1}{2}$ teaspoon black pepper

$\frac{1}{2}$ teaspoon nutmeg, freshly grated

1 cup milk

3 large eggs

2 pounds potatoes, peeled and shredded

$\frac{1}{2}$ pound Gruyere cheese, grated

Preheat oven to 350°. Melt butter in a large sauté pan over medium-high heat and add leeks; sauté until tender, about 10 minutes. Transfer leeks to large mixing bowl and set aside.

Blend cream cheese, salt, pepper and nutmeg in food processor or blender. Add milk and eggs to cream cheese mixture and process until just blended.

Pour cream cheese mixture over leeks and add potatoes and Gruyere. Stir to combine and transfer to greased 9x13-inch baking dish. Bake until cooked through and top is golden brown, about 1 hour.

RED WINE RISOTTO WITH ROASTED PUMPKIN

Serves 6 - 8

2 ½ cups pumpkin, peeled and cubed (substitute squash if necessary)

3 tablespoons olive oil, divided

1 teaspoon salt

¼ teaspoon black pepper

⅓ cup shallots, finely chopped

1 (8 ounce) package baby bella mushrooms

2 garlic cloves, minced

1 ½ cups brown Arborio rice

½ cup red wine

4 cups vegetable broth

¼ cup Parmesan cheese, freshly grated

2 tablespoons fresh basil, chopped

1 tablespoon fresh oregano, chopped

Preheat oven to 350°. Brush pumpkin cubes lightly with 1 tablespoon oil and season with salt and pepper. Sauté in large sauté pan over medium heat until golden, about 12 to 15 minutes. Transfer to baking sheet and roast for 4 to 5 minutes. Remove from oven and set aside.

Meanwhile, combine 2 tablespoons oil and shallots in sauté pan and cook about 1 minute over medium heat. Add mushrooms and garlic, cook an additional 3 minutes. Add rice and cook for 1 minute. Add red wine and cook until liquid has absorbed. Slowly add vegetable broth to rice mixture, ½ cup at a time, stirring constantly and allowing liquid to be absorbed before adding more broth, about 25 to 30 minutes. During last 15 minutes, mash ½ of the pumpkin cubes and stir into rice after the last broth addition. Add remaining cubed pumpkin, cheese, basil and oregano; stir to combine.

ROASTED GINGER MAPLE SWEET POTATOES

Serves 4 - 5

1 tablespoon butter

1 tablespoon fresh ginger, grated

$\frac{1}{2}$ cup maple syrup

1 cup orange juice

3 large sweet potatoes, unpeeled and sliced into $\frac{1}{2}$-inch rounds

$\frac{3}{4}$ teaspoon salt

$\frac{1}{4}$ teaspoon pepper

$\frac{1}{2}$ cup butter, melted

1 cup pecans, chopped

3 - 4 tablespoons demerara sugar

zest of 1 orange

Preheat oven to 450°. Melt 1 tablespoon butter in a large sauté pan over medium heat and add ginger; sweat until very high "perfume," about 4 to 5 minutes. Add maple syrup and cook until foamy and rising up the sides of the pan, about 3 to 4 minutes. Add orange juice and reduce liquid by half, about 10 to 12 minutes. Remove from heat and set aside.

In a large mixing bowl, toss potatoes with ginger maple mixture, season to taste with salt and pepper and then arrange in a single layer on a greased baking sheet. Bake uncovered for 15 minutes.

While potatoes are baking, combine melted butter, pecans, demerara sugar and orange zest. After potatoes have baked for 15 minutes, remove from oven and flip. Sprinkle with pecan topping and bake an additional 10 minutes.

Roasted Root Vegetable Medley

¼ cup olive oil

2 tablespoons maple syrup

1 garlic clove, minced

4 large beets, peeled and quartered

2 Yukon gold potatoes, cut into 1 ½-inch cubes

2 carrots, peeled and cut diagonally

2 parsnips, diced

1 large sweet potato, cut into 1 ½-inch cubes

1 rutabaga, cut into 1 ½-inch pieces

2 large onions, quartered lengthwise

salt and pepper, to taste

2 tablespoons clarified butter, melted

⅓ cup green onions, chopped

Preheat oven to 350°. In small mixing bowl, combine oil, maple syrup and garlic.

Place all vegetables on a heavy large-rimmed baking sheet. Pour oil mixture over vegetables and toss to coat. Spread vegetables out into a single layer and generously sprinkle with salt and pepper. Roast until tender and golden brown, about 1 ½ hours; stirring occasionally. Transfer vegetables to platter and drizzle with butter. Sprinkle with chopped green onions and serve immediately.

SAFFRON RICE WITH FRESH ASPARAGUS & RAISINS

Serve 10

2 tablespoons butter

$1/2$ medium sweet onion, minced

1 garlic clove, minced

1 $1/2$ cups basmati rice

2 $1/4$ cups chicken broth

$1/2$ teaspoon saffron strands

1 cup golden raisins

$1/2$ pound asparagus, cut into 1 $1/2$-inch pieces

fresh parsley, for garnish

Melt butter in a medium sauté pan over medium-high heat. Sauté onion and garlic until tender, about 5 to 6 minutes. Add rice and sauté for 1 minute, stirring constantly. Add chicken broth, saffron and raisins; bring to a boil. Reduce heat, cover and simmer for 15 minutes or until rice is tender and liquid is absorbed.

While rice is cooking, steam asparagus, about 4 to 5 minutes. To serve, combine rice and asparagus in a serving bowl and garnish with fresh parsley.

Smoky Corn Risotto

6 slices bacon

6 green onions, chopped

1 shallot, minced

2 garlic cloves, minced

1 cup Arborio rice

1 cup dry white wine

1 quart chicken broth

4 tablespoons butter

1/4 cup fresh parsley, chopped

1/8 cup Parmesan cheese, grated

1 1/2 cups canned corn kernels, drained

In a large saucepan, fry bacon until crispy. Remove bacon from pan and set aside.

Pour off half of the bacon fat and add onions, shallots and garlic. Cook 5 to 6 minutes or until tender. Add rice; cook for 3 minutes or until you hear a clacking noise (similar to glass beads knocking around). Add wine and stir constantly until the wine is absorbed. Add chicken broth one cup at a time; only adding the next cup after the first is completely absorbed. Continue this process until all chicken broth is absorbed and rice has a creamy consistency; about 20 to 25 minutes.

Remove from heat; stir in butter, parsley flakes, Parmesan and corn. Garnish with additional parsley flakes and crispy bacon.

SMOKY BAKED MARKET BEANS

½ pound Italian sausage

6 slices bacon

1 ½ cups onions, chopped

3 ½ tablespoons garlic cloves, chopped

1 tablespoon fresh thyme

¾ cup dark lager beer

¼ cup maple syrup

3 tablespoons Dijon mustard

3 tablespoons turbinado sugar

2 tablespoons Worcestershire sauce

1 tablespoon soy sauce

6 (15 ounce) cans Great Northern beans, drained

5 teaspoons chipotle chili in adobo sauce, minced

fresh Italian parsley, chopped

Preheat oven to 350°. In large frying pan, brown Italian sausage over medium heat; remove from pan, drain fat and set aside.

In same pan, add bacon and cook until crisp. Transfer to paper towels to drain fat then crumble. Transfer 2 ½ tablespoons bacon drippings from pan to large bowl and add chopped bacon, set aside.

In same skillet, with remaining ½ tablespoon bacon drippings, sauté onions, garlic and thyme over medium heat for 5 to 6 minutes or until tender.

In bowl with bacon, add beer, maple syrup, Dijon mustard, sugar, Worcestershire sauce, soy sauce and beans, whisk to blend. Add sausage, onion mix and chiles and stir to combine. Transfer bean mixture to a 9x13-inch baking dish. Bake uncovered until liquid begins to thicken and bubble, about 1 hour.

To serve, garnish with fresh parsley.

Soubise (Braised Rice & Onions)

Serves 10 - 12

4 quarts water

2 ½ teaspoons salt, divided

1 cup white rice

10 tablespoons butter, divided

5 - 7 yellow onions, finely diced

¼ teaspoon pepper

1 cup Swiss cheese, shredded

½ cup heavy cream

Preheat oven to 300°. In a large saucepan over high heat, bring water to a boil. Add 1 teaspoon salt and rice; boil 5 minutes and drain immediately. Set rice aside.

In the same saucepan over medium-high heat, melt 2 tablespoons butter. Add onions and stir to coat. Add rice, remaining salt and pepper and stir until combined. Transfer rice mixture to a casserole dish; cover and bake for 1 hour, stirring often. Remove from oven and stir in cheese, remaining butter and cream. Serve immediately.

STRING BEANS
WITH SHALLOT VINAIGRETTE

1 pound French beans

¼ cup pomegranate vinegar (or champagne vinegar)

2 teaspoons Dijon mustard

1 teaspoon kosher salt

pepper, to taste

2 shallots, minced

½ cup olive oil

In medium saucepan, steam French beans for 2 minutes. Remove from heat and strain in a colander, then submerge beans in a bath of ice water. Let cool in ice water 3 to 4 minutes and drain.

In separate mixing bowl, whisk together pomegranate vinegar, Dijon mustard, salt, pepper and shallots. Let sit for 15 to 20 minutes then whisk in olive oil. Pour over beans and serve or refrigerate for 1 hour and serve cold.

SUCCOTASH WITH WAX BEANS

¾ cup lima beans, shelled

4 ounces yellow wax beans

1 ear of corn, kernels removed and cob discarded

½ teaspoon baking soda

4 ounces French beans

3 tablespoons butter, divided

1 tablespoon olive oil

1 red bell pepper, finely diced

1 green bell pepper, finely diced

4 garlic cloves, minced

3 tablespoons water

1 ½ tablespoons fresh chives, finely chopped

salt and pepper, to taste

In large saucepan, bring salted water to a boil. Add lima beans, wax beans and corn and boil until tender, about 3 minutes. With a slotted spoon, remove beans and corn to an ice bath and cool, about 3 to 4 minutes. Remove from ice bath and drain, set aside.

In same saucepan, add baking soda to salted water and cook French beans then remove to ice bath and drain; set aside.

In large skillet, heat 1 tablespoon butter and oil over medium heat and sauté peppers and garlic until tender, but still crisp. Add beans and water and sauté until reheated, about 5 to 6 minutes. Finish with chives, reamining 2 tablespoons butter, salt and pepper before serving.

SWEET & SAVORY SWEET POTATOES

½ cup butter, melted

1 tablespoon dried basil

1 tablespoon chili powder

2 tablespoons brown sugar

1 teaspoon cinnamon

1 teaspoon cardamom seeds

3 large sweet potatoes, peeled and cut into 1-inch cubes

½ cup chicken broth

Preheat oven to 375°. In mixing bowl, combine melted butter, basil, chili powder, brown sugar, cinnamon and cardamom seeds; add potatoes and toss to coat. Pour chicken broth into 9x13-inch baking dish and add potatoes. Cover and cook for 35 minutes or until potatoes are tender. Remove cover and cook an additional 5 minutes, turning occasionally.

Excellent served with poultry and perfect for a holiday side dish.

SWEET ONION & TOMATO BAKE

Serves 10 - 12

• •

8 tablespoons butter, divided

6 sweet onions, quartered and sliced

6 ounces Swiss cheese, shredded

1 sleeve saltine crackers, crushed

6 ounces aged white Cheddar cheese, shredded

3 large eggs

1 ½ cups half & half

1 ½ teaspoons salt

½ teaspoon black pepper, freshly ground

4 - 5 roma tomatoes, sliced

Preheat oven to 350°. In large skillet, melt 6 tablespoons butter over medium heat. Add onions and sauté for 20 minutes, or until caramelized. Place half of cooked onions in a lightly greased 9x13-inch baking dish. Sprinkle evenly with grated Swiss cheese and ½ of crushed cracker crumbs. Top with remaining onions and shredded white Cheddar cheese.

In small mixing bowl, whisk together eggs, half & half, salt and pepper; pour over onion mixture. Arrange sliced tomatoes over casserole.

In small skillet, melt remaining butter over medium heat. Add remaining cracker crumbs and cook until slightly brown, stirring often. Sprinkle crumbs evenly over casserole and bake uncovered for 45 to 55 minutes, or until lightly browned and set.

SWEET POTATO SOUFFLÉ

3 cups sweet potatoes (canned or roasted)

1 cup sugar

$^1/_3$ cup milk

2 eggs, beaten

1 teaspoon vanilla extract

$^1/_2$ stick butter, softened

TOPPING

1 cup pecans, chopped

1 cup brown sugar, packed

$^1/_2$ stick butter, melted

$^1/_3$ cup all purpose flour

Preheat oven to 350° and grease a 9x9-inch baking dish.

In a food processor or blender, add sweet potatoes, sugar, milk, eggs, vanilla and butter; purée until smooth. Pour sweet potato mixture into greased baking dish.

In separate mixing bowl, combine pecans, brown sugar, butter and flour until well incorporated. Sprinkle nut topping over sweet potatoes. Bake uncovered for 30 minutes. Allow to cool slightly before serving.

DO IT YOURSELF

ROASTING SWEET POTATOES
Preheat oven to 425°. Arrange sweet potatoes in a single layer on a lightly greased baking sheet, bake for 45 - 50 minutes or until easily pierced with a knife.

THE BEST EVER
MACARONI & CHEESE

Serves 12

1 pound elbow macaroni

8 ounces white Cheddar, shredded

8 ounces garlic Cheddar, shredded

8 ounces Gruyere cheese

24 ounces cottage cheese

8 ounces Goat cheese crumbles

2 jumbo eggs, slightly beaten

1 teaspoon black pepper

1 teaspoon ground mustard

$1/2$ - 1 teaspoon nutmeg

$1/2$ teaspoon celery salt

$1 1/2$ - 2 teaspoons garlic salt

1 teaspoon kosher salt

3 medium tomatoes, sliced paper thin

2 cups breadcrumbs

$1/4$ cup Parmesan cheese, grated

$1/2$ stick butter, melted

Preheat oven to 350°. In large stockpot, boil macaroni according to package directions. Drain and set aside.

In a large mixing bowl, combine all cheeses except Parmesan, eggs, pepper, mustard, nutmeg, celery salt, garlic salt and kosher salt. Stir in macaroni and mix well. Pour mixture into a buttered 9x13-inch baking dish. Add sliced tomatoes to top.

In small mixing bowl, combine breadcrumbs and Parmesan cheese and sprinkle over macaroni and cheese. Drizzle with melted butter and then cook uncovered for 30 to 40 minutes.

THREE ONION RISOTTO

1 ½ cups + 3 tablespoons olive oil, divided

5 medium shallots

1 leek, thinly julienned

6 green onions, thinly sliced

1 yellow onion, diced

2 garlic cloves, chopped

pinch of fresh thyme, chopped

pinch of red pepper flakes

2 cups brown Arborio rice

pinch of salt

½ cup white wine

½ quart chicken broth

¼ cup heavy cream

4 tablespoons butter

Preheat oven to 450°. In a small mixing bowl, combine 1 cup oil and whole shallots. Place shallots on baking sheet, cover with aluminum foil and roast for 20 to 25 minutes. Once soft, allow to cool slightly; quarter and set aside

To fry leeks, toss with ¼ cup oil and place on baking sheet and bake until crispy, about 10 to 15 minutes; set aside.

In a frying pan over medium heat, toss green onions in ¼ cup oil and sauté for 2 minutes each side.

In separate large frying pan, heat 3 tablespoons oil over medium heat. Add onion, garlic, thyme and red pepper flakes and cook until onions are tender, about 5 to 6 minutes. Add rice and salt to onion mixture and cook for an additional 2 to 3 minutes. Stir in wine until fully absorbed, stirring constantly. Add chicken broth in ½ cup increments allowing broth to fully absorb before adding more. Once all broth is absorbed, remove pan from heat. Add cream and butter and allow to cool slightly before serving.

Top risotto with shallots, leeks and scallions before serving.

THYME GARLIC ROASTED SPAGHETTI SQUASH

Serves 8

1 spaghetti squash

4 tablespoons butter, cubed

10 sprigs fresh thyme

2 - 3 garlic cloves, sliced

salt and pepper, to taste

2 cups white wine

Preheat oven to 400°. Cut squash in half and place in roasting pan with butter, thyme, garlic, salt and pepper. Add wine to pan. Place pan in oven and bake uncovered for 1 hour, basting squash with liquid in pan every 10 to 15 minutes. Remove squash from oven and allow to cool slightly. Use fork to shred squash and serve immediately.

Toasted Pinenut Couscous with Mango & Avocado

1 cup pine nuts

1 box of couscous

chicken broth, substitute for water amount for couscous

$\frac{1}{2}$ cup mango, chopped

$\frac{1}{2}$ avocado, chopped

$\frac{1}{2}$ teaspoon lime juice

salt and pepper, to taste

$\frac{1}{2}$ bunch green onions, coarsely chopped

Preheat oven to 300°. Spread pine nuts on a baking sheet and bake for 15 to 20 minutes; stir halfway. Remove from oven when golden brown and set aside.

Prepare couscous as directed on the box, using chicken broth instead of water. Once broth has absorbed, add mango, pine nuts and avocado. Season with lime juice, salt and pepper and garnish with green onions to serve.

WILD RICE WITH BUTTERNUT SQUASH & DRIED CRANBERRIES

• •

1 cup wild rice

1 cup long-grain brown rice

2 tablespoons olive or salad oil

1 garlic clove, minced

1 cup onions, chopped

³/₄ cups carrots

1 tablespoon ginger, minced and peeled

3 cups butternut squash, peeled and cut into ¹/₂-inch cubes

1 Granny Smith or Fuji apple, peeled, cored and diced

1 cinnamon stick

¹/₄ cup water

¹/₂ cup dried cranberries

1 teaspoon dried thyme

¹/₂ teaspoon dried marjoram

¹/₄ cup Monterrey Jack cheese

2 teaspoons salt

1 teaspoon pepper

1 ¹/₄ cups walnuts, chopped

green onions, chopped, for garnish

Cook rice according to package directions. Set aside.

In medium skillet, heat oil, garlic, onions, carrots and ginger over medium heat, about 3 to 4 minutes. Add butternut squash, apple, cinnamon and water to vegetable mixture. Reduce heat to medium-low, cover and simmer until butternut squash is tender, about 10 to 15 minutes. Add cranberries, cook an additional 5 minutes. Fold in rice, season with thyme, marjoram, cheese, and salt and pepper. Remove cinnamon stick and top with walnuts and green onions before serving.

Zucchini Patties with Feta

2 tablespoons olive oil

1 vidalia onion, finely sliced

1 zucchini, shredded

1 carrot, grated

1 garlic clove, minced

3 fresh basil leaves, chopped

2 fresh oregano leaves, chopped

1/4 cup all purpose flour

2 egg whites

salt and pepper, to taste

1 tablespoon vegetable oil

8 ounces Feta cheese

Heat 2 tablespoons oil in a sauté pan over medium heat, sauté onions 5 to 6 minutes.

In a large mixing bowl, combine sautéed onions, remaining vegetables and herbs. Add in flour and stir to combine. In a small bowl, whip egg whites until foamy. Add egg whites to vegetable mixture until fully incorporated then season to taste with salt and pepper.

Heat 1 tablespoon vegetable oil in a skillet over medium-high heat. Make a zucchini patty with 1/3 to 1/2 cup of mix and place in skillet. Cook 4 to 5 minutes on each side.

Remove from skillet, top with crumbled feta and serve. Excellent served with fish or pork.

Cosmo Blood Orange Punch, page 354
and Old Salem Iced Tea, page 362

Sweet Grilled Peaches, page 330

Best Ever Carrot Cake, page 298

Grape Salsa, page 357

Marbled Mousse, page 320

Panna Cotta with Berry Gazpacho, page 322

Oatmeal Carmelitas, page 321

post

DESSERTS

BREAKFAST

EVERYTHING ELSE

APPLE CHEESECAKE

1 ²/₃ cups graham cracker crumbs

³/₄ cup butter, softened and divided

¹/₄ teaspoon cinnamon

³/₄ cup + 2 tablespoons sugar

3 medium Granny Smith apples,
    peeled, cored and thinly sliced

4 eggs

1 (8 ounce) package cream cheese,
    softened

¹/₄ teaspoon salt

1 (8 ounce) container cottage cheese

¹/₃ cup light brown sugar, packed

1 tablespoon lemon zest

2 teaspoons vanilla extract

1 cup heavy cream

8 ounces Mango Ginger Stilton, in
    dime-size crumbles

cinnamon, for garnish

Preheat oven to 450°. In a large bowl, combine graham cracker crumbs, ¹/₂ cup butter and cinnamon. Press mixture into a greased 9-inch springform pan, covering the bottom of pan and 1-inch up the sides; set aside.

In a large skillet over medium heat, add ¹/₄ cup butter and 2 tablespoons sugar. Once melted, add apple slices and cook until glazed and crisp tender, 4 to 5 minutes. Place apples over crust and reserve a few for decoration; set aside.

In a large bowl, combine ³/₄ cup sugar, eggs, cream cheese, salt, cottage cheese, brown sugar, lemon zest and vanilla extract. Using a mixer, beat on medium speed until smooth, about 1 minute. Reduce speed to low; gradually add heavy cream and beat 1 more minute. Pour mixture into springform pan over apples. Add crumbled Stilton cheese to pan, slightly pushing each crumble into the mixture. Top with remaining apple slices and sprinkle with cinnamon. Bake for 10 minutes. After 10 minutes, reduce heat to 300° and bake an additional 55 minutes. Remove from oven and cool for at least 30 minutes before removing sides of springform pan. Refrigerate until ready to serve.

BAKED PEAR DELIGHTS

1 (8 ounce) package cream cheese, softened

$\frac{1}{2}$ cup mayonnaise

$\frac{3}{4}$ cup pecans, finely chopped

$\frac{1}{4}$ cup confectioners' sugar

2 cups Riesling or sweet white wine

1 cup Demerara sugar

zest and juice of 1 lemon

2 cloves

pinch of cinnamon

4 whole pears, peeled, cored and cut in half

Preheat oven to 300°. In a mixing bowl, combine cream cheese, mayonnaise, pecans and powdered sugar; set aside.

In a large saucepan, combine white wine, Demerara sugar, lemon zest and juice, cloves and pinch of cinnamon. Bring to a boil and add pears; reduce heat. Turn pears after 10 minutes, then continue to cook 10 to 15 additional minutes. Remove pears from liquid and set aside; keep liquid in saucepan.

Turn heat to high and reduce remaining liquid to 1 $\frac{1}{2}$ cups. Let liquid cool completely and add to cream cheese mixture.

Bake pears for 10 minutes or until warmed through. Remove from oven and top with cream cheese mixture before serving.

BANANA CHOCOLATE HAZELNUT STUFFED CRÊPES

1 cup heavy cream

4 ounces white chocolate chunks or chips

1 cup all purpose flour

1 teaspoon sugar

$1/4$ teaspoon salt

3 eggs

2 cups milk

2 tablespoons butter, melted

1 cup chocolate hazelnut spread

4 bananas, sliced

In a medium saucepan, bring heavy cream to a simmer. Add white chocolate and remove from heat. Allow white chocolate to melt for approximately 5 minutes, stirring occasionally until combined. Cover and chill until cold, about one hour (may chill overnight).

Make crêpe batter by sifting together flour, sugar and salt; set aside. In a large bowl, beat eggs and milk together with an electric mixer. Beat in flour mixture until smooth; then stir in melted butter.

Heat a lightly oiled frying pan over medium-high heat. Pour or scoop crêpe batter into frying pan, using approximately 2 tablespoons for each crêpe. Tip and rotate pan to spread batter as thinly as possible over bottom of the entire pan. Brown on both sides and remove from pan.

Spread crêpe with chocolate hazelnut spread and a few banana slices and roll. Repeat with remaining crêpes, chocolate hazelnut spread and bananas. Top with white chocolate whipped cream. (When using whipped cream that has been chilling, refresh by whipping with a whisk until soft peaks form.)

BEST EVER CARROT CAKE

CARROT CAKE

³/₄ **cup sugar**

1 ½ **cups all purpose flour**

1 **teaspoon baking powder**

1 **teaspoon baking soda**

1 **teaspoon cinnamon**

½ **teaspoon salt**

²/₃ **cup vegetable oil**

2 **eggs**

2 **cups carrots, shredded**

½ **cup crushed pineapple with syrup**

1 **teaspoon vanilla extract**

CREAM CHEESE FROSTING

3 **ounces cream cheese, softened**

2 **cups confectioners' sugar**

1 **tablespoon butter, softened**

1 **teaspoon vanilla extract**

1 **tablespoon milk**

Preheat oven to 350°. In a medium bowl combine dry ingredients: sugar, flour, baking powder, baking soda, cinnamon and salt.

In separate bowl, combine vegetable oil, eggs, carrots, crushed pineapple with syrup and vanilla. Mix with a hand mixer at medium speed until all ingredients are combined (about 2 minutes). Gradually add dry mixture to wet ingredients; mix well after each addition. Grease a 9x9-inch or 11x7.5-inch pan (anything larger will come out too thin) and pour batter into the pan. Bake for 35 minutes or until golden.

To make cream cheese frosting, combine all ingredients in a bowl and mix until smooth. Let cake cool and top with frosting.

CAPPUCCINO BISCOTTI

Makes 20 - 24 cookies

2 large eggs

$^1/_3$ cup butter

$^1/_2$ cup brown sugar

$^1/_2$ cup sugar

1 tablespoon instant coffee

$^1/_4$ teaspoon cinnamon

2 cups all purpose flour

1 $^1/_2$ tablespoons baking powder

pinch of salt

$^1/_2$ cup chocolate chips

Preheat oven to 350°. In a medium bowl, cream eggs and butter. Add brown sugar, white sugar and instant coffee; mix until batter reaches a creamy consistency.

In a separate bowl, combine cinnamon, flour, baking powder and salt. Stir dry ingredient mixture into wet ingredients to form a sticky dough. Fold in chocolate chips.

Wet hands and form 2 or 3 logs on a parchment lined cookie sheet. Bake until firm, 30 to 40 minutes.

Remove from oven, slice diagonally into biscotti cookies, lay cut side down and bake an additional 5 minutes on each side.

CHARLESTON SQUARES

1 cup sugar

$\frac{1}{2}$ cup margarine

2 cups self rising flour

2 eggs, yolks and whites divided

1 $\frac{1}{2}$ teaspoons vanilla extract, divided

1 teaspoon almond extract

1 tablespoon water

1 cup brown sugar, packed

$\frac{1}{2}$ cup almonds, chopped

$\frac{1}{2}$ cup fresh cherries, pits removed and chopped

Preheat oven to 350°. In a large bowl, combine sugar, margarine, flour, egg yolks, 1 teaspoon vanilla, almond extract and water. Pour into a greased 9x9-inch baking dish.

In a separate bowl, beat egg whites until stiff peaks form. Add brown sugar and $\frac{1}{2}$ teaspoon vanilla and combine thoroughly. Spread over batter in baking dish and sprinkle with almonds and cherries. Bake for 30 minutes; remove from oven and allow to cool before serving.

CHERRY COFFEE CAKE

COFFEE CAKE

$^1\!/_2$ **cup butter**

1 cup sugar

2 eggs

1 cup sour cream

1 teaspoon vanilla extract

2 cups all purpose flour

$^1\!/_2$ **teaspoon salt**

1 $^1\!/_2$ teaspoons baking powder

$^1\!/_2$ **teaspoon baking soda**

1 (21 ounce) can cherry pie filling

TOPPING

$^1\!/_3$ **cup sugar**

$^1\!/_3$ **cup all purpose flour**

1 teaspoon cinnamon

$^1\!/_2$ **cup pecans, chopped**

3 tablespoons margarine, melted

Preheat oven to 350°. Grease and flour a 9x9-inch baking dish.

Cream butter and sugar together. Beat in eggs, sour cream and vanilla. In a separate mixing bowl, sift together flour, salt, baking powder and baking soda. Gradually add dry ingredients to butter/sugar mixture, beating well. Spread half of batter into prepared pan. Top with cherry pie filling. Add remaining batter over filling.

To prepare topping, mix together sugar, flour, cinnamon, pecans and margarine. Spread evenly onto batter.

Bake for 60 to 65 minutes or until top is golden.

CHERRY VANILLA BREAD PUDDING

1 day-old French baguette, cut into 1-inch pieces

3 cups milk

1 cup buttermilk

2 cups sugar

6 eggs, beaten

1 (16 ounce) jar of maraschino cherries, pitted (reserving 3 tablespoons juice for sauce)

1 cup pecans, chopped

2 tablespoons vanilla extract

1 teaspoon cinnamon

$\frac{1}{2}$ teaspoon nutmeg

SAUCE

1 stick butter

$\frac{1}{2}$ cup Demerara sugar

1 egg, beaten

1 tablespoon almond extract

3 tablespoons cherry juice

Preheat oven to 350°. Combine first 10 ingredients in a large bowl until well incorporated. Pour into a 9x13-inch glass baking dish. Bake for 1 hour and 15 minutes.

During the last 10 minutes of baking, place butter and sugar in a small saucepan over medium heat and whisk until butter is melted. Remove from heat and slowly add egg while whisking. Slowly add almond extract and cherry juice in the same manner. Serve sauce warm over bread pudding.

CHOCOLATE CHERRY COOKIES

Makes 30 cookies

1 cup dried cherries

$^1/_2$ cup cherry liqueur

$^1/_2$ cup butter

$^1/_2$ cup sugar

$^1/_2$ cup light brown sugar, packed

1 egg

1 $^1/_2$ teaspoons vanilla extract

$^1/_4$ teaspoon almond extract

$^1/_4$ teaspoon salt

$^1/_2$ teaspoon baking soda

1 $^1/_2$ cups all purpose flour

$^3/_4$ cup white chocolate chunks, coarsely chopped

$^1/_2$ cup semi-sweet chocolate chunks, coarsely chopped

$^1/_2$ cup macadamia nuts, coarsely chopped (optional)

Plump dried cherries by covering with boiling water; soak for 5 minutes, drain and toss with cherry liqueur. For best flavor, allow cherries to marinate in the cherry liqueur several hours or overnight.

In separate mixing bowl, cream butter with sugars; blend in egg, vanilla and almond extract. Fold in salt, baking soda and flour.

Drain cherries and fold into mixture with white and semi-sweet chocolate and macadamia nuts (optional). Refrigerate dough at least one hour before baking.

Preheat oven to 350°. Drop batter onto greased cookie sheet by the heaping teaspoon. Bake until lightly golden, 12 to 14 minutes. Remove from cookie sheet and place on wire rack to cool.

CHOCOLATE CHIP APPLE CAKE

1 cup vegetable oil

2 tablespoons hazelnut oil

3 eggs

1 teaspoon cinnamon

1 3/4 cups sugar

2 cups all purpose flour

1 teaspoon baking soda

1/2 teaspoon salt

1/2 cup walnuts, chopped

12 ounces mini chocolate chips

5 - 6 Granny Smith or Fuji apples, peeled, cored and diced

confectioners' sugar

Preheat oven to 350°. In a large bowl, whisk together oils, eggs, cinnamon and sugar. In a separate bowl, combine flour, baking soda and salt. Slowly add dry ingredients to wet ingredients and stir to combine. Fold in walnuts, chocolate chips and apples.

Spread batter into a greased 9x13-inch baking dish. Bake for 55 to 60 minutes; remove from oven and allow cake to cool completely. Remove from pan and sprinkle with confectioners' sugar.

CINNAMON APPLE TART

Serves 12 - 14

2 tablespoons sugar

$^3/_4$ teaspoon cinnamon, divided

1 sheet puff pastry, thawed

1 egg, beaten

8 tablespoons apricot preserves, divided

1 Granny Smith or Fuji apple, peeled, cored and thinly sliced

2 tablespoons lemon juice

1 $^1/_2$ tablespoons unsalted butter

$^1/_4$ teaspoon allspice

$^1/_4$ teaspoon nutmeg

1 teaspoon lemon zest

$^1/_4$ cup pecans

Preheat oven to 400°. In a small mixing bowl, combine sugar and $^1/_2$ teaspoon cinnamon; set aside.

Unfold pastry sheet on a lightly floured baking sheet. Brush egg on 1 inch border along all sides. Fold edge over to cover egg glaze and to create a raised border; press to adhere. Make $^1/_2$-inch cuts along the edge and pierce the inside of the puff pastry several times with a fork. Spread 2 tablespoons preserves in the center of the pastry. Arrange apple slices in 3 neat overlapping rows on the pastry. Brush folded edges with remaining egg glaze. Sprinkle entire pastry with cinnamon sugar.

Bake for 30 minutes or until apples are tender and pastry is golden brown; allow to cool on wire rack.

Meanwhile, mix remaining $^1/_4$ teaspoon cinnamon, 6 tablespoons preserves, lemon juice, butter, allspice, nutmeg, lemon zest and pecans all in a small saucepan over medium-low heat until hot. To serve, slice pastry and drizzle with sauce.

CRANBERRY PECAN ORANGE POUND CAKE

1 cup margarine

2 cups sugar

4 eggs

1 tablespoon vanilla extract

2 ¼ cups all purpose flour

½ teaspoon baking powder

¼ teaspoon salt

½ cup evaporated milk

1 cup pecans, chopped

1 cup dried cranberries, chopped

2 tablespoons orange zest

Preheat oven to 325°. Grease and flour a 10-inch Bundt pan and set aside. Using an electric mixer, cream together margarine and sugar. Continue mixing, adding eggs one at a time and then add vanilla.

In a separate bowl, combine flour, baking powder and salt. Using your mixer, alternate adding dry ingredients and milk to creamed mixture, incorporating completely with each addition until thoroughly combined. Carefully fold in pecans, cranberries and orange zest and pour into Bundt pan. Bake for 1 hour and 10 minutes or until a toothpick inserted in center comes out clean.

Allow cake to cool for 5 minutes, then invert onto wire rack and let stand for 10 minutes. Allow cake to cool completely before serving.

CREAMY CARAMEL & PEAR SUNDAES WITH TOASTED HAZELNUTS

¼ cup hazelnuts, chopped

1 tablespoon butter

2 Bartlett pears, peeled, cored and sliced

1 (56 ounce) container vanilla ice cream

4 tablespoons caramel sauce

Preheat oven to 350°. Spread hazelnuts on a baking sheet and toast for approximately 6 to 8 minutes. Be sure to watch the nuts as they approach 6 minutes because hazelnuts will quickly go from toasted to scorched. Remove hazelnuts from oven and set aside to cool.

In a sauté pan over medium heat, melt butter. Add sliced pears and sauté until pears are soft, about 5 to 7 minutes.

Scoop about 1 cup of ice cream into each serving dish and top with an equal portion of pears, toasted hazelnuts and 1 tablespoon of warmed caramel sauce. Serve immediately.

CREAMY MACADAMIA NUT COOKIES

Makes 24 cookies

½ cup unsalted butter, at room temperature

1 (8 ounce) package cream cheese, at room temperature

¾ cup dark brown sugar, packed

zest of 1 orange

2 teaspoons vanilla extract

1 ½ cups all purpose flour

2 teaspoons baking powder

¾ cup macadamia nuts, coarsely chopped

Preheat oven to 400°. In a large bowl using an electric mixer, cream together butter and cream cheese until light and fluffy. Beat in brown sugar, and add orange zest and vanilla extract.

In a separate bowl, sift flour and baking powder together. Add dry ingredients to butter mixture and combine with a wooden spoon. Carefully fold in macadamia nuts. Refrigerate dough at least 1 hour or overnight.

Drop heaping teaspoons of dough onto a greased cookie sheet, spacing the cookies 2 inches apart. Slightly flatten each cookie with the back of a spoon. Bake until lightly browned, 8 to 10 minutes. Cool completely on wire racks before serving.

DAIQUIRI CHIFFON CHEESECAKE

1 ¼ cups graham cracker crumbs

1 cup sugar, divided

4 tablespoons butter, melted

½ cup lime juice

1 envelope unflavored gelatin

4 eggs, yolks and whites separated

¼ cup rum

2 teaspoons lime zest

1 teaspoon lemon zest

2 (8 ounce) packages cream cheese, softened

1 cup heavy cream, whipped

1 lime, cut into wedges

In a large bowl, combine graham cracker crumbs, ¼ cup sugar and butter; reserve 2 tablespoons of the mixture and set aside. Press remaining crumbs into bottom and sides of a buttered 9-inch springform pan; chill 45 minutes.

Meanwhile, combine lime juice, gelatin and ½ cup sugar in a medium saucepan over low heat, about 8 to 10 minutes. In a large bowl, beat egg yolks until creamy; add gelatin mixture, rum, lime and lemon zest. Allow to cool for 30 minutes.

In separate bowl, beat cream cheese with an electric mixer at medium speed until smooth. Gradually add cooled gelatin mixture; beat until smooth. Set aside.

In a separate bowl, beat eggs whites until soft peaks form. Gradually add ¼ cup sugar, 1 tablespoon at a time. Add this egg mixture to the cream cheese gelatin mixture, stir to combine.

Pour into springform pan and refrigerate for 8 hours before serving.

Top with whipped cream and lime wedges before serving.

DIVINE CHOCOLATE CAKE

CAKE

2 cups cake flour

2 cups sugar

1 stick butter

¼ cup shortening

4 heaping tablespoons cocoa powder

1 cup water

1 teaspoon baking soda

½ cup buttermilk

⅓ teaspoon salt

1 teaspoon vanilla extract

2 large eggs

ICING

1 stick butter

4 tablespoons cocoa powder

6 tablespoons milk

1 (16 ounce) box confectioners' sugar

1 teaspoon vanilla extract

1 cup coconut flakes

Preheat oven to 350°. In a mixing bowl, sift flour and sugar; set aside.

In a saucepan, bring butter, shortening, cocoa and water to a rapid boil. Gradually pour melted mixture over flour and sugar and stir to combine.

In a separate bowl, combine baking soda, buttermilk, salt, vanilla and eggs; add to already combined ingredients and mix thoroughly. Pour batter into a greased 9x13-inch baking dish and bake for 35 minutes or until toothpick inserted in center comes out clean.

In a medium saucepan over medium-high heat, make icing by combining butter, cocoa and milk; stir constantly and bring to a boil. Remove from heat and add vanilla and confectioners' sugar; stir until sugar is completely dissolved. Fold in coconut flakes and pour icing over hot cake. Serve warm.

DOUBLE CHOCOLATE MINT BARS

CAKE

½ cup unsalted butter, softened

1 cup sugar

4 eggs

1 cup all purpose flour

1 teaspoon baking powder

⅛ teaspoon salt

1 teaspoon vanilla extract

1 (16 ounce) can chocolate syrup

MINT

½ cup unsalted butter, softened

2 cups confectioners' sugar

1 tablespoon water

½ teaspoon mint extract

3 dashes of green food coloring

CHOCOLATE TOPPING

6 tablespoons butter

1 cup mini semi-sweet chocolate chips

Preheat oven to 350°. In a large mixing bowl, beat butter and sugar until fluffy. Add eggs, one at a time. In a separate bowl, sift together dry ingredients; add to wet ingredients and stir in vanilla and chocolate until smooth. Pour into a lightly buttered 9x13-inch baking dish and bake for 25 to 30 minutes or until top begins to spring back when lightly touched. Allow to cool completely in pan.

Meanwhile, while cake is cooling, prepare mint cream layer. In a small mixing bowl, combine butter, sugar, water, mint extract and food coloring; beat until smooth. Spread mint cream over cake layer; chill in refrigerator for 15 to 20 minutes.

While first two layers are chilling, prepare chocolate topping by melting butter and chocolate chips in a small microwave-safe bowl; microwave for 30 seconds, stir and repeat until completely melted. Pour over mint layer and serve as is or chill and serve.

FARMHOUSE WALNUT PIE

Serves 12

1 cup all purpose flour

$^1/_4$ teaspoon salt

3 tablespoons butter, cold and cut into pieces

2 tablespoons shortening

3 tablespoons ice water

1 $^3/_4$ cups walnuts, chopped

4 large eggs

$^3/_4$ cup light brown sugar, packed

$^3/_4$ cup dark corn syrup

$^1/_2$ stick unsalted butter, melted

1 $^1/_2$ teaspoons vanilla extract

$^1/_4$ teaspoon salt

HONEY WHIPPED CREAM

1 cup heavy cream

3 tablespoons honey

Preheat oven to 350°. In a large mixing bowl, sift together flour and salt. Add butter and shortening and mix until coarse using a pastry blender or whisk. Add water 1 tablespoon at a time to dough, being careful not to allow dough to become sticky (more water may be used if necessary). Knead until dough becomes soft and crumbly. Wrap tightly in plastic wrap; refrigerate at least one hour.

On a lightly floured surface, roll out dough into an 11-inch crust. Place into a 9-inch pie pan, trim edges and refrigerate.

Spread walnuts on a baking sheet and toast for 15 minutes, tossing occasionally. Set aside to cool.

In a large bowl, whisk together eggs and brown sugar until smooth. Whisk in corn syrup, butter, vanilla and salt. Stir in toasted walnuts until evenly coated; pour into pie crust. Bake for 1 hour to 1 hour and 15 minutes.

While pie is baking, beat heavy cream and honey on high speed until stiff peaks form. Decorate cooled pie with honey whipped cream or add a dollop to each slice.

GEORGIA PEACH POUND CAKE

Serves: 12

1 cup + 2 tablespoons butter

2 ½ cups sugar, divided

4 eggs

1 teaspoon vanilla extract

3 cups all purpose flour, divided

1 teaspoon baking powder

2 cups fresh peaches, peeled, pitted
and chopped

½ teaspoon salt

Preheat oven to 350°. Grease a 10-inch Bundt pan with 2 tablespoons of butter and dust with ¼ cup of sugar; set aside.

Using an electric mixer, cream together remaining butter and sugar. Continue beating and add eggs one at a time. Once fully incorporated, gradually add 2 ¾ cups flour, baking powder and salt to mixture, beating until fully incorporated.

Dredge peaches with remaining ¼ cup flour and fold into batter. Pour batter into prepared pan and bake for 1 hour and 10 minutes. Remove from oven and allow to cool.

313

GRAHAM CRACKER PRALINES

24 - 30 graham cracker squares

1 cup butter

¾ cup light brown sugar, packed

½ teaspoon vanilla extract

2 cups almonds, chopped

12 ounces milk or semi-sweet chocolate chips

1 cup pecans (optional)

Preheat oven to 350°. Line a cookie sheet with foil and spray foil with cooking spray. Arrange graham crackers in a single layer on cookie sheet.

In a medium saucepan, combine butter, sugar and vanilla over medium-high heat. Once boiling, reduce heat and simmer 3 minutes; add almonds and pour sauce over crackers. Bake 6 to 8 minutes. Remove from oven. Sprinkle chocolate chips and allow chips to melt, spread to coat evenly. Sprinkle with pecans and refrigerate 2 hours. Break into squares before serving.

HAWAIIAN UPSIDE-DOWN MUFFINS

Makes 12 muffins

1 cup butter, melted and divided

1 ½ cups dark brown sugar, divided

1 cup pineapple, cubed

1 ¼ cups macadamia nuts, coarsely chopped

1 ½ cups all purpose flour

2 teaspoons baking powder

1 ½ teaspoons orange zest

1 teaspoon cinnamon

¼ teaspoon salt

2 eggs, beaten

½ cup milk

Preheat oven to 375°. Grease muffin tins with cooking spray.

In a small mixing bowl, combine ½ cup melted butter and 1 cup brown sugar. Divide mixture evenly between muffin cups. Evenly divide pineapple pieces over butter sugar mixture in the bottom of each muffin cup and sprinkle 1 tablespoon coarsely chopped macadamia nuts over pineapple.

In large mixing bowl sift flour, ½ cup brown sugar, baking powder, orange zest, cinnamon and salt. In separate bowl beat eggs together with remaining melted butter and milk then mix wet and dry ingredients until just combined. Divide batter evenly between muffin cups, pouring over pineapple and macadamia nuts. Bake 25 minutes then invert onto wire rack removing muffin tin carefully. If some of the pineapple pieces stay in the tin remove them and place on top of the muffins again.

Allow muffins to cool for 5 minutes before serving. Serve upside-down.

Holiday Pumpkin Bread with Orange Glaze

Serves 12 - 14

3 ⅓ cups all purpose flour

1 teaspoon baking powder

2 teaspoons baking soda

1 clove, ground (optional)

1 teaspoon cinnamon

1 teaspoon nutmeg

½ teaspoon salt

2 cups pumpkin puree

⅛ cup almond oil

¾ cup + 2 tablespoons vegetable oil

3 cups sugar

3 eggs

1 cup walnuts, chopped

1 cup raisins

Orange Glaze

1 ½ cups confectioners' sugar

1 teaspoon orange zest

6 teaspoons orange juice

walnuts, chopped

Preheat oven to 350°. In a medium bowl, mix flour, baking powder, baking soda, clove, cinnamon, nutmeg and salt; set aside.

In a separate bowl, beat pumpkin, oil, sugar and eggs until thoroughly blended. Add dry ingredients gradually to wet ingredients. Fold in walnuts and raisins. Divide batter evenly between two greased loaf pans. Bake 50 to 55 minutes. Cool in pans for 15 minutes then remove from pans and place on wire racks; allow to cool completely.

Combine confectioners' sugar, orange zest and orange juice in a small bowl; stir with a spoon until well blended. Spoon over cooled pumpkin loaves, allowing excess glaze to drizzle down the sides. Sprinkle with chopped walnuts before glaze hardens.

IRISH WHISKEY CAKE

Serves 8 - 10

1 cup + 2 tablespoons cocoa powder, divided

2 cups all purpose flour

1 ¼ teaspoons baking soda

½ teaspoon salt

1 cup butter, cubed

1 ½ cups coffee, brewed

½ cup Irish whiskey

2 cups sugar

2 eggs

1 teaspoon vanilla extract

Preheat oven to 325°. Butter and dust a Bundt pan with 2 tablespoons cocoa powder. Sift flour, baking soda and salt into a medium bowl; set aside.

In a saucepan over medium heat, combine butter, coffee, whiskey and cocoa powder. Heat until butter is melted. Whisk in sugar until thoroughly combined; remove from heat and allow to cool for 5 to 10 minutes.

In a large bowl, beat eggs and vanilla. Add cooled chocolate mixture to eggs and slowly add dry ingredients. Stir until thoroughly combined, being careful not to overmix. Pour batter into Bundt pan and bake for 40 to 50 minutes. Remove from oven and allow to cool completely (about 2 hours) before removing from pan.

ITALIAN SPONGE CAKE

Serves 8 - 10

CAKE

5 eggs, seperated

1 cup sugar

1 ½ cups all purpose flour, sifted

1 teaspoon vanilla extract

1 ½ teaspoons lemon zest

FILLING

1 (16 ounce) container Ricotta cheese

2 tablespoons chocolate chips

2 tablespoons candied orange peel

6 tablespoons sugar

1 tablespoon crème de cacao

2 (8 ounce) containers whipped topping

Preheat oven to 375°. Beat egg yolks and sugar until a ribbon consistency forms (when you lift the spoon out of the batter, a smooth ribbon should be created). Gradually add sifted flour, stirring as you add. Add vanilla extract and lemon zest, stir to combine.

In a separate bowl, beat egg whites until soft peaks form. Slowly stir egg whites into batter. Pour into two 9-inch cake pans. Bake for 40 minutes or until toothpick inserted in center comes out clean. Remove to wire rack. Cool completely and slice each layer in half horizontally.

Meanwhile, prepare Ricotta filling by combining cheese, chocolate chips, orange peel, sugar and crème de cacao. Pour Ricotta filling in between each layer of cake and cover entire cake with whipped topping.

DO IT YOURSELF

CANDIED ORANGE PEEL
Dissolve 1 cup sugar in ½ cup water Add orange peel from 2 oranges and simmer in a small saucepan for 15 to 20 minutes; allow to cool in pan then remove candied orange peel and store for up to 1 month.

MAMA'S UGLY APPLE CAKE

3 large eggs

2 cups sugar

1 cup vegetable oil

2 cups + 1 teaspoon all purpose flour, divided

1 teaspoon baking soda

2 teaspoons cinnamon

1 cup walnuts, chopped

1 teaspoon vanilla extract

4 cups apples, cored, peeled and thinly sliced

ICING

8 ounces cream cheese, softened

4 teaspoons butter, softened

2 cups confectioners' sugar

1 teaspoon lemon juice

Preheat oven to 350°. Butter and flour a Bundt pan.

In a large bowl, beat eggs with an electric mixer until frothy. Add sugar and beat until sugar is dissolved. Add oil and stir to combine.

In a separate bowl, combine 2 cups flour, baking soda and cinnamon; add egg mixture.

In a plastic bag, toss walnuts in 1 teaspoon flour. Add walnuts and vanilla to batter; stir until incorporated. Spread $1/2$ of the apples on the bottom of pan, pour $1/2$ the batter over apples and repeat with remaining apples and batter. Bake 1 hour and 15 minutes or until a toothpick inserted in the middle comes out clean. Remove cake from pan and allow to cool completely before adding icing.

While cake is cooling, beat together cream cheese and butter until fluffy. Gradually beat in confectioners' sugar followed by lemon juice. Spread icing evenly over cooled cake.

MARBLED MOUSSE

Serves 10 - 12

1 ³/₄ cups milk

¹/₄ teaspoon salt

3 egg yolks

1 cup sugar, divided

2 envelopes unflavored gelatin

2 (1 ounce) squares unsweetened
    chocolate, melted and cooled

3 teaspoons vanilla extract, divided

3 cups heavy cream

chocolate shavings, for garnish

In a saucepan, heat milk, salt, egg yolks and ³/₄ cup sugar over low heat for 2 to 3 minutes. Sprinkle gelatin evenly over mixture; let stand for one minute before stirring. Continue to cook, stirring constantly for 30 minutes or until gelatin dissolves completely and mixture coats a spoon.

In a medium mixing bowl, mix unsweetened chocolate with half of gelatin mixture and 1 teaspoon vanilla extract; whisk to blend.

In a separate bowl, pour remaining gelatin mixture and 2 teaspoons vanilla extract; whisk to combine. Cover both bowls in plastic wrap and refrigerate at least 25 minutes.

Once mixtures have chilled, beat cream and ¹/₄ cup sugar in a separate bowl until stiff peaks form. Using a rubber spatula, fold ¹/₂ of cream mixture into each gelatin mixture.

Alternately spoon the dark and white mixtures into a 9x13-inch pan creating a marbled appearance or, for a more elegant presentation, spoon into martini glasses; refrigerate at least 4 hours or until set. To serve, garnish with whipped cream and chocolate shavings.

320

OATMEAL CARMELITAS

2 cups all purpose flour

2 cups quick-cooking oats

1 ½ cups brown sugar

1 teaspoon baking soda

½ teaspoon salt

1 cup butter, melted

2 cups semi-sweet chocolate chips

1 cup walnuts, chopped

2 (11 ounce) jars caramel sauce

Preheat oven to 350°. Grease a 9x13-inch baking pan. In a medium bowl, stir together flour, oats, brown sugar, baking soda and salt. Add melted butter and stir to combine. Press ½ of batter into the bottom of baking pan. Bake for 10 minutes.

Remove from oven and sprinkle with chocolate chips and walnuts. Drizzle caramel sauce over top and crumble remaining oat mixture evenly on top, patting down lightly. Bake for an additional 15 to 20 minutes or until the top is golden; cool before cutting into bars.

PANNA COTTA WITH BERRY GAZPACHO

Makes 6 large ramekins

PANNA COTTA

¹/₃ cup milk

1 envelope unflavored gelatin

2 ¹/₂ cups heavy cream

¹/₂ cup sugar

1 ¹/₂ teaspoons vanilla extract

BERRY GAZPACHO

1 pint raspberries, stemmed

¹/₄ cup water

¹/₄ cup dry white wine

¹/₂ cup sugar

2 teaspoons fresh lemon juice

1 tablespoon cornstarch

2 tablespoons cold water

fresh berries, for garnish

In small mixing bowl, combine milk and gelatin. Set aside.

In a saucepan over medium heat, stir together heavy cream and sugar. Bring to a full boil, watching carefully, as the cream will quickly rise to the top of the pan. Once boiling, pour milk mixture into cream, stirring until completely dissolved. Cook for one minute, stirring constantly.

Remove from heat, add vanilla and pour into six individual ramekin dishes. Allow ramekins to cool uncovered at room temperature. When cool, cover with plastic wrap, and refrigerate for at least 4 hours, but preferably overnight.

Add raspberries and ¹/₄ up water to small saucepan over high heat, bring to a simmer, cover and simmer for 10 minutes or until mushy. Process berries in a food mill or blender at low speed until smooth, then press through a sieve to remove seeds. Return strained purée to pan, add remaining ingredients and heat to a boil, stirring constantly. Taste for sweetness and add sugar, if needed. Serve over Panna Cotta either hot or cold and top with fresh fruit toppings (optional).

PAVLOV'S MOUTHWATERING PAVLOVA

PAVLOVA

6 egg whites

1 ½ cups sugar

1 ½ teaspoons white wine vinegar

1 ½ teaspoons cornstarch

WHIPPED FILLING

1 cup heavy cream

1 tablespoon confectioners' sugar

1 teaspoon vanilla extract

1 cup Mascarpone cheese

strawberries, sliced

Preheat oven to 250°. In mixing bowl, whip egg whites with an electric mixer until stiff peaks form at the end of the beaters. Very slowly, add sugar. Fold in vinegar and cornstarch with a spatula.

To prepare filling, whip cream with sugar and vanilla until stiff using an electric mixer. Fold in Mascarpone cheese. Set aside.

Draw a 10-inch circle on a large piece of tin foil; using a dinner plate helps with accuracy. Scoop half egg white mixture into the circle. Scoop remaining egg whites on top of the edge, forming a bowl shape. Pour Whipped Filling inside the bowl and bake for 50 minutes. Leave in oven overnight to cool. Garnish with sliced strawberries.

DID YOU KNOW?

WHAT IS PAVLOVA?

Named after Anna Pavlova, a Russian ballet dancer in the early 20th century, this dessert consists of a crisp meringue base topped with sweet whipped cream and fresh fruit. Pavlova features a crispy exterior and moist interior which is the result of folding stiffly beaten egg whites into the other ingredients and cooking at a low heat for a long period of time.

PEACHES & CREAM PIE

3 egg whites

1 cup sugar

24 saltine crackers, crushed

$\frac{1}{4}$ teaspoon baking powder

$\frac{1}{2}$ cup pecans, chopped

1 teaspoon vanilla extract

1 pint whipped topping

1 peach, sliced

In a mixing bowl, beat egg whites with an electric mixer on high speed until soft peaks form. Add sugar and beat until stiff peaks form.

In a separate bowl, combine crackers, baking powder, pecans and vanilla. Fold in egg whites using a spatula. Pour into a 9-inch pie pan. Place in a cold oven, then heat to 325°. Bake 30 minutes, remove from oven and allow to cool completely.

In a mixing bowl, fold peaches into whipped topped and spread on top of cool pie. Allow to chill in refrigerator for 2 hours before serving.

PRIZED COFFEE CAKE

STREUSEL

½ cup brown sugar, packed

2 tablespoons all purpose flour

2 teaspoons cinnamon

2 tablespoons butter, melted

CAKE

1 ½ cups all purpose flour

2 teaspoons baking powder

½ teaspoon salt

¾ cup sugar

½ cup milk

1 egg, beaten

Preheat oven to 375°. Using a fork, combine all streusel ingredients; set aside.

In a mixing bowl, sift together flour, baking powder, salt and sugar. In a separate bowl, combine milk and egg; add to dry ingredients, stirring to combine.

Spoon ½ batter into a 8x8-inch baking dish. Sprinkle with ½ of streusel topping and repeat. Bake for 20 minutes. Serve warm.

RASPBERRY GANACHE TRUFFLES

CHOCOLATE GANACHE

1 pound semi-sweet chocolate chips

1 cup heavy cream

¼ cup Chambord

OPTIONAL COATINGS

crushed graham crackers

dark chocolate, finely chopped

DIPPING SAUCE

2 tablespoons raspberry jam

1 tablespoon Chambord

1 box pectin

3 oranges, juiced and zested

Place chocolate chips in a medium bowl; set aside. In a saucepan over medium-high heat, bring heavy cream to a boil. Pour cream over chocolate chips and let rest for 5 minutes. Stir until smooth, then add ¼ cup Chambord. Refrigerate at least 4 hours.

Using a small ice cream scooper or melon baller dipped in warm water, scoop out chocolate ganache and place on a cookie sheet. Roll each scoop between your hands into a neat ball and then roll through the coating of your choice. Refrigerate until ready to serve.

Optional Dipping Sauce

Bring jam, 1 tablespoon Chambord, pectin, orange juice and zest to a boil. Reduce heat to low and simmer 5 to 6 minutes. Drizzle over truffles or serve as a dipping sauce on the side.

SOUTHERN PECAN BLONDE

1 cup brown sugar, packed

1 cup sugar

4 eggs

1 cup hazelnut oil

1 teaspoon vanilla extract

1 ½ cups self-rising flour

2 cups pecans, coarsely chopped

Preheat oven to 350°. Grease a 9x13-inch baking pan. In a mixing bowl, beat both sugars, eggs, oil and vanilla together until smooth. Continue beating and slowly add flour until combined. Fold in pecans then pour batter into pan and bake for 35 minutes.

Cool before cutting. Excellent served with vanilla ice cream and caramel sauce.

Strawberry Rhubarb Crisp

1 cup flour

¾ cup old-fashioned oatmeal

1 cup brown sugar, packed

½ cup melted butter or oleo

1 teaspoon cinnamon

1 cup sugar

2 tablespoons cornstarch

1 cup water

1 teaspoon vanilla extract

3 cups rhubarb, chopped

1 cup strawberries, halved

Preheat oven to 350°. Mix flour, oatmeal, brown sugar, butter and cinnamon together until crumbly. Press half of crumb mixture into bottom of a 9x9 inch baking pan. Set aside remaining mixture.

In a saucepan over medium heat, combine sugar, cornstarch, water and vanilla; cook until thick and clear, about 5 minutes. Set aside.

Mix rhubarb and strawberries together gently and place on top of crumb mixture in prepared pan. Pour liquid over fruit and top with remaining crumbs. Bake until crisp, about 1 hour. Serve with whipped cream or ice cream.

SUPER EASY CHOCOLATE COOKIES

Makes 60 cookies

1 box of chocolate cake mix

1 egg, slightly beaten

1 cup mayonnaise

¼ cup water

1 (12 ounce) bag chocolate chips or white chocolate chips

1 (7 ounce) jar maraschino cherries, drained (optional)

Preheat oven to 350°. With a wooden spoon, blend cake mix, egg, mayonnaise and water. Fold in chocolate chips and drop by the teaspoon onto a lightly greased cookie sheet.

Bake for 11 minutes. Remove from oven and immediately put a cherry on top of each cookie and press lightly. Cool before serving.

SWEET GRILLED PEACHES

4 tablespoons unsalted butter, melted

2 tablespoons dark brown sugar

1 teaspoon ground cinnamon

4 peaches, unpeeled, halved and pitted

$\frac{1}{3}$ cup white baking chocolate, finely chopped

3 tablespoons toasted and salted pistachios, coarsely chopped (optional)

Heat grill to medium-high. Whisk together butter, brown sugar and cinnamon until well blended. Add peach halves and toss to coat.

Lightly oil grill grates to prevent sticking. Place peaches, cut side down on grill. Grill until slightly charred, about 2 minutes. Using tongs, turn peaches over carefully. Divide chopped chocolate among peach cavities and drizzle with remaining butter mixture from bowl. Grill until chocolate just begins to melt and peaches are charred, about 2 minutes.

To serve, sprinkle with pistachios or pair with vanilla ice cream.

Texas Praline Cheesecake

CRUST

1 ¼ cups graham cracker crumbs

4 tablespoons sugar

4 tablespoons margarine, melted

FILLING

3 (8 ounce) packages cream cheese, softened

⅔ cup brown sugar, packed

3 tablespoons all purpose flour

3 eggs

1 tablespoon vanilla

½ cup pecans, finely chopped

1 dozen pecan halves

1 cup pecans, chopped

Preheat oven to 350°. In a medium bowl, combine graham cracker crumbs, sugar and melted margarine. Press mixture into bottom of a greased 9-inch springform pan. Bake for 10 minutes and then remove from oven and cool completely.

Increase oven temperature to 450°. In a large mixing bowl, blend cream cheese, sugar and flour until well incorporated. Add eggs, one at a time, then vanilla. Pour batter over crust and bake for 10 minutes. Lower heat to 250° and bake for an additional 20 minutes. Cool and let stand for 5 minutes. Sprinkle top of cheesecake with chopped pecans and garnish sides with pecan halves. Refrigerate at least 4 hours before serving.

TEXAS SHEET CAKE

CAKE

2 sticks butter

2 tablespoons cocoa powder

1 cup water

2 cups sugar

2 cups all purpose flour

$\frac{1}{2}$ teaspoon salt

2 eggs

$\frac{1}{2}$ cup sour cream

1 teaspoon baking soda

FROSTING

1 stick butter

4 tablespoons cocoa

6 tablespoons milk

1 pound confectioners' sugar

1 teaspoon vanilla extract

1 cup nuts of your choice

Preheat oven to 375°. In a saucepan over high heat, bring butter, cocoa and water to a boil. In a large mixing bowl, combine sugar, flour and salt. Add butter mixture to dry ingredients and combine until incorporated. In a small bowl, combine eggs, sour cream and baking soda. Add to cake batter and beat well.

Pour into a greased 12x18-inch baking sheet and bake for 20 minutes.

In a saucepan, bring butter, cocoa and milk to a boil. Remove from heat and add confectioners' sugar and vanilla. Beat well then fold in nuts.

Pour frosting over cake as soon as it comes out of the oven; serve warm or chill and serve.

TRES LECHES CAKE

CAKE

6 large egg whites

½ cup sugar, divided

6 large egg yolks

1 cup all purpose flour

CREAM

1 (14 ounce) can sweetened condensed milk

1 cup heavy whipping cream

⅔ cup evaporated milk

1 teaspoon vanilla extract

ICING

1 cup heavy whipping cream

2 tablespoons sugar

½ teaspoon vanilla extract

Preheat oven to 375°. Grease and flour a 9-inch springform pan.

Beat egg whites and ¼ cup sugar in large mixing bowl until stiff peaks form, set aside.

Combine egg yolks and remaining sugar in medium bowl; beat until light yellow in color. Fold egg white mixture and flour alternately into egg yolk mixture. Pour into prepared pan.

Bake for 15 to 20 minutes or until just golden and toothpick inserted in center comes out clean. Remove from oven to wire rack.

Combine sweetened condensed milk, whipping cream, evaporated milk and vanilla extract in medium bowl; stir well. Using a toothpick, poke several holes in the top of cake. Pour 2 cups cream over cake allowing cream to soak into the cake. Spoon excess cream from side of pan over top of cake.

Let stand for 30 minutes or until cake absorbs cream. Remove side of pan.

Beat cream, sugar and vanilla in small mixing bowl until stiff peaks form. Spread over top and sides of cake.

Serve immediately with remaining cream sauce on the side.

WHITE CHOCOLATE CHEESECAKE

CRUST

1 cup graham cracker crumbs

3 tablespoons sugar

3 tablespoons butter, melted

FILLING

2 (8 ounce) packages cream cheese, softened

1/2 cup sugar

1/2 teaspoon vanilla extract

2 eggs

4 ounces white baking chocolate, melted

Preheat oven to 325°. In a small mixing bowl, combine graham cracker crumbs, sugar and butter. Press mixture into bottom and 1 inch up the side of a 9-inch springform pan.

Bake for 10 minutes; allow to cool at least 15 minutes before adding filling.

Meanwhile, mix cream cheese, sugar and vanilla with an electric mixer on medium speed until well blended. Add eggs, one at a time, until incorporated. In a small glass bowl, microwave white chocolate in 30 second intervals, stirring each time, until melted. Using a spatula, fold white chocolate into cream cheese mixture.

Pour filling into crust. Bake for 25 minutes or until center is set. Cool completely; refrigerate at least 4 hours before serving.

post

DESSERTS

BREAKFAST

EVERYTHING ELSE

APPLE NUT PANCAKES

Serves 8 - 10

1 cup all purpose flour

2 teaspoons salt

2 tablespoons baking powder

1 ½ tablespoons sugar

2 apples, peeled, cored and chopped

1 cup milk

2 egg whites

2 tablespoons applesauce

1 tablespoon vanilla extract

1 teaspoon pumpkin pie spice

1 cup walnuts, chopped for garnish

maple syrup

whipped cream

Preheat griddle over medium heat and coat with cooking spray.

In a medium bowl, combine flour, salt, baking powder, sugar and apples.

In a separate larger bowl, combine milk, egg whites, applesauce, vanilla extract and pumpkin pie spice. Pour dry ingredients into wet ingredients and stir to combine. Pour ¼ cup of batter at a time onto griddle; cook for 3 minutes. Once the sides and top of pancake begin to bubble, flip and cook another 3 minutes.

To serve, place pancakes on a serving dish and sprinkle with walnuts, maple syrup and a dollop of whipped cream.

AUTUMN GRITS

Serves 12 - 14

1 ½ cups yellow stone-ground grits, rinsed

3 cups water

salt, to taste

5 small apples, peeled, cored and thinly sliced

2 tablespoons brown sugar, packed

3 tablespoons butter

½ teaspoon salt

1 teaspoon cinnamon

¼ teaspoon nutmeg

½ teaspoon lemon juice

1 teaspoon vanilla

½ cup dried cranberries

dash of tapioca

1 (14 ounce) can sweetened condensed milk

dash of cinnamon

¼ pound Fontina cheese, shredded

1 cup mild Cheddar cheese, shredded

In a 6-quart stockpot, bring grits, water and salt to a boil. Cook until tender, about 5 to 6 minutes.

Meanwhile, in large saucepan, combine apples, brown sugar, butter and salt; cook over medium-high heat until apples are tender when pieced with a fork, about 10 minutes. Add cinnamon, nutmeg, lemon juice, vanilla, cranberries and tapioca; stir and cook an additional 2 to 3 minutes.

When grits are complete, stir milk, cinnamon and cheese into grits, adding gradually. Once cheese has completely melted, pour into a 9x13-inch baking dish and top with apple mixture. Serve for breakfast or as a side dish.

Banana Chocolate Chip Muffins

Makes 18 muffins

1 ¾ cups all purpose flour

¾ cup sugar

1 teaspoon baking powder

1 teaspoon baking soda

½ teaspoon salt

1 egg

¾ cup vegetable oil

½ cup plain yogurt

1 teaspoon vanilla extract

1 cup ripe bananas, mashed

¾ cup semi-sweet chocolate chips

Preheat oven to 350°. In a large bowl, combine flour, sugar, baking powder, baking soda and salt. In another bowl, combine egg, oil, yogurt and vanilla. Stir wet mixture into dry ingredients until just moistened, careful not to overmix. Fold in bananas and chocolate chips.

Fill greased or paper-lined muffin cups ⅔ full. Bake for 22 to 25 minutes or until a toothpick inserted in center of muffin comes out clean. Allow to cool for 5 minutes before removing to wire racks.

CASHEW BUTTER STUFFED FRENCH TOAST

• •

Serves 6 - 8

4 eggs

¼ cup milk

1 tablespoons sugar

½ teaspoon cinnamon

⅓ cup cashew butter

1 loaf of Challah Bread, sliced in
  ½-inch slices

butter, for frying

honey

confectioners' sugar

Preheat large skillet to medium heat. In a shallow bowl, whisk together eggs, milk, sugar and cinnamon.

Spread 1 tablespoon cashew butter between 2 slices of Challah bread and coat with egg mixture.

Melt desired amount of butter in skillet and add French toast. Fry for 5 minutes on each side or until golden brown. Drizzle with honey and dust with confectioners' sugar before serving.

Cherry Cinnamon Muffins

· ·

Makes 20 muffins

¼ cup vegetable oil

¼ cup almond oil

2 eggs

2 teaspoons vanilla extract

2 cups all purpose flour

2 cups sugar

2 teaspoons baking soda

2 teaspoons cinnamon

1 (21 ounce) can cherry pie filling

Preheat oven to 325°. In a large mixing bowl, whisk together oils, eggs and vanilla. In a separate bowl, combine flour, sugar, baking soda and cinnamon. Fold dry ingredients into wet, then add cherry pie filling and gently combine. Spread batter into greased or paper-lined muffin tins.

Bake for 30 to 40 minutes or until a toothpick inserted in center comes out clean.

COUNTRY
SAUSAGE DRESSING

● ●

Serves 8 - 10

2 eggs, beaten

1 cup milk

1 day-old French baguette, crumbled

1 stick butter

1 large onion, finely chopped

1 cup celery, chopped

salt and pepper, to taste

dried sage, to taste

poultry seasoning, to taste

dried thyme, to taste

dried basil, to taste

marjoram, to taste

2 pounds ground country sausage

1 tablespoon sugar

1 cup dried currants

Preheat oven to 325°. In shallow baking dish, combine eggs and milk; once blended, add bread. Allow to soak until softened.

In large sauté pan, melt butter and sauté onion, celery, salt, pepper, sage, poultry seasoning, thyme, basil and marjoram over medium-low heat until vegetables are slightly tender, about 8 to 10 minutes. Remove from heat.

Meanwhile, in separate frying pan, brown sausage over medium heat, about 8 to 10 minutes. Add sausage to vegetable mixture and mix well. Combine sausage mixture with soaked bread, sugar and currants; mix well. Place mixture in a 9x13-inch baking dish and bake for 20 minutes.

FALL HARVEST MUFFINS

1 ¼ cups sugar

2 cups all purpose flour

2 teaspoons cinnamon

2 teaspoons baking soda

½ teaspoon salt

½ cup coconut flakes

1 medium Granny Smith or Fuji apple,
   shredded

2 cups carrots, shredded

½ cup pecans, chopped

3 eggs

1 cup vegetable oil

2 tablespoons almond oil

½ teaspoon vanilla extract

½ cup raisins

Preheat oven to 375°. In a large mixing bowl, sift together sugar, flour, cinnamon, baking soda and salt. Add coconut, apple, carrots and pecans; stir to combine.

In a separate mixing bowl, beat eggs; add oil and vanilla and mix until well incorporated. Add dry ingredients to wet ingredients; being careful not to over mix. Fold in raisins and spoon batter into greased or lined muffin tins, about ⅔ full. Bake muffins for 20 minutes or until toothpick inserted in center comes out clean. Remove to iron racks to cool.

SALMON QUICHE WITH CUCUMBER SAUCE

Serves 8 - 10

CUCUMBER SAUCE

1 medium cucumber, peeled

1 tablespoon onions, grated

¼ cup mayonnaise

2 teaspoons red wine vinegar

1 tablespoon fresh parsley, chopped

½ cup sour cream

salt and pepper, to taste

SALMON QUICHE

2 eggs, beaten

½ cup milk

1 tablespoon butter, melted

¼ cup onions, peeled and chopped

2 tablespoons fresh parsley, chopped

¾ teaspoon dried basil

¼ teaspoon salt

⅛ teaspoon pepper

1 (14.5 ounce) can salmon, drained

1 (9-inch) frozen pie crust, thawed

Grate cucumber and using a paper towel, squeeze out any excess liquid. In a mixing bowl, combine cucumber, onions, mayonnaise, red wine vinegar, parsley, sour cream, salt and pepper, mixing well. Chill while quiche is baking.

Preheat oven to 425°. In a mixing bowl, combine eggs, milk, butter, onions and seasonings. Fold salmon into egg mixture and pour into pie crust. Bake for 25 minutes. Cool and serve with Cucumber Sauce.

STUFFED FRENCH TOAST

• •

Serves 10 - 12

1 ½ cups heavy cream

3 - 4 eggs, beaten

½ cup brown sugar

½ teaspoon nutmeg

2 teaspoons cinnamon

2 teaspoons vanilla extract

1 loaf French bread, cut into ½-inch
   slices

cream cheese, whipped

blueberries

strawberries

confectioners' sugar

maple syrup

In a mixing bowl, combine cream, eggs, brown sugar, nutmeg, cinnamon and vanilla extract. Preheat a non-stick skillet over medium heat and spray with cooking spray. Dip 2 to 3 slices of bread at a time into the batter and cook on skillet for 4 to 5 minutes per side, or until golden brown. Repeat with remaining slices.

Take 2 slices of cooked French toast and spread 3 to 4 tablespoons of whipped cream cheese between each slice. Drizzle with syrup and top with fresh berries and confectioners' sugar.

post

DESSERTS

BREAKFAST

EVERYTHING ELSE

APPLE COLESLAW

1 pound coleslaw mix

1 medium Granny Smith apple, julienned

2 tablespoons sugar

⅛ teaspoon salt

⅛ teaspoon apple pie spice

2 tablespoons apple cider vinegar

1 ½ tablespoons vegetable oil

2 tablespoons green onions, sliced (optional)

In a large serving bowl, combine all ingredients; toss to coat well. Refrigerate overnight. Sprinkle with extra apple pie spice just before serving.

Excellent served with pulled pork BBQ sandwiches.

DO IT YOURSELF

MAKE YOUR OWN APPLE PIE SPICE

To make your own apple pie spice, combine 1 teaspoon cinnamon, ½ teaspoon nutmeg, ¼ teaspoon allspice, ¼ teaspoon cardamom and ⅛ teaspoon ground clove. Not only good for adding to recipes, simmer Apple Pie Spice with water on the stove top for a fragrant Fall aroma to fill your home.

BANANA PUNCH

3 cups water

1 ½ cups sugar

1 ½ cups pineapple juice

1 ½ cups orange juice

2 large bananas, mashed

juice of 1 lemon

1 liter lemon-lime soda

Mix together first 6 ingredients; freeze until solid. Four hours before serving, take frozen mixture out of freezer and allow to thaw partially at room temperature.

Once soft, mash with a potato masher until slushy. Add soda or liquor of choice; serve.

SERVING SUGGESTION

Banana Punch is a great base for dark rum and/or triple sec. Garnish with pineapple wedges or orange slices for a festive treat!

CHIVE RÉMOULADE

2 garlic cloves, minced

2 - 3 large shallots, minced

½ (3 ounce) jar capers, crushed with 3 teaspoons juice reserved

3 tablespoons dill relish

pinch of thyme, chopped

2 anchovy fillets, chopped

1 cup mayonnaise

1 cup sour cream

½ teaspoon Worcestershire sauce

salt and pepper, to taste

2 teaspoons citrus champagne vinegar (or champagne vinegar)

2 (.75 ounce) packs fresh chives

In a food processor, combine all ingredients. Adjust seasoning, if needed.

SERVING SUGGESTION

Excellent served with our
Truffle Chips, page 369.

351

CINNAMON PITA CHIPS

Makes 24 chips

3 pitas or flour tortillas

4 tablespoons butter, melted

1 tablespoon cinnamon

8 tablespoons sugar

Preheat oven to 400°. Brush both sides of each tortilla with butter and cut into eighths. In a small bowl, mix cinnamon and sugar together with a fork. Sprinkle over tortillas and bake for 8 to 10 minutes or until golden brown.

CITRUS, HONEY & JALAPEÑO MARINADE

juice and zest of 1 lime

juice and zest of 1 lemon

juice and zest of 1 orange

1 teaspoon hot sauce

$\frac{1}{2}$ teaspoon red pepper flakes

2 jalapeños, finely chopped and seeded

3 tablespoons fresh Italian parsley, chopped

2 tablespoons fresh basil, chopped

2 tablespoons fresh thyme, chopped

salt and pepper, to taste

3 tablespoons honey

4 tablespoons olive oil

3 tablespoons white wine

1 tablespoon unsalted butter, melted

In a bowl, whisk together all ingredients until well combined.

Pour over salmon or other fatty fish (mackerel, tuna or swordfish) and marinate for 15 minutes at room temperature before cooking.

COSMO BLOOD ORANGE PUNCH

Makes 18 cups

8 cups cranberry juice

1 (12 ounce) container frozen limeade

$\frac{1}{3}$ cup orange liqueur

8 cups lemon-lime soda

1 blood orange, thinly sliced

Combine cranberry juice, limeade and orange liqueur in a large bowl. Refrigerate 24 hours.

Right before serving, add lemon-lime soda and garnish with orange slices.

FRUIT SALSA

3 kiwis, peeled

¼ cup pepper jelly

1 mango, finely diced

2 pints strawberries, chopped

2 tablespoons black sage honey

1 yellow bell pepper, finely diced

1 green bell pepper, finely diced

2 tablespoons turbinado sugar

To slice kiwis, cut in half, then cut halves into 4 wedges. Thinly slice each wedge and place in mixing bowl.

Add remaining ingredients and toss to combine. Refrigerate 1 hour or until ready to serve.

SERVING SUGGESTION

Excellent served with Cinnamon Pita Chips, page 352.

FRESH FIESTA SALSA

Makes 6 cups

juice of 2 limes

1 bunch fresh cilantro, chopped

1 tablespoon garlic, minced

6 jalapeños, seeded and diced

3 bell peppers, seeded and diced

1 large red onion, diced

6 roma tomatoes, diced

1 teaspoon kosher salt

2 cups white vinegar

¼ cup water

In a large bowl, combine all ingredients. Refrigerate before serving with your favorite tortilla chips.

GRAPE SALSA

Makes 2 ½ cups

¾ cup green seedless grapes, quartered

¾ cup red seedless grapes, quartered

½ cup red bell pepper, chopped

¼ cup green onions, chopped

2 tablespoons fresh cilantro, finely chopped

2 tablespoons olive oil

1 tablespoon lime juice

2 teaspoons jalapeños, chopped

½ teaspoon salt

¼ teaspoon hot sauce

In a large mixing bowl, combine all ingredients. Serve with tortilla or pita chips.

SERVING SUGGESTION

Excellent served with Cinnamon Pita Chips, page 352.

HOT VEGETABLE GARLIC BREAD

1 stick butter

3 tablespoons olive oil

1 cup baby carrots, shredded

1 cup zucchini, shredded

5 - 6 garlic cloves, minced

1 loaf Italian bread

1/2 cup Parmesan cheese, grated

Preheat oven to 350°. Heat butter and oil in small sauté pan over medium heat. Add vegetables and garlic and sauté for 5 to 10 minutes, or until tender.

Slice loaf in half lengthwise. Spread hot vegetable and garlic mixture on each half and sprinkle with Parmesan cheese. Put halves back together and wrap in foil; bake for 20 to 25 minutes.

Margarita & Avocado Salsa

Makes 2 cups

½ avocado, diced

1 mango, diced

½ red bell pepper, seeded and finely diced

juice of ½ lime

1 teaspoon Triple Sec

1 tablespoon tequila

salt and pepper, to taste

Combine avocado, mango, bell pepper, lime juice, Triple Sec and tequila. Season with salt and pepper to taste and serve with chips or over grilled chicken or fish.

MARINATED MUSHROOMS

¼ cup + 1 tablespoon olive oil, divided

4 large portabella mushroom caps, cleaned and diced

¼ cup blackberry balsamic vinegar with pears (or balsamic vinegar)

¼ cup fresh parsley, minced

2 garlic cloves, minced

3 teaspoons sugar

salt and pepper, to taste

Heat 1 tablespoon olive oil in a sauté pan over high heat. Cook mushrooms until golden, about 8 to 10 minutes. Place in a medium serving bowl and set aside.

In a separate mixing bowl, whisk together ¼ cup olive oil, vinegar, parsley, garlic, sugar, salt and pepper. Pour over mushrooms and toss to coat. Cover with plastic and refrigerate for 4 hours.

SERVING SUGGESTION

Excellent served over our Asiago Stuffed Veal Chops, page 235.

MOJO COCONUT SAUCE

½ cup orange juice

1 teaspoon lime zest

1 teaspoon honey

1 teaspoon soy sauce

1 tablespoon sweet chili sauce

1 cup coconut milk

In a medium saucepan over high heat, add orange juice, lime zest, honey, soy sauce and chili sauce. Bring to a boil, reduce heat to medium and simmer for 15 to 20 minutes. Add coconut milk, increase heat to high and bring to a boil. Turn off heat and let stand for 5 minutes.

Serve with grilled chicken, shrimp or any flaky fish.

OLD SALEM ICED TEA

Makes 18 cups

4 sprigs of fresh mint

8 - 12 cloves

3 quarts water

4 (1 ounce) tea bags

juice of 8 lemons

juice of 6 oranges

1 (46 ounce) can pineapple juice

1 pound sugar

In a large stockpot over high heat, add mint and cloves to water, bring to a boil. Simmer for 10 to 15 additional minutes. Remove from heat, add tea bags and steep for 10 to 15 minutes. Strain while still hot to remove cloves and tea bags. Add fruit juice and sugar. Stir thoroughly to dissolve sugar; chill.

Serve garnished with fresh mint and thin lemon slices.

PEACH BRUSCHETTA

Serves 8

4 peaches, halved with pits removed

1 teaspoon canola oil

1 tablespoon honey

1 teaspoon cinnamon

Preheat grill to high heat. Prepare peaches by brushing with canola oil. Place on grill for 3 minute per side or until grill marks are visible.

In a small microwave safe dish, microwave honey 10 to 15 seconds to warm; remove and add cinnamon. Stir until evenly distributed.

Remove peaches from grill, dice and toss with warm honey and cinnamon.

SERVING SUGGESTION

Serve on shortbread cookies, with Cinnamon Pita Chips (page 352) or over grilled chicken, pork or ice cream.

Pesto Hummus

· ·

½ cup tahini

½ cup water

3 - 4 garlic cloves

3 (15 - 16 ounce) cans garbanzo beans, rinsed and drained

5 tablespoons olive oil

2 tablespoons lemon juice

1 teaspoon cumin

BASIC HUMMUS

In a food processor, add tahini, water and garlic; puree until smooth. Add remaining ingredients and process until smooth.

For a twist, try one of the variations below:

SUN-DRIED TOMATO HUMMUS

Add 1 ¼ cup sun-dried tomato pesto to 5 cups prepared basic hummus. Serve with pitas or on a sandwich of turkey, provolone and fresh basil.

LEMON GARLIC HUMMUS

Add ¼ cups lemon juice and the zest of 4 lemons to 5 cups of basic hummus. Serve with pitas or on a grilled chicken sandwich

CHEESE & WALNUT HUMMUS

Add 1 ¼ cups of Gourmandise Cheese with ¼ cup chopped walnuts to 5 cups of basic hummus and process in a blender or food processor.

ROASTED GARLIC & ONION HUMMUS

Add ¼ cup of Roasted Garlic Onion Jam to 5 cups of basic hummus; stir to combine.

PIMENTO CHEESE DEVILED EGGS

Makes 12 portions

½ pound Cheddar cheese

½ cup pimentos

3 tablespoons mayonnaise

2 tablespoons relish

2 teaspoons relish juice

2 tablespoons fresh chives, chopped

1 teaspoon brandy

2 teaspoons olive oil

1 tablespoon hot sauce

salt and pepper, to taste

6 eggs, hard boiled, halved with yolks and whites separated

fresh chives, chopped for garnish

In a food processor or blender, combine all ingredients except egg whites and blend until smooth. Place blended ingredients in a piping bag and pipe into egg whites. Garnish with chives and serve.

POMODORO SAUCE

. . . .

2 tablespoons olive oil

3 garlic cloves, finely chopped

1 medium onion, finely chopped

6 - 7 medium to large tomatoes, peeled
  and chopped

2 tablespoons tomato paste

10 fresh basil leaves, chopped

3 - 4 fresh parsley sprigs, chopped

1 tablespoon salt, to taste

1 tablespoon seasoned salt

1 tablespoon garlic salt

2 tablespoons sugar

1 tablespoon black pepper, coarsely
  ground

Heat olive oil in a large saucepan over medium heat; lightly brown garlic and onion, approximately 4 to 5 minutes. Add tomatoes, tomato paste, seasonings and herbs. Stir to combine.

Simmer for 30 minutes over medium heat without lid until liquid has reduced by $1/4$.

Serve over your favorite pasta, in lasagna or as a pizza sauce.

SHISH KABOB MARINADE

Marinades 8 kabobs

2 garlic cloves, minced

1 medium onion, chopped

¼ cup fresh parsley, minced

½ cup olive oil

1 (8 ounce) can tomato sauce

1 cup vinegar

⅔ cup Worcestershire sauce

¾ cup brown sugar, packed

1 teaspoon dried rosemary

½ teaspoon dried thyme

In a sauté pan over medium heat, sauté garlic, onions and parsley in oil for 5 minutes. Add remaining ingredients and simmer for 20 minutes over low heat; remove from heat and allow to cool completely.

Marinate shish kabobs for 1 to 2 hours before grilling.

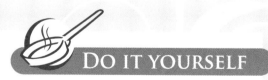

DO IT YOURSELF

TRY THESE UNIQUE KABOB IDEAS
- pork tenderloin, red bell pepper and onion
- ham, apple and onion
- lamb, baby bella mushrooms and cherry tomatoes
- turkey, zucchini, green pepper and onion
- eggplant, onion, cherry tomatoes and green pepper
- scallops, cherry tomatoes, green peppers

SPICY PUMPKIN MOLE SAUCE

Makes 5 ½ cups

1 tablespoon olive oil

1 onion, sliced into rings

2 garlic cloves, minced

¾ cup diced tomatoes, drained

2 ancho chile, seeded and coarsely
   chopped

4 chipotle chiles in adobo sauce

3 ½ cups chicken broth

1 cup pumpkin purée

1 tablespoon brown sugar

2 ounces semi-sweet chocolate chips

Heat olive oil in a medium saucepan over medium heat. Sweat onions and garlic until translucent, about 5 to 6 minutes. Add tomatoes and chiles and sauté for 5 to 6 minutes. Stir in broth and pumpkin purée and bring to a boil. Remove to a blender and purée until smooth. Return to saucepan and simmer for 20 minutes. Before serving, stir in brown sugar and chocolate until melted.

Excellent served with grilled pork, duck or chicken.

TRUFFLE CHIPS

2 cups vegetable oil

5 large red or brown potatoes, thinly sliced

¼ cup Parmesan cheese, grated

sea salt, to taste

1 teaspoon truffle oil

Preheat deep fryer or frying pan with 3 inches of oil to 350°. Add sliced potatoes and fry until they float. Remove and pat dry with a paper towel.

Place chips in a large bowl and toss with Parmesan cheese, salt to taste and truffle oil.

SERVING SUGGESTION

Serve with Chive Rémoulade, page 351, or your favorite dip.

ZESTY CORN SALSA

Makes 4 ½ cups

2 cups fresh corn

2 cups canned corn

1 ½ tablespoons fajita seasoning

1 red bell pepper, chopped

½ jalapeño, chopped and seeded

½ cup green onions, chopped

¼ cup fresh cilantro, chopped

¼ cup lime juice

¾ cup black beans, drained and rinsed

¾ teaspoon salt

½ teaspoon pepper

2 avocados, diced

In a large sauté pan over medium-high heat, cook fresh corn, canned corn and fajita seasoning for 6 to 8 minutes or until corn is slightly golden. Remove from heat; let cool.

In a mixing bowl, stir together corn mixture, bell pepper, jalapeño, green onions, cilantro, lime juice, black beans, salt and pepper. Cover and chill for at least 30 minutes. Stir in avocado just before serving.

SERVING SUGGESTION

Serve with chips, over fish or with Tequila Fajitas, page 144.

CONTRIBUTORS

Denise Adams
Shelly Adams
Chris Aho
Lili Akerson
Kathy Alberts
Geraldine Alfano
Ann Allnutt
Mary Alspaugh
Robyn Alton
Okasinski Ami
Juan Amorini
Alice Anastasia
Pat Andres
Carol Andrews
Miriam Andrews
Kathy Anthony
Aleida Arbona
Shari Ardis
Barbara Argonis
Stephen Armellini
David Armstrong
Margaret Ashworth
Lu Astrene II
Jennifer Atkins
Jennifer Ault
Ann Austin
Carla Austin
Suzanne Austin
Sabohi Ayaz
Peggy Ayscue
Linda Baer
Leslie Bailey
Ann Bailey
Raye Bane
Vicci Bane
Carolyn Banister
Linda Barbrow

Rosanne Barker
Virginia Barlow
Carrie-Ellen Barnes
Lucy Barre
Linda Bartley
Brenda Basham
Millicent Bauer
Lori Baum
Elanor Baumner
Lisa Bazzanella-Smith
Theresa Beck
Penny Beckham
H. Behnice
Ann Belk
Harry Belk
Doreen Bell
Jill Bell
Laura Bell
Nicole Bellemare
Beman
Amy Bendekovits
Lori Bennett
Shelia Bennett
Lou Benton
Sonja Benz
Connie Berg
Beverly Bergstrom
Angelo Bersani
Edith Bevill
Lauren Biggs
Whitney Binzel
Nikki Bird
Becky Bishop
Mary Bishop
Frankie Bissell
Ginny Bissell
Tracy Bissen

Susan Black
Liz Blackwell
Dayne Blair
Alex Blake
Judith Blake
Elizabeth Blakeman
Katy Blankenhorn
Linda Blevins
Andrea Block
Anne Bloomer
Audrey Bodenhamer
Susan Bohn
Carol Borchardt
Marilyn Bosworth
Cheryl Bousson
Ariel Bouvier
Tracey Boyd
Dolores Boyer
Mary-Louise Boyer
Sara Gwynn Brackett
Diane Bradley
Noel Bradley
Linda Brammett
Emily Braswell
Susan Brener
Mary Brickheimer
Sonia Briere
Sonja Brine
Debra Britton
Aileen Broaddus
Eleni Brooks
Ashley Brown
Ashley Brown
Fran Brown
Gladys Brown
Ken Brown
Patsy Brown

Steve Brown
Susan Brown
Kate Brown
Kathy Browning
Kim Bruce
Hope Bruens
Bailey Buchanan
Brittany Buchanan
Mary Buchanan
Mindi Sue Buchanan
T.J. Buchanan
Teisha Buchanan
Pat Buchinski
Linda Buckley
Emily Bull
Liz Burford
Gloria Burg
Mary Ellen Burke
Elizabeth Burress
Georgina Burton
John & Nina Bye Jr.
Marty Byrne
Loretta Cadell
Shana Cain
Joseph Calia
Lana Calton
Geraldine Campbell
Marilyn Campbell
Mary Cancemi
Carol Candora
Elena Canler
Nancy Canoy
Agnes Canzona
Yolanda Capo
Margaret Capp
Lourdes Carasa
Craig Carolean
Susan Carothers
Carol Carrara
Marcie Carrier
Emma Jane Carroll
Roni Carroll
Courtney Carter
Rosemary Carter

Jennifer Cash
Dave Casper
Emma Casperite
Amy Castellani
Gloria M. Castro
Ana Maria Causillas
Barbara Cave
Debbi Cella
Patricia Certisimo
Socha Chadwick
Alison Chapman
Wanda Chapman
Joan Chase
Meredith Chehardy
Majeur Chery
Grace Childers
Helen Christman
Angela Cihiwsky
Tyler Cintron
Chris Cirule
Debora Clark
Nancy Clark
Beth Clarkson
Judi Clifford
Arlene Clifton
Tina Clowney
Desiree Cluett
Mitchel Coats
Jerry Coker
Anita Collins
Leketha Collins
Marcia Collins
Mary Connick
Veda Connolly
Amy Cook
Karen Cook
Susan Coomer
Bonnie Cooper
Omagene Cooper
Sandye Copeland
Wanda Cordoba
Kim Corley
Craig Cornwell
Jorge Corrales

Ann & Mel Cosgrove
Debbie Courte
Joanie Covell
Jennifer Cowan
Madeleine Coyra
Robert Crane
Ruth Crane
Cheryl Crawford
Diane Craycraft
Sandra Crossley
Dora Crow
Nan Crowder
Renee Crowson
Rita Gale Cruise
Donald & Doris Cuddihee
Rita Cullen
Mary Cummings
Caroline Cundiff
Janet Cunningham
Scott Curtis
Patricia Cutcher
Jill Dabbs
Marjorie Dahl
Judi Dahlen
Brenda Dailey
Rita Danker
Sharon Daqiel
Holly Dartez
John Dartez
Eric Dattler
Brenna Davenport-Leigh
Jackie Davidson
Joan Davis
Karen Davis
Mary Beth Davis
Barbara Dawkins
Christy Day
Sandra De Jong
Nancy DeBord
Heather DeDona
Kim Deese
Janice DeGree
Shari Deitchman
Carol Demartini

Debbie Dempsey

Julia Denson

Barbara Dettelbach

Sandy Sue Devries

Dale DeWood

Betty Dickson

Emily Dixon

Linda Doan

Warner Dobbins

Willa Dodd

Debi Dodson

Harriet Dodson

Susie Donley

Jenny Donnelly

Angie Dormuth

Fran Down

Melanie Duan

Kathy Dubé

Catherine Duke

Jane Duralia

Betsy Durrenberger

Betty Duteau

Debbie Dyer

Venus Dyer

Terri Dyson

Caroline Eager

Julia Eanes

Vivian Earnhardt

Sandy Easley

Peggy Ebert

Heather Echols

Charlene Echols-Barnes

Melanie Economou

Robin Edgar

Janet Edwards

Sherry Edwards

Carol Eiber

Susan Eifert

Alison Ellis

Janet Ellison

Maryann English

Natalie English

Margaret Ensley

Dottie Erickson

Judith Erickson

Barbara Erway

John Esposito

Ann Estes

Janet Evans

Pamela Evans

Cheryl Everhart

Elizabeth (Libby) Everhart

Paul Ezelle

Nick Fabiano

Kimberly Falck

Gladys Falk

Tura Farish

Cheryl Farrow

Joy Fatigate

Lynn Fauser

Kristen Faust

Bonnie Fauver

Ann Feldman

Freddi Felt

Tres Fenton

Marianne Ferris

Beth Fields

Dorothy Finkelstein

Sharon Finlon

Veronica Fischer

Jean Fisher

Ashley Fisk

Elizabeth Fite

Patricia Fitzgerald

Richard Fiumara

Pam Floyd

Cheryl Fogel

Donna Folgarelli

Greg Fontenot

Charlotte Ford

Renée Ford

Richard Ford

Brenda Fradette

Monica France

Nathan Frazier

Linda Freireich

Elaine French

Cynthia Fridlich

Janice Friend

Silke Fritz

Dori Fritzinger

Geri Frusterio

Barbara Fry

Gayle Fulcher

Jamie Fulghum

Melissa Fuller

Mindy Gaebel

Sue Gaither

Karen Galiger

Paula Gallagher

Janet C. Ganote

Tina Garber

Lori Garner

Noah Garrett

Jayne Geier

James Geyer

Nancy Geyer

Bonnie Ghosh

Frances Gibbes

Lil Gibson

Katie Gilbert

Katherine Gilland

Janet Gillespie

Susan Gladwin

Beth Gloss

Betty Glower

Sheila Goff

Linda Gogreve

Paul Goldberg

Bonnie Goldfarb

Mayra Gonzalez

Linda Goodwin

Pearl Gopoian

Martin Gordon

John Grace

Marilyn Grace

Maureen Grady

Brittany Graffagnino

Patricia Graham

Jennifer Grant

Linda Grassa

Stacy Grassa

Alyson Graves
Steve Graves
Marion Greenbelt
Myra Greene
Jason Greer
Betty Lou Gresham
Astrid Griffin
Aaron Grogan
David Gross
Amy Grossenbacher
Bonnie Gurnham
Judi Guy
Sharon Haas
Carl Hackerman
Dolly Hadden
Ann Hageseth
Dakota Haggerty
Shirley Haggerty
Barbara Haik
Leslie Hakanson
Kim Halbert
Lorna Hale
Barbara Hall
MiChal Hall
Pamela Hall
Rebecca Hamby
Emily Hamilton
Lena Hamrick
Brian Harbach
Allison Hardin
Laura Hardy
Andrea Harper
Cynthia Harper
Dianne Harper
Jennett Harrell
Vista Harrington
Barbara Harris
Dede Harris
Sabine Harris
Joe Haskins
Katy Hassen
Connie Hassler
R. Hastings
Nancy Hatch

Sandra Hawkins
Shirley Hawkins
Joe Hawthorne
Gretel Hecht
Denise Held
Alexa Hellstrom
Boog Henderson
Carla Hennett
Jean Henriksen
Deanie Hermann
Joan Hettinger
Sally Hewitt
Carla Hibbard
Lili Highsmith
Harriet Hill
Mark Hines-Cobb
Thomas Hingle
Sherri Hinkle
Linda Hodges
Phyllis Hoffman
Susan Hoffman
Carolyn Hogue
Kathryn Hollins
Wanda Hollowell
Pat Holt
JoAnne Holva
Jayne Homsher
David Hoover
Stephanie Horacek
Joanne Horton
Angela Hough
Helen Houghton
Anne Houston
Ashley Houston
Katie Houston
Janice Howard
M.W. Howard
Katherine Howland
Stacy Hoyt
Charles Hubbard
Nyoka Huddlestone
Donna Hudson
Natalie Huffaker
Jean Hundley

Audrey Hunt
Carol Hunter
Meredith Hunter
Judy Husick
Suzie Huth
Mark Hutter
Kenneth Ide
Lisa Inabinet
Mary Isaacson
Rocky Ivanov
Laura Jackson
Paul Jackson
Vivian Jackson
JoAnn Jacobsen
Sue Ellen Jameson
Meredith Jamieson
Chris Janow
Edward Janow
Eleanor Jasper
Sandra Jaster
Beulah Jayalatha
Cynthia Jennings
Gloria Jennings
Cindy Jessup
Thomas Jevcak
Joanne Johanson
April Johnson
Betty Johnson
Chelsea Johnson
Jere Johnson
Kindle Johnson
Martha Johnson
Nancy Johnson
Rosemary Johnson
Sharon Johnson
Sharon Johnson
Shirley Johnson-Nelson
Shirley Johnston
Nancy Joines
Debbie Jones
Joyce Jones
Kelly Jones
Marc Jones
Millie Jones

Sally Jones

Sherry Jones

Shirley Jones

Tom Jones

Betty Jordan

Tammie Jordan

Nada Jovanovich

Linda Joynes

Lisa Julius

Karen Jumonville

Janis Jung

Kathryn Kading

Millie Kaempfer

Jerry Kahn

Sadia Kahn

Donald Kalina

Jo Anne Kampschroeder

Regina Kane

Ann Kann

Teresa Kara

Carol Karszes

Jeff Kaslofsky

Mary Anne Kearns

Judy Keen

Doris Keiger

Twila Keirns

Renate Kellner

Tracey Kennedy

Jim Keown

Rosie Kereczman

Rorie Kerns

Linda Kerr

Nelda Kersey

Lauren Kershner

Thomas Keshian

William (Bill) Kilpatrick

Carmen Kimbrell

Susan Kimbrough

Joan Kimmel

Stanley Kimmel

Janet Kindred

Judy King

Kaye King

Betty P. Kjera, Ph.D.

Chelsy Klein

Velva Knapp

Radelle Knappenberger

Richard Knoll

Paula & Casey Knynenburg

Josette Konczeski

Tim Koon

Susan Koren

Karen Koslowski

Kristin Kouka

Dave Kral

Jean Kral

Marilyn Kraut

Doris Kreager

Jessica Kreamer

James Krems

Judy Kruzan

Ann Kuehnel

Sylvia Kwee

Kellie LaCour

Debbie Ladd

Pamela Lafoe

Pat LaHote

Gail LaMagna

Philip LaMarche

Anthony Lance

Chris Lapienski

Andra Larson

James Larson

Florence LaShomb

Christian Laver

Jul LaVera

Kim Lawton

Paul LeBlanc

Joni Lee

Julie Lee

Brenda Lenkway

Toni Lennie

Kit Leppert

Teresa Lesher

Maryann Leslie

Tony Lesniak

Michael Levy

Barri Lewis

Kate Lewis

Susan Lineback

Cindie Linhart

Mary Jayne Linhart

Sue Linhart

Angie Liollio

Susan Lippman

Larry Lipscomb

Anna Christina Little

Ellen Ljung

Carrie Long

Jorge Lorrales

James Lowers

Margaret Lucas

Diana Luckhardt

Ginny Luckhardt

Karlyn Luckhardt

Rachel Luckhardt

Virginia Luckhardt

Jeanne Lund

Thomas Lunney

Matt and Holly Lytle

Betty MacCloud

Terry Macey

Maria MacGowan

Pauline MacQueen

Dottie MacVicar

Lynn Mahbubani

Crystal Maleski

Ginny Maloney

Mary Maloney

Connie Manahan

Dolores Manning

Maria Mantek

Doris Mantooth

Cynthia Marcotte

Judie Marcum-Holley

Marty Marlatt

Jan Marshall

Betty Sue Martin

Debby Martin

Margaret Ann Martin

Vivian Martin

Wendy Martin

Wendy Martz
Sarah Marvel
Peyton Mathis
Paula Matthews
Joan Mattingly
Susan Mazzella
James McClain
Susan McClugage
JP McCormick
Judith McCune
Beth McDonald
Sally McFaddon
Julie McGuire
Cindy McIntosh
Judy McKay
Lisa McKinnon
Elaine McLane
Thomas McLeod
Candace Mcmenamin
Janet McNeal
Joyce McNeill
Jennie McShea
Sylvia McSwain
W. Mae McTier
Linda Meek
G. Frank Meekins
Sherry Meluskey
Ervin Menant
Lucyle Merriwether
Betsy Metcalf
Eve Metz
Jane Mika
Ed Mikulski
Alice Miller
Belinda Miller
Betty Miller
Janet Miller
Judy Miller
Lee Anne Miller
Teresa Miller
Jane Miller
Susan Miller
Tom, Meslissa, Chance & Hailey Millon
Cynthia Milton

Cheryl Mire
Frances Mitchell
Jean Mitchell
Susan Mizober
Jessica Modeen
Grace Modey
Freddie Moffett
Marilyn Mokray
Donna Monagle
Marsha Montgomery
Barbara Moore
Joan Moore
Michelle Moore
Wilma Moore
Erin Moorehead
Thomas Morgan
Tracy Morgan
Nicole Mortimer
Joan Morton
P. Alden Mount
Susan Murphy
Anne Murray
Connie Murray
Maxine Murray
Catherine Musella
Carolyn Musgrave
James Musumeci
Bonnie Myers
Bonnie Myers
Bonnie Myers
Lisa Myers
Garrett Mynatt
Carly Mys
Julia Nameth
Sarah Napier
Beth Natividad
Bob Nawalanioe
Jackie Nelson
Clara Newman
Pamela Newman
Janet Niblick
Brian Nicholson
Kim Nixon
Beverly Noles

Tina Novit
Sharon Nystrom
Linda O'Brien
Pat O'Keefe
Emily Olson
Chuck Ortego
Brenda O'Shields
Mustafa Osman
Charlene Ottinger
Trish Otto
Edilia Ovies
Beth Pafford
Carol Page
Martha Pahl
Leslie Palmer
Imelda Panzer
Lavon Paré
Judy Parker
Lisa Parker
Karen Parks
Amy Parsons
Christopher Partovi
Jeanne Pastrnak
Laura Payne
Trisha Pearson
Michael Peceri
George Pecuch Jr.
Mara Pederzani
Mara Pederzani
Renee Pellati
LaVonne Peller
Joyce Penley
Alice Perry
Julia Perry
George Perry
Nan Peszko
Carolyn Peterson
Nancy Peterson
Trang Pham
John Phillips
Marilyn Phillips
Matthew Phillips
Elizabeth Pickerill
Ben Pierce

Martha Pierce
Sally Pierce
Trudilynne Pina
Corey Pitz
Corinne Pluchon
Patricia Plummer
Elaine Polino
Bridget Pople
Debbie Pratt
Julie Prescott
Elaine Preston
Amy Price
Erika Price
Nicky Puccio
Mariana Pundsack
C. Pupillo
Tina Pupillo
Ann Quist
Elliot Rabone
Annette Rachlin
Gerald Radford
Janie Radford
John Raushenbush
Marcia Raushenbush
Carol Rawson
Jane Reding
Patsy Reeves
Jennifer Regan
Sandy Reiser
Pamela Reiss
Joyce Remenowsky
Jacalyn Resman
JoAnn Bonfiglio Reyes
Linares Reynaldo
Mary Reynolds
Kathy Reynolds-Weaver
Patricia Rhoden
Ross Rhodes
Jason Rice
Katy Richards
Jane Ries
Cody Rifkin
Barbara Riley
Barbara Rink

Rhonda Ritchie
Marian Rizza
Roselyn Robertson
Deborah Robinson
Don Robinson
Joann Robinson
Dawn Rock
Sandra Rocks
Jean Roden
Judith Rogers
Kathleen Rohde
Denise Rohrbach
Selenia Roldan
V.M. Rose
Bonnie Rosemeier
Lori Rosenberg
Patricia Roth
Erin Rudd
Elizabeth Ruggles
Doris Rule
Judith Rush
Lisa Russ
Kathy Russell
Keli Rylance
Maggie S.
Gloria Sacco
Bridget Salvi
Linda Samples
Bonnie Samuel
Mary Ann Sanborn
Christina Sanders
Phyllis Sanders
Susan Sanders
Natalie Sargent
Pamela Sattari
Cathy Ann Sauer
Nicole Saunders
Gypsy Savvides
Debra Schaben
Angie Schemm
Ruth Schlafer
Jennifer Scholbrock
Janet Schramm
Sally Schreiber

Nonie Schuler
Loretta Schult
Joan Schulz
Paula Marie Schwartz
Jennifer Schwarz
Paula Scifres
Mary Scott
Sandra Lee Scott
Jacy Seaman
Edward Sedlmeier
Anna Seeto
Anne Seippel
Patti Seippel
Charlotte Shake
Martha Sharron
Rae Shatto
Ralph Sheets Jr.
Marti Shelby
Sue Sherwood
Barbara Shoener
Sarah Shoffner
Kay Shore
Melissa Short
Heather Showstead
Ann Marie Sides
Leona (Lee) Silgado
Thomas Silva
Beatrice Silverman
Cathy Simmons
Diana Sims
Susan Sinclair
Thomas Singarella
Chris Sizemore
Donald Sjaarda
Mona Skidmore
Janine Skraban
Steve Slack
Gail Sloan
Susan Small
Barbara Smith
Barry Smith
Carol Smith
Davis Smith
Leah Smith

Marie W. Smith
Mary Snyder
Linda Soeder
Barbara Soiref
Lynda Somers Donahue
Susan Sommerkamp
Jan Soto
Robert Southard
Sharon Southard
Rebecca Sovern
Mildred Soyars
Julia Spainhour
Kathleen Spencer
Kenny Spencer
Robert Spencer
Sue Spencer
Cathy Sperr
Barbara Spitzer
Wendy Squitero
Tim Sroka
Amy Stanis
Bonnie Stark
Amy Stavish
Gerri Stavish
Joy Steadman
Judith Steinbeck
Kimberly Steinke
Ann Steitz
Kathleen Stephens
Richa Stevens
Kristen Stevenson
Priscilla Stewart
Virginia Stibbe
Robin Stickney
Patty Stilwell
Ruth Stolting
Carolyn Storrs
Angela Strickland
Cheryl Strickland
Andrea Strzelec
Myrel Sullivan
Sherry Sullivan
Violet Summerall
William Sutara

Denise Swan
Carol Sue Swann
Tanya Swann
Laszlo Szatmari
Christine T.
Sue Tako
Greg Talamantez
David Talazs
Joan Tarkington
Luminita Tat
Rhona Tavernia
Diane Taylor
Julie Taylor
Lara Taylor
Herb Teitelman
Wayne Thagard
Marjatta Thamm
Deborah Thomas
Heide Thomas
Judith Thomas
Tani Thomas
Nicole Thompson
Eyvind Thor
Glenda Thrift
Carol Tighe
Susie Tilton
Anne Tinkel
Connie Todd
Rhonda Toich
Robert Tomko
Pat Toth
Debbie Touchton
Jon Traurig
Joyce Travis
Stephanie Troia
Brenda Trowbridge
Lila Trudel
Angie Tucker
May Tudor
Donald Tulaldie
Glenda Turner
Ryllis Turner
Millie Turner-Tyson
Betty Tyson

Frannie Ugarte
Sharon Uhrmacher
Richard Ulmer
Shari Upchurch
Sherry Upshaw
Betty Valachovic
Renee Valentine
Eudoro van der Biest
Kristie van Gaalen
Ellen VanDervort
Dannielle VanGuilder
Katherine Varnell
Ellen Verre
Maya Vincelli
Deland Vitty
Regina von Kamp
Chris Wagner
Ginger Wald
Gabe Walden
Donald Waldie
Jan Waldt
Autumn Walker
Edy Walters
Shamus Walters
Sherry Walters
Elayne Ware
Vernon Warner, Jr.
Nancy Warren
Craig Weaver
Nancy Weaver
Lorraine Webber
Elizabeth Weber
Sandie Weeks-Pendley
Dolores Wehling
Ouida Welborn
Sherry Wellman
Donna Welsh
Ward Welty
Dave Wessinger
Diane West
Val Weymouth
Regina Whaley
Sandy Wheeler
Beverly Whiddon

Martha Whitaker

Mary Lou White

Bonnie Whitehead

William Wiedrich

Rita Wilber

Josie Wilkins

Lisa Willard

Allison Williams

Debi Williams

Kim Williams

Lillan Williams

Linda Williams

Pam Williams

Pauline Williams

Renn Williams

Shirley Williams

Wendy Williams

Melissa Wilmoth

Charles Wilson

Kathy Wilson

Nannette Wilson

Patti Wilson

Stan Wilson

Carol Wilson-Yontz

Irene Windsor

Judith Winkley

Aysim Wisco

Allison Woerner

Candice Wohlfeil

Patricia Wojcik

Mikki Wolfberg

Brenda Woodie

Sandra Woodis

Katherine Wratchford

Susan Wright

Winkie Wright

Dee Wydnyk

Doris Wylee-Becker

Nan Yablong

Mary Yager

Erin Yasenchak

Chris & Lori Yerington

Nathan E. Young

Tanya Young

Debby Zagerman

Ursula Zamora

Jennifer Zarrinnam

Peter Zasowski

Jianhua Zhang

Ron Ziegler

Judy Zoldowski

Leah Zwang

Tiffany Zylstra

INDEX

ACCOMPANIMENTS

Asparagus in a Fig Balsamic Vinaigrette 247

Baby Artichoke Ragoût 248

Baked Potatoes Stuffed with Crabmeat 249

Barley Stuffed Portabella Mushrooms 250

Braised Leeks 251

Coconut Mashed Sweet Potatoes 252

Corn Pudding 253

Costa Rican Tostada 254

Couscous with Mint, Pinenuts & Cranberries 255

Curried Chickpeas and Black Beans 256

Filled Roasted Tomatoes 257

Green Beans with Peppered Goat
    Cheese & Toasted Walnuts 258

Grilled Garlic Baby Artichokes 259

Herbed Asparagus Sauté 260

Indian Style Curry Potatoes, Cauliflower & Chickpeas 261

Lobster Truffle Risotto 262

Mashed Cauliflower 263

Poblano Crème Fraîche Mashed Potatoes 264

Polenta & Spinach Casserole 265

Potatoes with Leeks & Gruyère 266

Red Wine Risotto with Roasted Pumpkin 267

Roasted Ginger Maple Sweet Potatoes 268

Roasted Root Vegetable Medley 269

Saffron Rice with Fresh Asparagus & Raisins 270

Smoky Baked Market Beans 272

Smoky Corn Risotto 271

Soubise (Braised Rice and Onions) 273

String Beans with Shallot Vinaigrette 274

Succotash with Wax Beans 275

Sweet & Savory Sweet Potatoes 276

Sweet Onion & Tomato Bake 277

Sweet Potato Soufflé 278

The Best Ever Macaroni & Cheese 279

Three Onion Risotto 280

Thyme Garlic Roasted Spaghetti Squash 281

Toasted Pinenut Couscous with Mango & Avocado 282

Wild Rice with Butternut Squash & Dried Cranberries 283

Zucchini Patties with Feta 284

ALMONDS

Charleston Squares 300

Chicken Marrakech with Jeweled Couscous 186

Fall Salad 86

Grand Chicken Salad Dulaine 90

Green Bean Salad with Soy Glazed Almonds 92

Tuna in Lemon Butter Dill Sauce with Almonds & Capers 231

Turkey Almond Salad with Herb Dressing 104

Wild Rice Salad with Arugula 106

APPETIZERS

Asiago Cheese Dip 19

Bacon-Wrapped Oysters 20

Baked Brie Bread Boule 21

Bourbon Pecan Brie Pastries 22

Chipotle Black Bean Empanadas 23

Coquilles St. Jacques 24

Crab Cakes with Cucumber Salad 25

Crab Crostini 26

Crab Puffs with Lime Sauce 27

Crunchy Potato Wedges with Pecan Romesco Sauce 28

Fig Mascarpone Pizza 29

Goat Cheese Canapés 30

Grilled Halloumi Open Faced Sandwiches 31

Herbed Cheese Canapés 32

Maple Rum Chicken Drummettes 33

Mediterranean Sun-Dried Tomato Spread 34

Neptune's Sea Cakes 35

Onion Apple Tartlets 36

Oriental-Style Chicken Drummettes 37

Pecan Dip 38

Pepperoni Stuffed Mushrooms...39

Phyllo Chicken Triangles...40

Pickled Shrimp...41

Pimento Cheese Deviled Eggs...365

Portabella Paradise...43

Prosciutto & Swiss Dip..42

Roasted Red Pepper & Goat Cheese Appetizer.........................44

Rosemary Shrimp Skewers with Lemon Garlic Pesto.................45

Shrimp Quesadilla Palenque...46

Smoked Gouda & Wild Mushroom Dip......................................47

Smoked Salmon Pillows with Old Bay Aioli..............................48

Smokey Cheddar Mini Burgers..49

Spicy Bombay Sliders..50

Spicy Panko Chicken Strips..51

Stuffed Baked Pears..52

Stuffed Grape Leaves..53

Tomato Pesto Tart...54

Tropical Shrimp Fiesta...55

Turkey Burgers with Goat Cheese..56

Veal Stuffed Mushrooms...57

Water Chestnut Dip...58

APPLES

Apple Cheesecake..295

Apple Chicken Salad with Rosemary Pecans.............................79

Apple Coleslaw..349

Apple Nut Pancakes...337

Autumn Grits...338

Baked Chicken with Cinnamon Braised Apples........................184

Candied Pecan & Apple Salad...83

Chocolate Chip Apple Cake...304

Cinnamon Apple Tart..305

Fall Harvest Muffins...343

Fall Salad...86

Grand Chicken Salad Dulaine..90

Mama's Ugly Apple Cake...319

Onion Apple Tartlets..36

Phyllo Chicken Triangles...40

Turkey Almond Salad with Herb Dressing................................104

Wild Rice with Butternut Squash & Dried Cranberries............283

APRICOTS

Apricot Chicken with Mushroom Cream Sauce........................183

Macadamia Crusted Jerk Pork with Apricot Relish..................172

ARTICHOKES

Artichoke Hearts with Shiitake Cream
Sauce over Linguini..147

Baby Artichoke Ragoût...248

Big Bang Chicken...185

Grilled Garlic Baby Artichokes...259

Pasta Corona...157

Potato Artichoke Salad with Horseradish Dressing....................98

Shrimp, Crab & Artichoke Casserole.......................................226

ASPARAGUS

Asparagus in a Fig Balsamic Vinaigrette.................................247

Asparagus Salad with Roasted Red Peppers
& Asiago Cheese..80

Herbed Asparagus Sauté...260

Saffron Rice with Fresh Asparagus & Raisins..........................270

AVOCADO

Avocado Tomato Salad..81

Margarita and Avocado Salsa...359

Salmon Steaks Veracruz-Style...222

Toasted Pinenut Couscous with Mango & Avocado...................282

Tortilla Soup with Fresh Avocado...74

Zesty Corn Salsa..370

BACON

Avocado Tomato Salad..81

Bacon-Wrapped Oysters...20

BBQ Ranch Chicken Salad...82

Beef Tips & Pearl Onion Pinot Noir Sauce...............................130

Colorado Green Chili..63

Creamy Lemon Garlic Scallops..213

Daube de Boeuf Provençale...133

Gnocchi with Bacon and Brussels Sprouts..............................151

Gorgonzola Pear Salad...89

Mâche & Goat Cheese Salad...95

Pacific Rim Meatballs with Spiced Glass Noodles....................156

Smokey Cheddar Mini Burgers..49
Smoky Baked Market Beans.. 272
Smoky Corn Risotto 271
Whiskey Chili..76

BANANAS

Banana Chocolate Chip Muffins.................................... 339
Banana Chocolate Hazelnut Stuffed Crêpes................ 297
Banana Punch.. 350

BEANS

Chipotle Black Bean Empanadas.......................................23
Costa Rican Tostada 254
Curried Chickpeas and Black Beans............................. 256
Indian Style Curry Potatoes, Cauliflower & Chickpeas............. 261
Sistafriend's Bean Salad...99
Smoky Baked Market Beans.. 272
Spicy Black-Eyed Pea Salad with Tomatoes,
   Cucumbers & Cilantro 100
Succotash with Wax Beans.. 275
Three Bean Stew 73

BEEF

Asian Pasta Salad with Beef, Broccoli & Bean Sprouts 148
Beef Casalinga... 127
Beef Filets with Cherry Ancho Espresso Sauce 128
Beef Tenderloin with Fennel and Ancho..................... 129
Beef Tips & Pearl Onion Pinot Noir Sauce 130
Black Fig Filet with Sweet Potato Pancakes................ 131
Citrus Ginger Strip Steaks 132
Daube de Boeuf Provençale 133
Grilled Halloumi & Steak Kabobs 134
Pacific Rim Flank Steak... 135
Pacific Rim Meatballs with Spiced Glass Noodles..................... 156
Pear Balsamic Flank Steak 136
Petite Filets with Port Shallot Sauce &
   Roquefort Peppercorn Crust...................................... 137
Picadillo Style Enchiladas 138
Polynesian Meatballs.. 139
Smokey Cheddar Mini Burgers.......................................49
Spiced Beef Tenderloin Steaks with Mango Salsa 140
Spiced Honey Porterhouse Steaks................................ 141

Sun-Dried Tomato & Brazil Nut Wellington............................. 142
Sweet N' Spicy Brisket.. 143
Tequila Fajitas 144
Whiskey Chili..76

BERRIES

Fruit Salsa 355
Panna Cotta with Berry Gazpacho............................... 322
Pavlov's Mouthwater Pavlova.. 323
Pecan Chicken Roll-Ups with Raspberry Currant Sauce 195
Raspberry Ganache Truffles 326
Strawberry & Onion Salad with Cashew Lime Dressing........... 103
Strawberry Rhubarb Crisp 328
Stuffed French Toast 345

BEVERAGES

Cosmo Blood Orange Punch.. 354
Old Salem Iced Tea... 362

BREAKFAST

Apple Nut Pancakes 337
Autumn Grits.. 338
Banana Chocolate Chip Muffins................................... 339
Cashew Butter Stuffed French Toast 340
Cherry Cinnamon Muffins 341
Country Sausage Dressing.. 342
Fall Harvest Muffins... 343
Salmon Quiche with Cucumber Sauce 344
Stuffed French Toast 345

CAKES

Best Ever Carrot Cake.. 298
Chocolate Chip Apple Cake 304
Divine Chocolate Cake 310
Irish Whiskey Cake 317
Italian Sponge Cake 318
Mama's Ugly Apple Cake 319
Texas Sheet Cake... 332
Tres Leches Cake... 333

Carrots

Asian Pasta Salad with Beef, Broccoli & Bean Sprouts 148

Best Ever Carrot Cake... 298

Chicken Marrakech with Jeweled Couscous 186

Creamy Tomato Basil Soup 66

Crunchy Chinese Chicken Salad 84

Fall Harvest Muffins 343

Hot Vegetable Garlic Bread.. 358

Italian Sausage and Harvest Vegetable Soup 68

Italian Turkey and Spinach Meatball Soup..................................69

Roasted Root Vegetable Medley 269

Sweet N' Spicy Brisket.. 143

Veal Osso Bucco 243

Zucchini Patties with Feta... 284

Cashews

Mâche & Goat Cheese Salad..95

Strawberry & Onion Salad with Cashew Lime Dressing........... 103

Cauliflower

Indian Style Curry Potatoes, Cauliflower & Chickpeas.............. 261

Mashed Cauliflower 263

Celery

Apple Chicken Salad with Rosemary Pecans.................................79

Candied Pecan & Apple Salad...83

Country Sausage Dressing.. 342

Creamy Tomato Basil Soup 66

Curried Chicken Salad 85

Gazpacho Salad 88

Grand Chicken Salad Dulaine 90

Italian Turkey and Spinach Meatball Soup..................................69

Marinated Mashed Potato Salad 96

Phyllo Chicken Triangles..40

Potato Artichoke Salad with Horseradish Dressing 98

Sistafriend's Bean Salad 99

Surinam Chicken Curry.. 198

Thai Style Peanut Shrimp with Noodles.................................... 163

Turkey Almond Salad with Herb Dressing................................. 104

Veal Osso Bucco 243

Cheese

Artichoke Hearts with Shiitake Cream Sauce over Linguini 147

Asiago Cheese Dip..19

Asparagus in a Fig Balsamic Vinaigrette 247

Asparagus Salad with Roasted Red Peppers & Asiago Cheese....80

Autumn Grits... 338

Baked Blue Cheese & Lime Shrimp 204

Baked Brie Bread Boule 21

Bourbon Pecan Brie Patries..22

Butternut Squash and White Cheddar Soup................................61

Coquilles St. Jacques 24

Cream of Tomato and Parmesan Soup 65

Fennel and Creamy Tomato Soup 67

Fig Mascarpone Pizza..29

Four Cheese and Shrimp Angel Hair.. 149

Four Cheese Ravioli with Tomato-Basil Cream Sauce 150

Goat Cheese Canapés...30

Greek Chicken on Flatbread with Feta-Yogurt Sauce 192

Green Beans with Peppered Goat
   Cheese & Toasted Walnuts 258

Grilled Eggplant Rigatoni with Peppered Goat Cheese............ 152

Grilled Halloumi & Steak Kabobs 134

Grilled Halloumi Open Faced Sandwiches 31

Herbed Cheese Canapés 32

Lemon Herb Chicken with Gruyére and Pancetta 194

Lobster Lasagna 154

Mâche & Goat Cheese Salad..95

Onion Apple Tartlets...36

Parmesan Baked Halibut.. 219

Pecan Chicken Roll-Ups with Raspberry Currant Sauce 195

Pecan Dip..38

Pepperoni Stuffed Mushrooms..39

Phyllo Chicken Triangles..40

Pimento Cheese Deviled Eggs.. 365

Potatoes with Leeks & Gruyère.. 266

Prosciutto & Swiss Dip..42

Pumpkin Soup with Gruyere 70

Roasted Poblano Chicken... 197

Roasted Red Pepper & Goat Cheese Appetizer............................44

Roasted Shrimp with Tomatoes & Feta....................................... 221

Roasted Vegetable & Four Cheese Lasagna................................ 161

Sausage & Gorgonzola Stuffed Pork Chops 178

Smokey Cheddar Mini Burgers..49

The Best Ever Macaroni & Cheese 279

Turkey Burgers with Goat Cheese 56

Zucchini Patties with Feta 284

CHEESECAKE

Apple Cheesecake 295

Daiquiri Chiffon Cheesecake 309

Texas Praline Cheesecake 331

White Chocolate Cheesecake 334

CHERRIES

Beef Filets with Cherry Ancho Espresso Sauce 128

Charleston Squares 300

Cherry Cinnamon Muffins 341

Cherry Coffee Cake 301

Cherry Vanilla Bread Pudding 302

Chocolate Cherry Cookies 303

Duck Breast with A Warm Cherry-Pineapple Relish 238

Mâche & Goat Cheese Salad 95

Pork Tenderloin with Cherry Pecan Stuffing 176

Super Easy Chocolate Cookies 329

Winter Chery Salad with Crispy Pancetta 107

CHICKEN

Apple Chicken Salad with Rosemary Pecans 79

Apricot Chicken with Mushroom Cream Sauce 183

Baked Chicken with Cinnamon Braised Apples 184

BBQ Ranch Chicken Salad 82

Big Bang Chicken 185

Chicken Marrakech with Jeweled Couscous 186

Chicken with Mushrooms and Herbs 187

Chicken with Tomatillos and Poblanos 188

Chipotle Black Bean Empanadas 23

Cilantro Chicken Soup 62

Crunchy Chinese Chicken Salad 84

Curried Chicken Salad 85

Feta Chicken Rolls 190

Garlic Chicken with Sherry Butter 191

Grand Chicken Salad Dulaine 90

Greek Chicken on Flatbread with Feta-Yogurt Sauce 192

Grilled Chicken Quarters with a Grilled Fennel Slaw 193

Lemon Herb Chicken with Gruyére and Pancetta 194

Maple Rum Chicken Drummettes 33

Oriental-Style Chicken Drummettes 37

Pecan Chicken Roll-Ups with Raspberry Currant Sauce 195

Phyllo Chicken Triangles 40

Regal Curried Chicken 196

Roasted Poblano Chicken 197

Spicy Panko Chicken Strips 51

Surinam Chicken Curry 198

Tender Yogurt Chicken 199

Tortilla Soup with Fresh Avocado 74

Tropical Curried Chicken 200

CHIPS AND SNACKS

Cinnamon Pita Chips 352

Truffle Chips 369

Zesty Corn Salsa 370

CHOCOLATE

Banana Chocolate Chip Muffins 339

Banana Chocolate Hazelnut Stuffed Crêpes 297

Cappuccino Biscotti 299

Chocolate Cherry Cookies 303

Chocolate Chip Apple Cake 304

Divine Chocolate Cake 310

Double Chocolate Mint Bars 311

Graham Cracker Pralines 314

Irish Whiskey Cake 317

Italian Sponge Cake 318

Marbled Mouse 320

Raspberry Ganache Truffles 326

Super Easy Chocolate Cookies 329

Texas Sheet Cake 332

White Chocolate Cheesecake 334

COCONUT

Coconut Mashed Sweet Potatoes 252

Coconut-Panko Crusted Tilapia with Mango Chutney 210

Divine Chocolate Cake 310

Fall Harvest Muffins 343

Indian Style Curry Potatoes, Cauliflower & Chickpeas 261

Mojo Coconut Sauce 361

Polynesian Meatballs.. 139

Spiced Beef Tenderloin Steaks with Mango Salsa 140

Spicy Shrimp and Coconut Soup.......................................72

Tropical Shrimp Fiesta 55

COD

Chipotle Fish Wraps 209

Neptune's Sea Cakes 35

COFFEE

Beef Filets with Cherry Ancho Espresso Sauce 128

Cappuccino Biscotti.. 299

Irish Whiskey Cake 317

COOKIES & BARS

Charleston Squares.. 300

Chocolate Cherry Cookies.. 303

Creamy Macadamia Nut Cookies 308

Oatmeal Carmelitas 321

Southern Pecan Blonde.. 327

Super Easy Chocolate Cookies 329

CORN

Corn Chowder 64

Corn Pudding 253

Lobster Lasagna 154

Salmon with Heirloom Tomato Crab Salsa............................. 223

Smoky Corn Risotto 271

Succotash with Wax Beans 275

Tortilla Soup with Fresh Avocado 74

CRAB

Baked Potatoes Stuffed with Crabmeat 249

Crab Cakes with Cucumber Salad 25

Crab Crostini..26

Crab Puffs with Lime Sauce 27

Crab Stuffed Eggplant 211

Crab Stuffed White Fish 212

Salmon with Heirloom Tomato Crab Salsa............................. 223

Seafood Chowder..71

Shrimp, Crab & Artichoke Casserole 226

CRANBERRIES

Autumn Grits.. 338

Couscous with Mint, Pinenuts & Cranberries 255

Cranberry Pecan Orange Pound Cake................................. 306

Cranberry Pecan Turkey Roulade 189

Curried Chicken Salad 85

Fall Salad...86

Pork Chops with a Cranberry Port Sauce 173

CRÈME FRAÎCHE

Bacon-Wrapped Oysters 20

Poblano Crème Fraîche Mashed Potatoes............................. 264

CUCUMBER

Bacon-Wrapped Oysters 20

Crab Cakes with Cucumber Salad 25

Fresh Dill Salad 87

Gazpacho Salad 88

Greek Chicken on Flatbread with Feta-Yogurt Sauce 192

Salmon Quiche with Cucumber Sauce 344

Spicy Black-Eyed Pea Salad with
    Tomatoes, Cucumbers & Cilantro.................................. 100

DESSERTS

Apple Cheesecake 295

Baked Pear Delights... 296

Banana Chocolate Hazelnut Stuffed Crêpes........................... 297

Best Ever Carrot Cake... 298

Cappuccino Biscotti... 299

Charleston Squares.. 300

Cherry Coffee Cake 301

Cherry Vanilla Bread Pudding.. 302

Chocolate Cherry Cookies.. 303

Chocolate Chip Apple Cake 304

Cinnamon Apple Tart 305

Cranberry Pecan Orange Pound Cake................................. 306

Creamy Caramel & Pear Sundaes with Toasted Hazelnuts 307

Creamy Macadamia Nut Cookies 308

Daiquiri Chiffon Cheesecake 309

Divine Chocolate Cake 310

Double Chocolate Mint Bars 311

Farmhouse Walnut Pie 312

Georgia Peach Poundcake 313

Graham Cracker Pralines 314

Hawaiian Upside Down Muffins 315

Holiday Pumpkin Bread with Orange Glaze 316

Irish Whiskey Cake 317

Italian Sponge Cake with Cream Cheese 318

Mama's Ugly Apple Cake 319

Marbled Mouse 320

Oatmeal Carmelitas 321

Panna Cotta with Berry Gazpacho 322

Pavlov's Mouthwater Pavlova 323

Peaches and Cream Pie 324

Prized Coffee Cake 325

Raspberry Ganache Truffles 326

Southern Pecan Blonde 327

Strawberry Rhubarb Crisp 328

Super Easy Chocolate Cookies 329

Sweet Grilled Peaches 330

Texas Praline Cheesecake 331

Texas Sheet Cake 332

Tres Leches Cake 333

White Chocolate Cheesecake 334

DIPS

Chive Rémoulade 351

Fresh Fiesta Salsa 356

Fruit Salsa 355

Grape Salsa 357

Margarita and Avocado Salsa 359

Peach Bruschetta 363

Pesto Hummus 364

Zesty Corn Salsa 370

DUCK

Duck Breast with A Warm Cherry-Pineapple Relish 238

EGGPLANT

Crab Stuffed Eggplant 211

Grilled Eggplant Rigatoni with Peppered Goat Cheese 152

EVERYTHING ELSE

Apple Coleslaw 349

Banana Punch 350

Chive Rémoulade 351

Cinnamon Pita Chips 352

Citrus, Honey & Jalapeño Marinade 353

Cosmo Blood Orange Punch 354

Fresh Fiesta Salsa 356

Fruit Salsa 355

Grape Salsa 357

Hot Vegetable Garlic Bread 358

Margarita and Avocado Salsa 359

Marinated Mushroom 360

Mojo Coconut Sauce 361

Old Salem Iced Tea 362

Peach Bruschetta 363

Pesto Hummus 364

Pimento Cheese Deviled Eggs 365

Pomodoro Sauce 366

Shish Kabob Marinade 367

Spicy Pumpkin Mole Sauce 368

Truffle Chips 369

Zesty Corn Salsa 370

FENNEL

Baked Tilapia with Tomato Fennel Sauce 205

Beef Tenderloin with Fennel and Ancho 129

Fennel and Creamy Tomato Soup 67

Flounder with a Candied Ginger Butter Sauce 214

Grilled Chicken Quarters with a Grilled Fennel Slaw 193

Roasted Tomato Pasta with Grilled Fennel Ragout 160

GREEN BEANS (INCLUDES FRENCH BEANS)

Green Bean Salad with Soy Glazed Almonds 92

Green Beans with Peppered Goat Cheese & Toasted Walnuts 258

Sistafriend's Bean Salad 99
String Beans with Shallot Vinaigrette 274
Succotash with Wax Beans 275

HALIBUT
Parmesan Baked Halibut.. 219
Proscuitto Wrapped Halibut... 220
Smoked Fish with Tequila Cilantro Sauce................... 229

LAMB
Marinated Smoked Leg of Lamb 240
Perfect Rack of Lamb 241
Praline Pecan Lamb Chops.. 242

LEEKS
Braised Leeks 251
Fennel and Creamy Tomato Soup 67
Potatoes with Leeks & Gruyère................................... 266
Three Onion Risotto 280

LOBSTER
Brandied Shrimp & Lobster 206
Lobster Lasagna 154
Lobster Truffle Risotto 262

MACADAMIA NUTS
Chocolate Cherry Cookies.. 303
Creamy Macadamia Nut Cookies 308
Hawaiian Upside Down Muffins 315
Macadamia Crusted Jerk Pork with Apricot Relish 172

MAHI MAHI
Panko Mahi-Mahi with Hawaiian Soy Butter Sauce ... 218

MANGOES
Coconut-Panko Crusted Tilapia with Mango Chutney............. 210
Fruit Salsa 355

Margarita and Avocado Salsa 359
Regal Curried Chicken... 196
Shrimp Quesadilla Palenque..46
Spiced Beef Tenderloin Steaks with Mango Salsa 140
Surinam Chicken Curry.. 198
Toasted Pinenut Couscous with Mango & Avocado................. 282
Tropical Shrimp Fiesta 55

MUFFINS
Cherry Cinnamon Muffins 341
Fall Harvest Muffins 343
Hawaiian Upside Down Muffins 315

MUSHROOMS
Apricot Chicken with Mushroom Cream Sauce 183
Artichoke Hearts with Shiitake Cream Sauce over Linguini 147
Barley Stuffed Portabella Mushrooms 250
Chicken with Mushrooms and Herbs........................... 187
Coquilles St. Jacques..24
Marinated Mushroom 360
Pasta Corona 157
Pepperoni Stuffed Mushrooms.......................................39
Portabella Paradise 43
Seared Scallops with Mushroom Truffle Oil 225
Smoked Gouda & Wild Mushroom Dip.........................47
Veal Stuffed Mushrooms 57

OLIVES
Crunchy Potato Wedges with Pecan Romesco Sauce...................28
Daube de Boeuf Provençale 133
Gazpacho Salad..88
Greek Style Plum Tomatoes...91
Mediterranean Pasta... 155
Mediterranean Sun-Dried Tomato Spread.....................34
Pasta Corona 157
Picadillo Style Enchiladas 138
Sun-dried Tomato Pasta 162

OYSTERS
Bacon-Wrapped Oysters 20
Seafood Chowder..71

Pancetta

Asiago Stuffed Veal Chops.................................. 235
Lemon Herb Chicken with Gruyére and Pancetta 194
Winter Chery Salad with Crispy Pancetta.................................. 107

Pasta

Artichoke Hearts with Shiitake Cream Sauce over Linguini 147
Asian Pasta Salad with Beef, Broccoli and Bean Sprouts 148
Bucatini & Grilled Scallops with a
 Rosemary & Lemon Sauce 208
Creamy Lemon Garlic Scallops.................................. 213
Four Cheese and Shrimp Angel Hair 149
Four Cheese Ravioli with Tomato-Basil Cream Sauce 150
Gnocchi with Bacon and Brussels Sprouts............................. 151
Grilled Eggplant Rigatoni with Peppered Goat Cheese........... 152
Grilled Sweets and Garden Pea Ravioli 153
Italian Turkey and Spinach Meatball Soup................................69
Lobster Lasagna 154
Mediterranean Pasta.................................. 155
Pacific Rim Meatballs with Spiced Glass Noodles..................... 156
Pasta Corona 157
Penne Pasta with Italian Sausage in a
 Garlic Tomato Cream Sauce.................................. 158
Proscuitto Pasta 159
Roasted Tomato Pasta with Grilled Fennel Ragout.................... 160
Roasted Vegetable & Four Cheese Lasagna............................. 161
Sun-dried Tomato Pasta.................................. 162
Thai Style Peanut Shrimp with Noodles.................................. 163
The Best Ever Macaroni & Cheese.................................. 279

Peaches

Georgia Peach Poundcake 313
Peach Bruschetta.................................. 363
Peaches and Cream Pie 324
Sweet Grilled Peaches.................................. 330

Pears

Baked Pear Delights.................................. 296
Creamy Caramel & Pear Sundaes with Toasted Hazelnuts 307
Gorgonzola Pear Salad.................................89
Pear Balsamic Flank Steak 136

Pork Chops with Sweet Potato & Pear Crisps............................ 174
Spicy Pear Salad.................................. 101
Spinach & Grilled Pear Salad.................................. 102
Stuffed Baked Pears.................................52

Pecans

Apple Chicken Salad with Rosemary Pecans.................................79
Bourbon Pecan Brie Pastries 22
Candied Pecan & Apple Salad.................................83
Cherry Coffee Cake 301
Cherry Vanilla Bread Pudding.................................. 302
Cinnamon Apple Tart 305
Cranberry Pecan Orange Pound Cake............................. 306
Cranberry Pecan Turkey Roulade 189
Crunchy Potato Wedges with Pecan Romesco Sauce..................28
Fall Harvest Muffins.................................. 343
Graham Cracker Pralines 314
Peaches and Cream Pie 324
Pecan Chicken Roll-Ups with Raspberry Currant Sauce 195
Pecan Dip.................................38
Phyllo Chicken Triangles.................................40
Pork Chops with Sweet Potato & Pear Crisps............................ 174
Pork Tenderloin with Cherry Pecan Stuffing.................................. 176
Praline Pecan Lamb Chops.................................. 242
Roasted Ginger Maple Sweet Potatoes 268
Southern Pecan Blonde 327
Spicy Pear Salad.................................. 101
Spinach & Grilled Pear Salad 102
Sweet Potato Soufflé.................................. 278
Texas Praline Cheesecake.................................. 331

Peppers & Chiles

Arroz Con Camarones 203
Asian Pasta Salad with Beef, Broccoli and Bean Sprouts 148
Asparagus Salad with Roasted Red Peppers & Asiago Cheese....80
Big Bang Chicken.................................. 185
Chicken Marrakech with Jeweled Couscous 186
Chicken with Tomatillos and Poblanos 188
Chipotle Fish Wraps 209
Citrus, Honey & Jalapeño Marinade 353
Colorado Green Chili.................................63
Couscous with Mint, Pine Nuts, & Cranberries........................ 255

Crab Cakes with Cucumber Salad 25
Crab Crostini 26
Crab Puffs with Lime Sauce 27
Creamy Lemon Garlic Scallops 213
Crunchy Potato Wedges with Pecan Romesco Sauce 28
French Veal Sauté 239
Fresh Dill Salad 87
Fresh Fiesta Salsa 356
Fruit Salsa 355
Gazpacho Salad 88
Grape Salsa 357
Grilled Lime Center Cut Pork Chops 171
Macadamia Crusted Jerk Pork with Apricot Relish 172
Margarita and Avocado Salsa 359
Mediterranean Pasta 155
Pepperoni Stuffed Mushrooms 39
Picadillo Style Enchiladas 138
Poblano Crème Fraîche Mashed Potatoes 264
Polynesian Meatballs 139
Potato Artichoke Salad with Horseradish Dressing 98
Roasted Poblano Chicken 197
Roasted Red Pepper & Goat Cheese Appetizer 44
Salmon Steaks Veracruz-Style 222
Salmon with Sesame & Orange-Ginger Relish 224
Shrimp Étouffée 227
Smoky Baked Market Beans 272
Spiced Beef Tenderloin Steaks with Mango Salsa 140
Spicy Black-Eyed Pea Salad with
    Tomatoes, Cucumbers & Cilantro 100
Spicy Shrimp and Coconut Soup 72
Strawberry & Onion Salad with Cashew Lime Dressing 103
Succotash with Wax Beans 275
Tequila Fajitas 144
Three Bean Stew 73
Tropical Curried Chicken 200
Tropical Shrimp Fiesta 55
Zesty Corn Salsa 370

PIES

Farmhouse Walnut Pie 312
Peaches and Cream Pie 324

PINE NUTS

Bucatini & Grilled Scallops with a Rosemary & Lemon Sauce 208

Couscous with Mint, Pine Nuts, & Cranberries 255
Mediterranean Pasta 155
Pasta Corona 157
Rosemary Shrimp Skewers with Lemon Garlic Pesto 45
Sausage & Gorgonzola Stuffed Pork Chops 178
Stuffed Grape Leaves 53

PINEAPPLE

Banana Punch 350
Best Ever Carrot Cake 298
Duck Breast with A Warm Cherry-Pineapple Relish 238
Hawaiian Upside Down Muffins 315
Macadamia Crusted Jerk Pork with Apricot Relish 172
Old Salam Iced Tea 362
Panko Mahi-Mahi with Hawaiian Soy Butter Sauce 218
Polynesian Meatballs 139
Tropical Shrimp Fiesta 55

PORK

Balsamic Vinegar & Sage Pork 168
Bourbon & Honey Smoked Pork Chops 167
Carribean Spice Pork Tenderloin 169
Colorado Green Chili 63
Garlic Studded Dijon Pork Tenderloin 170
Grilled Lime Center Cut Pork Chops 171
Macadamia Crusted Jerk Pork with Apricot Relish 172
Pacific Rim Meatballs with Spiced Glass Noodles 156
Pork Chops with a Cranberry Port Sauce 173
Pork Chops with Basil Cream Sauce 175
Pork Chops with Sweet Potato & Pear Crisps 174
Pork Tenderloin Medallions with
    Black Pepper Cream Sauce 177
Pork Tenderloin with Cherry Pecan Stuffing 176
Sausage & Gorgonzola Stuffed Pork Chops 178
Tangy Baby Back Ribs 179
Whiskey Chili 76

POTATOES

Baked Potatoes Stuffed with Crabmeat 249
Black Fig Filet with Sweet Potato Pancakes 131
Corn Chowder 64
Crunchy Potato Wedges with Pecan Romesco Sauce 28
Indian Style Curry Potatoes, Cauliflower, & Chickpeas 261

Italian Sausage and Harvest Vegetable Soup 68

Marinated Mashed Potato Salad 96

Marinated Potato Salad 97

Neptune's Sea Cakes 35

Poblano Crème Fraîche Mashed Potatoes 264

Potato Artichoke Salad with Horseradish Dressing 98

Potatoes with Leeks & Gruyère 266

Roasted Root Vegetable Medley 269

Surinam Chicken Curry 198

Sweet N' Spicy Brisket 143

Truffle Chips 369

POULTRY

Apricot Chicken with Mushroom Cream Sauce 183

Baked Chicken with Cinnamon Braised Apples 184

Big Bang Chicken 185

Chicken Marrakech with Jeweled Couscous 186

Chicken with Mushrooms and Herbs 187

Chicken with Tomatillos and Poblanos 188

Cranberry Pecan Turkey Roulade 189

Feta Chicken Rolls 190

Garlic Chicken with Sherry Butter 191

Greek Chicken on Flatbread with Feta-Yogurt Sauce 192

Grilled Chicken Quarters with a Grilled Fennel Slaw 193

Lemon Herb Chicken with Gruyére and Pancetta 194

Pecan Chicken Roll-Ups with Raspberry Currant Sauce 195

Regal Curried Chicken 196

Roasted Poblano Chicken 197

Surinam Chicken Curry 198

Tender Yogurt Chicken 199

Tropical Curried Chicken 200

POUND CAKES & COFFEE CAKES

Cherry Coffee Cake 301

Cranberry Pecan Orange Pound Cake 306

Georgia Peach Poundcake 313

Holiday Pumpkin Bread with Orange Glaze 316

Prized Coffee Cake 325

PROSCIUTTO

Beef Casalinga 127

Fig Mascarpone Pizza 29

Mediterranean Sun-Dried Tomato Spread 34

Prosciutto & Swiss Dip 42

Proscuitto Pasta 159

Proscuitto Wrapped Halibut 220

Stuffed Baked Pears 52

PUMPKIN

Holiday Pumpkin Bread with Orange Glaze 316

Honey Roasted Butternut Squash Salad
with Pomegranate Vinaigrette 93

Pumpkin Soup with Gruyere 70

Red Wine Risotto with Roasted Pumpkin 267

Spicy Pumpkin Mole Sauce 368

RAISINS

Apple Chicken Salad with Rosemary Pecans 79

Chicken Marrakech with Jeweled Couscous 186

Fall Harvest Muffins 343

Grand Chicken Salad Dulaine 90

Holiday Pumpkin Bread with Orange Glaze 316

Regal Curried Chicken 196

Wild Rice Salad with Arugula 106

RICE & GRAINS

Barley Stuffed Portabella Mushrooms 250

Chicken Marrakech with Jeweled Couscous 186

Couscous with Mint, Pinenuts & Cranberries 255

Filled Roasted Tomatoes 257

Lobster Truffle Risotto 262

Red Wine Risotto with Roasted Pumpkin 267

Saffron Rice with Fresh Asparagus & Raisins 270

Smoky Corn Risotto 271

Soubise (Braised Rice and Onions) 273

Stuffed Grape Leaves 53

Three Onion Risotto 280

Toasted Pinenut Couscous with Mango & Avocado 282

Wild Rice Salad with Arugula 106

Wile Rice with Butternut Squash & Dried Cranberries 283

SALAD

Apple Chicken Salad with Rosemary Pecans.................................79

Asparagus Salad with Roasted Red Peppers & Asiago Cheese....80

Avocado Tomato Salad..81

BBQ Ranch Chicken Salad 82

Candied Pecan & Apple Salad..83

Crunchy Chinese Chicken Salad 84

Curried Chicken Salad 85

Fall Salad..86

Fresh Dill Salad 87

Gazpacho Salad 88

Gorgonzola Pear Salad 89

Grand Chicken Salad Dulaine..90

Greek Style Plum Tomatoes...91

Green Bean Salad with Soy Glazed Almonds 92

Honey Roasted Butternut Squash Salad
   with Pomegranate Vinaigrette...93

Italian Tomato Bread Salad..94

Mâche & Goat Cheese Salad..95

Marinated Mashed Potato Salad 96

Marinated Potato Salad 97

Potato Artichoke Salad with Horseradish Dressing 98

Sistafriend's Bean Salad 99

Spicy Black-Eyed Pea Salad with Tomatoes,
   Cucumbers & Cilantro 100

Spicy Pear Salad 101

Spinach & Grilled Pear Salad 102

Strawberry & Onion Salad with Cashew Lime Dressing.......... 103

Turkey Almond Salad with Herb Dressing................................ 104

Watermelon Salad with Balsamic Vinaigrette 105

Wild Rice Salad with Arugula.. 106

Winter Chery Salad with Crispy Pancetta.................................. 107

SALMON

Salmon Steaks Veracruz-Style 222

Salmon with Heirloom Tomato Crab Salsa................................ 223

Salmon with Sesame & Orange-Ginger Relish 224

Sweet Salmon with a Kick 230

SAUCES

Mojo Coconut Sauce 361

Pomodoro Sauce 366

Spicy Pumpkin Mole Sauce 368

SAUSAGE

Arroz Con Camarones 203

Baby Artichoke Ragoût 248

Bread Pudding with Shrimp & Sausage.. 207

Corn Chowder...64

Country Sausage Dressing.. 342

Four Cheese Ravioli with Tomato-Basil Cream Sauce 150

Italian Sausage and Harvest Vegetable Soup 68

Mediterranean Pasta... 155

Penne Pasta with Italian Sausage
   in a Garlic Tomato Cream Sauce.. 158

Sausage & Gorgonzola Stuffed Pork Chops 178

Smoky Baked Market Beans.. 272

Turkey and Andouille Sausage Stew..75

SCALLOPS

Bucatini & Grilled Scallops with a
   Rosemary & Lemon Sauce 208

Coquilles St. Jacques 24

Creamy Lemon Garlic Scallops.. 213

Seared Scallops with Mushroom Truffle Oil 225

SEAFOOD

Arroz Con Camarones 203

Baked Blue Cheese & Lime Shrimp.. 204

Baked Tilapia with Tomato Fennel Sauce 205

Brandied Shrimp & Lobster 206

Bread Pudding with Shrimp & Sausage....................................... 207

Bucatini & Grilled Scallops with a
   Rosemary & Lemon Sauce 208

Chipotle Fish Wraps 209

Coconut-Panko Crusted Tilapia with Mango Chutney............. 210

Crab Stuffed Eggplant 211

Crab Stuffed White Fish 212

Creamy Lemon Garlic Scallops.. 213

Flounder with a Candied Ginger Butter Sauce.......................... 214

Grilled Blacked Red Snapper.. 215

Mussels Extraordinaire... 216

Pan Seared Tuna Steaks with Wasabi Butter Sauce.................... 217

Panko Mahi-Mahi with Hawaiian Soy Butter Sauce 218

Parmesan Baked Halibut.. 219

Proscuitto Wrapped Halibut.. 220

Roasted Shrimp with Tomatoes & Feta....................................... 221

Salmon Steaks Veracruz-Style 222

Salmon with Heirloom Tomato Crab Salsa 223

Salmon with Sesame & Orange-Ginger Relish 224

Seared Scallops with Mushroom Truffle Oil 225

Shrimp Étouffée 227

Shrimp with Tomato Rice 228

Shrimp, Crab & Artichoke Casserole 226

Smoked Fish with Tequila Cilantro Sauce 229

Sweet Salmon with a Kick 230

Tuna in Lemon Butter Dill Sauce
with Almonds & Capers 231

SHRIMP

Arroz Con Camarones 203

Baked Blue Cheese & Lime Shrimp 204

Brandied Shrimp & Lobster 206

Bread Pudding with Shrimp & Sausage 207

Crab Stuffed White Fish 212

Four Cheese and Shrimp Angel Hair 149

Neptune's Sea Cakes 35

Pickled Shrimp 41

Roasted Shrimp with Tomatoes & Feta 221

Rosemary Shrimp Skewers with Lemon Garlic Pesto 45

Seafood Chowder 71

Shrimp Étouffée 227

Shrimp Quesadilla Palenque 46

Shrimp with Tomato Rice 228

Shrimp, Crab & Artichoke Casserole 226

Spicy Shrimp and Coconut Soup 72

Thai Style Peanut Shrimp with Noodles 163

Three Bean Stew 73

Tropical Shrimp Fiesta 55

SMOKED SALMON

Salmon Quiche with Cucumber Sauce 344

Smoked Salmon Pillows with Old Bay Aioli 48

SOUPS

Butternut Squash and White Cheddar Soup 61

Cilantro Chicken Soup 62

Colorado Green Chili 63

Corn Chowder 64

Cream of Tomato and Parmesan Soup 65

Creamy Tomato Basil Soup 66

Fennel and Creamy Tomato Soup 67

Italian Sausage and Harvest Vegetable Soup 68

Italian Turkey and Spinach Meatball Soup 69

Pumpkin Soup with Gruyere 70

Seafood Chowder 71

Spicy Shrimp and Coconut Soup 72

Three Bean Stew 73

Tortilla Soup with Fresh Avocado 74

Turkey and Andouille Sausage Stew 75

Whiskey Chili 76

SPINACH

Butternut Squash and White Cheddar Soup 61

Flounder with a Candied Ginger Butter Sauce 214

Honey Roasted Butternut Squash Salad
with Pomegranate Vinaigrette 93

Italian Turkey and Spinach Meatball Soup 69

Roasted Vegetable & Four Cheese Lasagna 161

Smoked Gouda & Wild Mushroom Dip 47

Spinach & Grilled Pear Salad 102

Thyme Garlic Roasted Spaghetti Squash 281

Wile Rice with Butternut Squash & Dried Cranberries 283

SWEET POTATOES

Black Fig Filet with Sweet Potato Pancakes 131

Coconut Mashed Sweet Potatoes 252

Grilled Sweets and Garden Pea Ravioli 153

Pork Chops with Sweet Potato & Pear Crisps 174

Roasted Ginger Maple Sweet Potatoes 268

Roasted Root Vegetable Medley 269

Sweet & Savory Sweet Potatoes 276

Sweet Potato Soufflé 278

TILAPIA

Baked Tilapia with Tomato Fennel Sauce 205

Coconut-Panko Crusted Tilapia with Mango Chutney 210

TOMATOES

Asiago Cheese Dip..19
Avocado Tomato Salad..81
Baked Tilapia with Tomato Fennel Sauce 205
BBQ Ranch Chicken Salad...82
Chipotle Fish Wraps... 209
Colorado Green Chili..63
Costa Rican Tostada 254
Cream of Tomato and Parmesan Soup 65
Creamy Tomato Basil Soup 66
Daube de Boeuf Provençale 133
Fennel and Creamy Tomato Soup 67
Filled Roasted Tomatoes.. 257
Four Cheese Ravioli with Tomato-Basil Cream Sauce 150
French Veal Sauté.. 239
Fresh Fiesta Salsa 356
Gazpacho Salad..88
Greek Chicken on Flatbread with Feta-Yogurt Sauce 192
Greek Style Plum Tomatoes..91
Grilled Eggplant Rigatoni with Peppered Goat Cheese............ 152
Indian Style Curry Potatoes, Cauliflower, & Chickpeas 261
Italian Tomato Bread Salad..94
Mediterranean Pasta 155
Mediterranean Sun-Dried Tomato Spread.................................34
Mussels Extraordinaire 216
Pasta Corona... 157
Penne Pasta with Italian Sausage in a Garlic Tomato Cream Sauce
    158
Pomodoro Sauce 366
Proscuitto Pasta 159
Roasted Red Pepper & Goat Cheese Appetizer...........................44
Roasted Shrimp with Tomatoes & Feta.................................... 221
Roasted Tomato Pasta with Grilled Fennel Ragout.................... 160
Roasted Vegetable & Four Cheese Lasagna 161
Salmon Steaks Veracruz-Style 222
Salmon with Heirloom Tomato Crab Salsa.............................. 223
Sausage & Gorgonzola Stuffed Pork Chops 178
Shrimp Étouffée... 227
Shrimp with Tomato Rice 228
Spicy Black-Eyed Pea Salad with
    Tomatoes, Cucumbers & Cilantro....................................... 100
Spicy Pumpkin Mole Sauce 368
Sun-Dried Tomato & Brazil Nut Wellington............................ 142

Sun-dried Tomato Pasta.. 162
Surinam Chicken Curry... 198
Sweet Onion & Tomato Bake 277
The Best Ever Macaroni & Cheese... 279
Three Bean Stew...73
Tomato Pesto Tart..54
Veal Osso Bucco 243
Whiskey Chili...76

TRUFFLE OIL

Lobster Truffle Risotto 262
Seared Scallops with Mushroom Truffle Oil 225
Truffle Chips.. 369

TUNA

Pan Seared Tuna Steaks with Wasabi Butter Sauce.................... 217
Tuna in Lemon Butter Dill Sauce with Almonds & Capers...... 231

TURKEY

Cranberry Pecan Turkey Roulade... 189
Italian Turkey and Spinach Meatball Soup.................................69
Spicy Bombay Sliders...50
Turkey Almond Salad with Herb Dressing............................... 104
Turkey and Andouille Sausage Stew..75
Turkey Burgers with Goat Cheese...56

VEAL

Asiago Stuffed Veal Chops... 235
Citrus Peppercorn Veal Chops 236
Dill Veal 237
French Veal Sauté 239
Veal Osso Bucco 243
Veal Stuffed Mushrooms 57

WALNUTS

Apple Nut Pancakes 337
Asparagus in a Fig Balsamic Vinaigrette 247
Chocolate Chip Apple Cake 304
Curried Chicken Salad..85
Farmhouse Walnut Pie 312
Gorgonzola Pear Salad..89

Grand Chicken Salad Dulaine 90

Green Beans with Peppered Goat Cheese & Toasted Walnuts 258

Herbed Cheese Canapés 32

Holiday Pumpkin Bread with Orange Glaze 316

Mama's Ugly Apple Cake 319

Oatmeal Carmelitas 321

Wile Rice with Butternut Squash & Dried Cranberries 283

YOGURT

Curried Chicken Salad 85

Fresh Dill Salad 87

Greek Chicken on Flatbread with Feta-Yogurt Sauce 192

Tender Yogurt Chicken 199

ZUCCHINI

Chicken Marrakech with Jeweled Couscous 186

Crab Puffs with Lime Sauce 27

Hot Vegetable Garlic Bread 358

Zucchini Patties with Feta 284

Cook's Notes

COOK'S NOTES

COOK'S NOTES